Praise for *Women, Wealth, and Giving*

"*Women, Wealth, and Giving* is an inspirational must-have book! If you want to explore how your talents, values, and emotions can be guided, shaped, and created into significant contributions for your family, friends, community, and yourself, buy this book. It enlightens, informs, and empowers you to realize your unique talents and gifts—a powerful book that is truly a personal journey of discovery and transformation."

—Sherron Long, President, Creating Executive Options Inc.

"*Women, Wealth, and Giving* will be of interest to any financial advisor or fundraiser who works with women or with couples, particularly Boomers, around their giving. The book gets to "the heart of the matter." It would make a great present for key donors or clients."

—Philip Cubeta, CLU, ChFC, MSFS, CAP, Sallie B. and William B.
Wallace Chair of Philanthropy, The American College

"*Women, Wealth, and Giving* demonstrates how women can move from home and community and deploy their wealth and their hearts in a time when compassionate leadership is desperately needed. Every generation faces its own urgent issues, but rarely in human history have we been on the precipice of irreparable harm to things as large as the world's environment or as local as the loss of civility and caring for the overwhelmed. Margaret and Niki put forth a call for—and the means to achieve—a more harmonious world, "… healing a world crying for serenity and salvation."

—Richard M. Weber, MBA, CLU, AEP®, President—The Ethical Edge, Inc.

"Some people have jobs. Some have careers. And then there are those who have callings. Niki Nicastro McCuistion and Margaret May Damen have a calling to share their love and passion about the joys of philanthropy with others. What makes their sharing so profound is that they come from it with their breadth of experience as fundraisers, donors, financial planners, storytellers, wives, mothers, daughters, and recipients. You will be fascinated, inspired, and moved to action by their stories."

—Carol Weisman, MSW, CSP, author of *Raising Charitable Children*
and *Transforming Ordinary People in Fundraising Superheroes*

"This book speaks right to the heart of every Baby Boomer, women and men too, by reminding us of why we are here and what sort of legacy we want to leave for our children and grandchildren. Speaking to women in the middle stage of life, Margaret and Niki remind us of the real wealth—spiritual, intellectual and financial—that we have to share with others. Their book will help many women to find their "voice and place" in this 21st century world. It will help us all to become active participants in change for good. Women long to make a difference with their wealth and talents and this book shows us a path towards that difference."

—Abbie J von Schlegell, Editor, *Women as Donors, Women as Philanthropists*

"*Women, Wealth, and Giving* is much more than a book on philanthropy. It reaches to the soul and addresses life's purpose. Women at every stage of life will find this book both fascinating and rewarding."

—G. Roger Schoenhals, Founder and Editor, *Planned Giving Today®*

"From the beginning of time to now, women have been givers. The generosity of women coupled with influence, intellect, and insight is a force that propels societal transformation and advancement. The "women effect" is another gradation upon which to build "compassion in action.""

—Thelma Morris-Lindsey, Founding Director, Earning By Learning

"Margaret and Niki take the reader on a transformative journey. If you are a boomer woman, you will feel empowered to take up the mantle of philanthropy with vigor and purpose. If you are a development officer, you will more successfully tap this rich and growing universe of donors. Don't even think of targeting the generation of boomer women for fundraising until you have read this book."

—Debra Ashton, author, *The Complete Guide to Planned Giving*

"Damen and McCuistion hit the nail on the head with this provocative book that challenges boomer women to connect to their inner core values, open their hearts and then put their money where their hearts are. Women do have the power, both financially and politically, to lead us out of these dark times and into a new culture based on loving, caring, and sharing. *Women, Wealth, and Giving* is a wonderful guidebook to help all women, no matter what their financial situation, to find their path to becoming leaders, healers, and creators of a bright new world."

—Barbara Wilder, author of *Money is Love: Reconnecting to the Sacred Origins of Money, Embracing Your Power Woman*, and *Power Woman Magic—The Play*

"For many nonprofits today, women represent a growing generation of gatekeepers of the philanthropic purse strings. Every fundraiser and development officer who wants to partner with women to achieve their mission needs to read this book."

—Suzanne Horstman, FAHP, Executive Director, Library Foundation of Martin County

"This is a powerful and inspirational book that engages women's hearts and minds in ways to make a true and vital difference with their time, talent, and treasure. This book is a must read for all of us who care about the future of our planet."

—Lynne Twist, author, *The Soul of Money*

"*Women, Wealth, and Giving* provides valuable insights about philanthropy that are refreshingly embedded in an historic context. Arming the reader with an arsenal of practical information, Niki and Margaret illustrate how the "power of the purse" can have a profound impact on our economy and our cultural values, as well as help define the "new spirit in America." A book that provides this kind of inspiration about the powerful potential of giving should be required reading for members of the Association of Fundraising Professionals and any other organization in a position to pave the way for informed, innovative giving."

—Pam Gerber, Executive Director, Entrepreneurs Foundation of North Texas

"Forty-three million boomer woman have been pioneers in their own right since the 60s. They're all grown up and desire more than ever to contribute as mentors and volunteers. They also have financial wealth to share. The authors capture the philanthropic hearts of this spirited generation of women who yearn to make a difference in the lives of others by leaving a legacy that will speak for generations to come."

—Dotsie Bregel, Founder, National Association of Baby Boomer Women, www.NABBW.com

"I'm reminded of the many decades of medical research, conducted on male subjects, but assumed to apply equally to women. Margaret May Damen and Niki Nicastro McCuistion demonstrate that women have a unique perspective on legacy and giving, different than that traditionally defined by the actions of men. Our hearts may be in the same place anatomically, but the passions that inspire us are distinct. The authors guide women toward a very personal understanding of their values and potential as philanthropists."

—Tanya Howe Johnson, President and CEO, Partnership for Philanthropic Planning

"Most men and women, boomers or not, do not know the chronological history of women in America especially as it relates to wealth and giving. *Women, Wealth, and Giving* changes this dramatically. We can now understand the struggle and appreciate and accept where women are in relation to status, influence and significance. Kudos to Damen and McCuistion for giving us this gift. It is truly a treasure."

—Bob Hopkins, Founder, *Philanthropy World Magazine*

Women,
Wealth, and Giving

THE VIRTUOUS LEGACY OF
THE BOOM GENERATION

Margaret May Damen
and
Niki Nicastro McCuistion

WILEY

John Wiley & Sons, Inc.

Illustrations by Elizabeth Huggins-Thompson.

For general information on our other products and services or for technical
support, please contact our Customer Care Department within the United States
at (800) 762-2974, outside the United States at (317) 572-3993 or fax (317)
572-4002.

Wiley also publishes its books in a variety of electronic formats. Some content that
appears in print may not be available in electronic books. For more information
about Wiley products, visit our Web site at www.wiley.com.

Library of Congress Cataloging-in-Publication Data

Damen, Margaret May.
    Women, wealth & giving : the virtuous legacy of the boom generation /
  Margaret May Damen and Niki Nicastro McCuistion.
        p.   cm.
    Includes bibliographical references and index.
    ISBN 978-0-470-23064-0 (cloth)
        1. Women—United States.   2. Women employees—United
States.   3. Baby boom generation—Economic aspects—United
States.   4. Generosity.   I. McCuistion, Niki Nicastro.   II. Title. III. Title:
Women, wealth and giving.
  HQ1421.D36   2010
  171'.8—dc22
                                                           2009031701

Printed in the United States of America
10 9 8 7 6 5 4 3 2 1

God could not be everywhere, so he created Mothers and Grandmothers.

—Author Unknown

This book is dedicated to Lillian M. May, Mother, 1912–2007, and Mary H. Strassburg, Grandmother, 1887–1982, forever alive in my heart, two loving, empowering, and pragmatic women with vision far ahead of their generations. Memories of their courage, compassion, and creativity continue to inspire me each day of my life.

—Margaret May Damen

This work is dedicated to my Mom, who until almost her last day gave her talent, and time, and treasure. She was honored, loved, and respected by many. I am grateful for all she taught me.

And to my extraordinary grandchildren who share the same spirit of giving: Carissa, a kind, caring soul, full to the brim with true compassion for others, and Bianca and Chiara, my personal role models for giving from the heart with their loving generosity toward others. They are our hope for the future.

—Niki Nicastro McCuistion

Ode

Your virtuous legacy
starts with you…

Respect thyself and thy spiritual life.

Respect thyself and thy physical body.

Respect thyself and thy steadfast faith.

Respect thyself and the purity of thy soul.

Respect thyself and thy compassion for others.

Respect thyself and thy harvest of well-sown seeds.

Respect thyself and thy accomplishments and unique talents.

Respect thyself and cherish the love of thy family and friends.

Respect thyself and share thy gratitude for blessings received.

Respect thyself and thy infinite quest for knowledge and wisdom.

Respect thyself and the sanctity of thy hopes, aspirations and dreams.

Respect thyself and honor thy abundant virtues each day of your life.

Margaret May Damen © 2006

Contents

Foreword

There are moments in history when breakdowns happen and so, too, do breakthroughs. This book, collected by a woman who has had her own breakthrough, Margaret May Damen, and shaped by another remarkable soul, Niki Nicastro McCuistion, is full of caring interviews with powerful women ready and committed to serve and lead for the greater good.

Here you will find stories that will move you to impactful action; here are women sharing, which women have come to know is essential, revealing stories of their evolution for the future of humankind and for those they mentor and guide.

Women, Wealth, and Giving is about the transformation, influence, and leadership of women. It is also about their resourcefulness and their multiple forms of capital—courage capital, influence capital, financial capital, and social capital—as they are moved intentionally to make personal and community change.

"The women effect," as this new wave of women stepping up is called, is about the heart cracked open in the face of great loss, grief, hope, and fear. What you will read here is about those who did not dwell in fear; instead, when the rest of the world cocooned, these women transcended their personal difficulties and the culture of anxiety around them to serve and make change happen. These thriving and generous community and family leaders stand out because of their contributions and generosity, and you will find them resilient and infinitely more hopeful than their peers who were less giving. For it is their very giving that has supported their leaps to personal healing or greater leadership. And who cannot be moved by reading stories of inspiration and impact?

In only a short half century, women have taken their places as creative forces for shifting the constructs of families and communities and are shaping the world they want. Nearly 150 public and private women's foundations in the United States and globally have

been created, and women are heads of over 60% of family foundations. As women rise or inherit the role of primary decision maker
in stewarding larger sums of money, their advisors will also benefit
from seeing what motivates these women managers.

Only a short time ago, a group of women donors I was part
of, led by two sisters, Swanee and Helen Hunt, invited a group
of women worldwide to step up to their giving and leadership
potential and form a community through the Women's Funding
Network, called Women Moving Millions (www.womenmovingmil-
lions.org). In two short years, just 80 women donated lifetime and
legacy gifts to women's foundations of $180 million, breaking the
ambitious goal that had been created of $150 million. While you
may or may not have this level of financial wealth, we all can understand this surge even during the economic downturn that the campaign faced. "This is the time when we know as hard as it may be to
face our own losses, there are always those who are in much greater
need," proclaimed one donor in making her substantial pledge
while offering to raise more from others. You are not alone. There
is a force between us now, and a collective understanding about
our responsibilities and moral imperative to lead so as to save the
planet, and so we are doing it.

Born into a world that did not value them, the boom generation of women has made known already its intentions and determination for a world that will work for everyone. Propelled by the
injustices they have seen and experienced, the passionate commit-
ments of these women will rock you to tears. We are reminded also
of the sacrifices of our own mothers, as well and their guidance.
"There is no greater gift than service to community," said my own
exemplary mother, Pat deBary, when I was 14, and so, too, I had the
guidance and mandate from her that has moved in me for some 40
years since. I could see the joy it brought her amid many shadows
of other difficulties.

Readers will be aided by the authors' *Three Principles of
Abundance* and tools such as the *Seven Covenants*. These weavers of
wisdom share the steps of just who and how we can count on this
generation and how best to cheer and support them.

Faithful to their call to build community, these are the queen
bees of our action, in their homes and hives. They are the builders
of a new culture and a new generosity consciousness. Here is the

generosity generation. Watch and listen to them shaping our future with love and remarkable compassion. Readers can step forward expecting remarkable opportunities.

Women, Wealth, and Giving is an inspiring story of how we enrich our lives on every level when we give to others. It is a call to action, for each one of us to get involved, to join hands and hearts in collaboration with others, to share, to give what we can, to volunteer, and to strengthen our commitment to our communities.

Join me in making a deep bow to our writers for gathering the wisdom found here and showcasing these inspired women. May we all seek to join them and, by doing so, create a lasting legacy and make a great leap forward for the love of humankind.

Tracy Gary
Author, *Inspired Philanthropy*
Founder, Inspired Legacies

Preface

This book is for and about you, your time, your happiness, and your values. It is frankly about your soul and what really matters to you. It is about awakening purpose and instilling a passion in the pursuit of happiness. *Women, Wealth, and Giving* leads you on an uplifting path to the freedom of giving, of yourself and your spirit, of your time and your blessings. It opens the door to the true joy, peace, and harmony that giving brings.

Women, Wealth, and Giving is neither a magic wand nor the only solution to the challenges of living and leaving a legacy. It is not a technical text of the tools and techniques of gift planning or a saga of the history of women and philanthropy, two subjects covered extensively by several highly qualified and respected authors and colleagues in the field. Rather, it is a perspective seen through many different lenses, the personal lens of women whose stories tell how they have found fulfillment through giving and our own lens as the storytellers. No matter what your age or circumstances, consider these stories a helping hand, which will inspire and lead you to create your own path; a path we believe necessary for women to follow as we look for solutions to a more humane and sustainable world; a journey we believe imperative for boom-generation women if they are to lead as mentors for Generations X and Y and those to follow.

Both of us have long been immersed in the world of philanthropy; this has been our life. It has been our vocation and our avocation. In writing this book, it was our intent to share what we have learned and experienced over the more than three decades we have each been speaking, writing, and consulting on philanthropic issues and women's giving and trends. Margaret brings her perspective and expertise as a Certified Financial Planner, investment advisor, and endowment gift planning design specialist, and Niki as a nonprofit founder and chief executive, a consultant, and a strategist who has put the principles we share with you into practice for her own organization and those of her clients.

We have been leaders in philanthropic endeavors, fund raising and investing money for our clients in nonprofits we have been involved in as trustees, leadership consultants, board members, and grantors. We have spoken internationally, talking to leaders of industry and finance, in the corporate and the nonprofit world. And we share a deep commitment to empower humanity, most especially women, to live their lives philosophically, financially, and philanthropically to the fullest extent possible. In the process of searching our souls, we found ourselves more open to thoughts about how not only we, but our generation, the boomers, were preparing to leave a legacy of values as well as valuables. We began to question, how an idealist generation, especially one in which women control substantial wealth, thinks about and acts out what significance means in their lives. We sought to explore reasons why women approaching the final chapters of their life would take time out to focus and redirect their lives in more meaningful ways, building on decades of idealistic and individualistic experiences that challenged their courage and molded their character. In each story, each experience, unknowingly at the time, we found the setting of one more brick in the right place at the right time, building the firm foundation upon which we find ourselves and a generation approaching midlife and beyond.

We have visited many cultures and have firsthand experience of what love of humankind and giving to make a difference really means, when it really matters. And we can personally attest to the difference giving means to both the giver and the recipient. Giving has its own rightful place, and in a world full of challenges, bankrupt economies, and declining morality, it provides a place that feeds our soul. Giving has measurable, proven benefits to our spiritual and physical well-being; it is a path to holistic wholeness and connectedness. It is about securing for ourselves a meaningful existence. While our pursuit of material happiness leads us away from a path of meaning, it is in giving we find our personal mission. Giving enriches lives, most especially our own. It is an act of love that frees and strengthens us. We believe we, having had so much—not necessarily financially, but spiritually—have a deep sense of responsibility to share our principles and our path.

This book is about integrity of the soul. It is about building a life that is worthwhile, with respect, compassion, and caring for the rights of others. It is about living life fully, joyfully, and with a consciousness of the good we practice in our daily lives, sometimes without fully knowing the extent that difference makes in the lives of others. Living as virtuous philanthropists has transformed our lives and opened our hearts to the possibility of a more compassionate world; we know it holds the promise of doing the same for you. We wrote this book to open a window in your heart, to kindle a flame, and to light your spirit with a passion for living a purposeful life. We believe that it is the true joy of giving that leads to peace of mind and full prosperity, the wealth within each of our souls. We cannot imagine a more exciting and vibrant time for us and our generation to be alive and entering a season in life that affords us opportunities to reflect, recharge, and renew convictions for a safer, saner, more just and harmonious world. There is no better time for each of us to become torchbearers for compassionate change and light the way for others to follow.

Come with us on this journey to knowing yourself and what you stand for and how you personally can make a difference. We trust you will find empowerment and a new way to look at yourself and life through a different lens, the lens of being a virtuous philanthropist. And that by living the Three Principles of Abundance and subscribing to the Seven Covenants, you will transform every aspect of your life with the true joy of giving with compassion and responsibility as you walk your journey.

Acknowledgments

The seeds for this book were sown in January 1999 when my friend and colleague Suzanne Horstman and I traveled from the east to the west coast of Florida to hear Andrea Kaminski speak on women and philanthropy at a workshop sponsored by the Venice Foundation. Now, 10 years later, those seeds have been nurtured to harvest by many colleagues and friends. All have brought the richness of their own special talents and perspective into my life, and I am blessed by their willingness to share and support my work.

I want to express my gratitude to Carol Weisman, whose persistent encouragement in her ubiquitous style for me to complete this work led to the collaboration with my coauthor, Niki Nicastro McCuistion. It is a memorable moment when instantaneously a stranger becomes a trusted friend and professional ally, and that moment was September 24, 2008, the best birthday present a woman could wish to have in her lifetime. Niki's quick wit, worldly outlook, tenacious spirit, and writing acumen succeeded in setting the tone for us to fine-tune and realize this book. Yes, indeed, we are a good team; together we possess the best of the yin and yang.

A special thanks to Susan McDermott, senior editor at John Wiley & Sons, Inc., for her conviction and compassion to stand by her resolve that this book be written. Her much-needed encouragement, understanding, and faith in the message lifted me through moments of doubt and life-changing experiences while writing. Also my praise goes to Elizabeth Huggins-Thompson and her talents to bring words to life through her illustrations. Liz began this book project with me before a word was written. She has a special enthusiasm and skill to masterfully capture a vision from the written word, as well as the fortitude to try various perspectives.

I want to thank Suzanne Wentley and Peggy Payne for their invaluable feedback and critique of earlier drafts of this manuscript. Their writing expertise and coaching helped craft my skills to more freely express on paper what is in my heart, as did the moral support of Gary J. Damen. During the past three years I could not have asked for a better set of cheerleaders than Barbara Carraway, Carol Compton, Debra Ashton, Lynn Wagner, Sherron Long, Suzanne Horstman, Jessica Crosby, Nancy M. Vrechek, PhD, Martha Boisvert, and Danie Victor Laguerre to keep my spirit fueled with optimism and remind me at the end of a pensive day of research to focus on the silver lining. Much of the inspiration for my work comes from the teaching and writing of Paul Schervish, Tracy Gary, Scott Farnsworth, Phil Cubeta, and Barb Culver, to whom I owe gratitude and thanks for sharing their wisdom one on one with me.

A sincere thank you to Barbara Yeager, editor of the *Journal of Gift Planning*, for the opportunity early on to publish excerpts of my preliminary work, and to Andrea Pactor, associate director of the Women's Philanthropy Institute at the Center on Philanthropy at Indiana University, for providing the venue at the 2008 symposium on women's philanthropy to express and refine my views. My appreciation to Tanya Howe Johnson, president and chief executive, and the staff of Partnership for Philanthropic Planning (formerly the National Committee on Planned Giving) and the leadership of the Association of Fundraising Professionals for having the occasion at several national conferences as a presenter to articulate my working theories that have become the foundation of this book.

Every action in life is inspired by the graciousness and love of others, especially my family, including my brother Donald and my now-departed mother and father, Lillian and Thomas May, and my grandparents, Herman and Mary Strassburg.

Thank you one and all, named and unnamed. Know by being in my life that your spirit has added to the shaping of this book. Hugs to K.C. and Marshall.

—Margaret

———

Writing *Women, Wealth, and Giving* was a gift to me from a community of dedicated, talented people who have a unique passion for their mission. Its journey began with the nonprofit I co-started and its mission, which I still work to fulfill, the role models I met along the way, and the clients I worked with who so deeply believed and worked for their organization's purpose, and who taught me so much about giving. It takes a community to write a book like this one, and I am very grateful to each and every one of our contributors, who with their stories will inspire others in their life work.

I want to especially acknowledge my coauthor, Margaret May Damen. Her keen insights, intellect and intuition, and cheerful, supportive stewardship made the writing a joy. She has my highest respect. We make quite a team. Our work is better for our collaboration and friendship, and I hope it is one of many to come.

A special thank you to Carol Weisman, a dear friend to us both. Carol, herself a gifted and prolific writer and nonprofit consultant, brought Margaret and me together. She knew our work would be richer as a result.

A heartfelt thank you to Karla Williams, ACFRE, an extraordinary teacher, and my advisor in the St. Mary's University Master's in Philanthropy and Development program, in Winona, Minnesota. Karla, an accomplished and successful writer and consultant in the nonprofit world, has been my coach and my mentor. She has provided encouragement when I needed it, as well as a lecture or two. And she planted the seed from which my participation in this work took root.

I want to thank each and every one of the numerous nonprofits I have served on. They have been my classroom. To name just a very few that have taught me philanthropy in action because of their leadership and attention to their mission: Avance-Dallas, the Children's Cancer Fund, and most especially the World Affairs Council of Dallas/Fort Worth, whose leaders are generous with their spirit, time, and treasure. They are my role models, as is Jim Falk, its president and chief executive, who is a walking example of what a nonprofit executive needs to be. He has taught me a great deal about truly making a difference.

And very heartfelt thank-yous must go to my dear friends for their advice and encouragement, Mary Handley and Mary Baker. They have given me unconditional support as well as hands-on contributions in every project and venture I am involved in. And to all of my friends and associates who really believe in me and encourage me and cheer me on, thank you so very much. To all those friends I am so grateful to, you know who you are and you know how much I value each and every one of you. Your kindness and caring are part of my heart.

Finally, I want to acknowledge my family. They have taught me so much. My late, beloved mother, who was truly an inspiration of giving in action; my treasured daughter Lisa, who opens her heart and empties her pockets. Her warmth is a beacon for me. And my son's family, who truly give for the joy of it: Danya, generosity of spirit is her middle name; the girls they taught so well; and my son Nick, a truly amazing person, who daily works to make the world a better place to be.

—Niki

CHAPTER 1

A Generation in the Right Place at the Right Time

The raising of extraordinarily large sums of money given voluntarily and freely by millions of our fellow Americans is a unique American tradition. . . . Philanthropy . . . charity, giving, call it what you like, but it is truly a jewel of American tradition.
——John F. Kennedy (1917–1963)
35th President of the United States

Women need
To utilize their superior intelligence
About Love
So that their hour's legacy
Can make us all stronger and more clement.
——*Hafiz: The Great Sufi Master**

In 2030, of the 57.8 million American Boomers, 54% will be women.[1] And it is women worldwide who make the largest slice of

---

* Excerpt from "The Mule Got Drunk And Lost In Heaven"
From the Penguin publication, *The Gift: Poems by Hafiz, the Great Sufi Master*, copyright 1999, Daniel Ladinsky, and used with his permission

the pie when it comes to making consumer purchasing decisions, estimated at $20 trillion annually, including 91% of homes, 60% of automobiles, and 51% of consumer electronics.[2] Today, women control almost 60% of the nation's wealth, and evidence indicates they will inherit and manage even more wealth in the future. And since women outlive men by an average of five years, in the next twenty years, it is predicted that 80% to 90% of women will be in charge of their families' financial affairs sometime in their life.[3] With the majority of the estimated $41 trillion that is expected to be transferred through estate settlements and trusts passing through their hands, women will have a defining role in the reshaping of the American Dream for future generations. There is no question; women are indeed where the money is.[4]

Even better, they are using the "power of the purse" to profoundly influence our economy and our society. The Center for Women's Business Research states that 54% of businesswomen make all of their philanthropic decisions independent of advice or counsel from anyone.[5] And since women are the key decision makers in the managing and disposing of wealth, they will be, as management guru Tom Peters affirms, "the largest 'national' economy on earth."[6]

While men may still earn more money, women give as much to charity, yet they do so differently. In today's challenging economic, political, and sociological times, women have the power to accelerate their ability to do good and change the face of society. A case in point is the 2008 national elections. Women made contributions to candidates in unprecedented numbers. Women increasingly realize their own tremendous potential to apply their charitable dollars to shaping the future of society and the world. Women are where the money is; they matter. "If you don't get more women in politics," says Marie C. Wilson, founder and president of the White House Project, "you won't get more women on boards that have the possibility for change. If you don't fund political work and power, you don't get the change you need."[7]

More and more women are becoming aware of the power of money to truly make a difference in their local and global community. One of our interviewees, Dallas boomer Brenda Pejovich, an entrepreneur who devotes significant time to serving on state agency and nonprofit boards and supporting political causes, says that one of the reasons she gives to political organizations is to be heard and to raise awareness for women's issues, She emphasizes, "We [women] need to understand that while volunteering time is important, we need to support the causes we believe in with our checks so that we have a seat at the table. Women have a major impact on policy and the more involved we are, the more effectively we can influence decisions that are important to us and our families. By increasing our participation in the competition for ideas, women will continue to contribute to a better society. It's our checks that influence and it's never been more important to open our wallets and give."[8]

For women born between 1943 and 1964, the first decade of the twenty-first century is a defining time. Women of this generation are entering the next phase of their biological life. This fresh vigor—as anthropologist Margaret Mead calls it, the "post menopausal zest"—brings with it new assets, freedom, networks, and knowledge that allow boomer women to take on unique challenges, give more creatively, become even more authentic, and engage in pursuits that can bring a greater sense of meaning, joy, and balance. For boomer women, the rite of passage to "post menopausal zest" is a signal to reconnect with the voice of their soul, to find original songs from the heart, to dance to an unfamiliar beat, and to create authentic ways of making those challenging situations better.

"Our time on this earth is so short," says Vi Nichols Chason, co-president of the Martin County Women Supporting the Arts. "I think often of how important taking action is every time I hear the lyrics of the Beatles' song 'Hey Jude.'" She runs through a few lines of that familiar boomer-generation song that urges us to give sad songs happy endings. "There are so many, many, sad songs that we encounter in our daily lives," Chason laments. "Why not find your passion—the passion that rises up from your belly and consumes you! Make the decision you are going to make a difference in someone else's life."[9]

For many boomers, the desire to shape their lives to their deepest values, to take charge of their time and money, and to contribute, each in their own distinctive way, to the greater good becomes even stronger as they reach midlife. In short, many of us begin to speak out and take action as we have never done before. In those of our generation, "moral priorities are growing," according to a recent Yankelovich Inc. survey, "with interests running the gamut from social causes to spiritual revivals to personal charity." Now and in the coming decades as boomers repurpose their lives, it will be the "righteous self," the report continues, "that is dominant among aging boomers.[10]

And it has long been known that women over 50 often make some sort of fresh start. The psychoanalyst Carl Jung notes that middle-age women, having submerged their identity for decades, take off their "personas" at midlife, drop their masks, and find new meaning in their lives. Of course, women traditionally have been helpers and caregivers, at home and in schools, their churches and neighborhoods. Many charities came about because women saw a need and fulfilled it and believed it was their role to do so. In every generation, pioneering women sought large-scale causes and led public reforms that truly changed society for the better. What is new today is an entire generation of women with unprecedented independence, assets, and experience beginning to take the lead in reshaping the larger world, through highly individual and carefully focused giving of time, talent, and money. Many have begun to design the changes they want in the world; and some, such as Meg Whitman, former president and chief executive of eBay and a 2010 candidate for governor of California, and Darla Moore, president of Rainwater, Inc., a private investment firm, even ask for and get their names on the buildings they are now funding.[11]

The Big Picture

The term "Boomer Generation," a phrase coined by Landon Y. Jones, applies to those born between 1946 and 1964,[12] although other experts, such as William Strauss and Neil Howe, prefer to set the generation parameters to those born between 1943 and 1960.[13] We chose to accept the wider time frame, and invite readers at each end of the age spectrum to make their own decisions based on how they identify with the boomer personality. In our focus groups, a significant number of women born between 1943 and 1945 told us they consider themselves boomers while several women we interviewed born between 1960 and1964 expressed a much closer affinity in attitude and values to Generation X. Jones uses the term "Boomer Generation" to define the "boom" in births in unprecedented numbers after World War II. In 1946, 2.2 million couples married, a record not equaled for 33 years. Today, this birth explosion includes 29% of the population, 78-plus million boomers in the United States alone.[14] It is one of the most polled, analyzed, interviewed, and criticized generations ever. From the media to ad agencies, who they are, what they want, and how they have influenced America continues to be news.

It is of this boomer group we are writing. Their strength in numbers alone has changed our world and how we function. We believe that the better the understanding we have of their thinking, their decision making, and their values, the more effectively we can harness and use this incredibly focused energy for the public good. Our research shows that Americans are the most generous people on earth. In fact, more Americans donate money than vote. And of this group, the most generous are women, many of whom are of the boomer generation and have focused their energy on the public good.

The first wave of boomers (those born before 1957) grew up in relative luxury, luxury previously unknown to their parents, who were products of the Great Depression. They were spoiled, petted, pampered, and became the so-called self-absorbed generation. J. Walker Smith, president of Yankelovich, Inc., and Ann Clurman, a senior partner, sum up the boom generation with this classic statement: "For decades baby boomers have been chided for being self-centered, self-absorbed and self-confident, even narcissistic. There is no argument there. Guilty as charged, but so what?"[15]

This was a generation that to a large degree rejected and then refined the traditional values of their post–World War II parents. The boomers grew up genuinely and optimistically expecting the world to improve with time. Brought up to believe they were special, they had no doubt that they themselves would be the ones to change the world. Growing up in the golden era of the 1950s, their upbringing contributed to an assumption of lifelong prosperity and entitlement.

It was/is a generation widely associated with privilege. The golden era was a time of affluence, and it bred the healthiest, wealthiest generation in the history of the world. Boomers grew up with the exploding of the feminine mystique and took to heart the message that women could and should find fulfillment outside the home. The myth and belief was that childbearing, doing house-work, and waiting on their husbands hand and foot was not what real women, the women growing up in this generation, did. In the 1940s, in their parents' generation, one in six marriages ended in divorce. Divorce had strong stigmas against it. The boomers pushed the divorce rate to 50-plus % and made it a norm that today is pretty much acceptable. The music, lifestyle, politics, and social changes of the era all had an impact. Yet while there is much that ties this generation together, there is also much that separates them. Older boomers were affected by the deaths of President Kennedy and his brother Robert and that of Martin Luther King. The Vietnam War took its toll. Boomers participated in protests, of which there were many. Some avoided the draft and took off to Canada. The Beatles, Woodstock, Haight Ashbury, and Flower Power; this generation grew up with a freedom and affluence never seen before.

Glued to their transistor radios, boomers set out to conquer the world while listening to the Beatles and Motown. Those born in the first wave of boomers may have marched to a different drum, but march they did. Boomers born between 1943 and 1955 epito-mize the cultural change of the 1960s, with its social experimenta-tion, civil rights, activism, environmentalism, sexual freedom, the pill, recreational drug use, and women's rights. This was a free-wheeling, free-spirited, individualistic group oriented to social causes that believed in their capacity to change the world.

Younger boomers absorbed the messages of the oil embargo, gasoline shortages, inflation, Watergate, and the shock of a presi-dent forced to resign. They grew up with the Cold War and MTV and a lowered expectancy of life's beneficence. This half of the boom generation is more cynical, less optimistic, and much more distrustful of government.

In 1967, *Time* magazine selected the boomer generation as its "man" of the year, truly cementing the me generation's concept of importance. This was an idealized generation that today is the major force in the economy. Boomers represent the vast major-ity of today's workforce. Statistically 78 million strong, they *are* the workforce. The strength in the economy in the 1990s was due in no small part to these 78 million Americans working up to their peak earning and spending years. It is to the boomers that most of consumerism sings—SUVs, high-end cars, vintage wines, vacations and vacation homes, travel of any kind anywhere, cosmetic surgery, teeth whitening, Lasik surgery, the list goes on. It is the boomers who have the money to spend.

Today, the producers of most TV shows and movies are boomers. The chief executives of most major companies that influence our economy and consumption habits are boomers. Our technology wizards, from Bill Gates to Steve Jobs, are boomers. The president of the Federal Reserve, Ben Bernanke, is a boomer, as is the president of the United States, Barack Obama. And just about every potential candidate for the Supreme Court for the next 20 years will be a boomer.

Ann Mulcahy, Hilary Clinton, Oprah, Madonna, Michelle Obama, and Condoleezza Rice have in common the ideals that baby boomers brought to the social landscape. Every hour, 330 baby boomers turn 60 years of age, 50.8% of these women. In 1946, the U.S. population was estimated at 141 million. In 2006, our population was over 298 million. In 1947, only 5% of our population had a bachelor's degree, and 33% had a high school diploma. Today, over 85% of our population has a high school diploma and 28% a bachelor's degree, and since the late 1970s, more of these graduates have been women than men.[16]

Retirement age is fast approaching for many of this generation. Roughly two-thirds of boomers are 50 years old or older. Their influence, using their $3 trillion in income to boost consumerism, has been felt in every area of society. Baby boomers rank as the wealthiest generation in history. Their sheer size boosted output and outgrowth rates. And for the first time in history, women have been an integral part of the workforce, working outside the home, not just on the farm or in cottage industries. This group married later, had children later, divorced at higher rates, or remained single. It was this generation that took advantage of their housing and investment wealth to fund their lifestyles. Yet a 2008 survey by Key Bank and Zogby International found that 67% of boomers believe they will run out of money in their lifetimes.[17]

For the oldest boomers, this fear may significantly impact their ability to retire, their current spending, and their charitable contributions. Out of necessity comes an urgency to be more strategic and transformative in the use of resources and gifting to meet both altruistic and self-interest values, two goals quite complementary through philanthropy.

Boomers' higher levels of education enabled them to capitalize on economic changes in technology and globalization. During their working lives, they consumed more and saved less. Today boomers spend more than they make. In 2005, boomers had 47% of all disposable income yet they contributed only 7 percentage points to overall household savings. In the mid-1980s, the U.S. household savings rate was at 10-plus %; today it is less than 2%, and some say it stands at 5%. Boomer attitudes toward savings and spending are decidedly different from those of their parents. In fact, a boomer ratio of debt to net worth is 50% higher than the generation before them.[18] The economic downturn of 2008 may well impact boomers' spending and giving. Stock market dips and decreasing home equity have changed the financial landscape, yet boomer resilience is not to be undervalued.

No group is cut from a cookie-cutter mold, and the characteristics we talk about are general tendencies. Nevertheless, there are common values and characteristics that the boomer generation shares. Boomers have been described as hardworking and basically a live-to-work generation. They tend to put in long hours and have a strong high work ethic. Work is a very important part of their sense of self-worth. They tend to define themselves by what they do and *how successful* they are at what they do. This is a competitive group that tends to do what it takes to get it done even if it means sacrificing nights, weekends, and holidays, regardless of the toll it may take on the family.

While boomers may have started out as unambitious, somewhere along the way money became their driving force. It measured their success and served as their reward for hard work. This is a group that values promotions and looks for more responsibility. The tokens of success—awards, plaques, certificates, and trophies— demonstrate to the outside world that, yes, indeed, they have done good work. From praise to tangible rewards, they need acknowledgment. Middle-class boomers by and large denied themselves nothing and, in turn, denied their latch-key kids nothing, except close relationships with their parents. The boomer workaholics striving to continually build their careers value a person's worth by his or her accomplishments and net worth.

This is a group known for having changed the world and for believing that not only could one do so but that one *had* to. Women especially have changed not only society in the past 50 years; they have changed their own roles in that society. All of us can remember major life dramas, when they occurred and what we were doing at the time. For the first wave of boomers, it was the assassination of John F. Kennedy. For the second wave, it may have been the resignation of Richard Nixon. Regardless, we knew the times they were a changing. Members of the me generation came of age in the aftermath of World War II and called into account every single value their parents—the silent generation—considered sacred. In fact, so many of the boomers were born in the same year that competition became the norm, whether for resources, attention, jobs and education, or recognition. Today more people are alive who were born after World War II than those who were born before it. The midlife boomer is the largest general grouping in the developed world.

Whether we are raising money to fund our cause or nonprofit or marketing our products or services, we need to understand what makes an individual or group act similar to or different from one another. There are distinct generational differences in lifestyles and life stages. The me generation was acculturated in the chaos of Watts, the TET offensive, and Chappaquiddick. Of this generation, 70% do not remember life before television. And while boomers may be classified as greedy—spend, not save—as a group they also absorbed the culture and were shaped by the experiences of their youth, their formative years.

The public events we witnessed shaped our values, and while some chose to drop out, more of us somehow understood that we had to make changes. We knew we could and would do anything we set our minds to. Our inner absorption crafted a voyage of self-discovery that fueled individual self-esteem. As Barbara Caplan, vice president of Yankelovich, Clancy and Shulman, said of this generation, "They had a higher level of optimism and a sense that the world is their oyster."[19] The boomers' financial style of buy now, pay later resulted in happy days but also a narcissistic perspective.

Why Women Are So Crucial

Boomer women have successfully—in fact, dramatically—built on the legacy of their foremothers. In a period of three years, from 1963 to 1966, social reforms and legislation enacted by Congress forever changed women's role in charting the course of our nation's history. In 1963, Congress passed the Equal Pay Act, requiring equal pay for equal work without regard to sex. This was also the year the President's Commission on the Status of Women, with Eleanor Roosevelt as chair, issued its report titled *American Woman.* That same year marked the debut of Betty Friedan's book *The Feminine Mystique,* which talked about the lack of fulfillment in women's lives—"the problem that had no name."

In 1964, Congress passed the historic Title VII of the Civil Rights Act, the law that prohibits employers from discrimination of employment based on race, color, and national origin. In 1966, the National Organization for Women (NOW) formed, with an ambitious agenda for women's rights and stated in their purpose "to bring women into full participation in the mainstream of American Society now, exercising all privilege and responsibilities thereof in truly equal partnership with men."

Over the next four decades, women's "firsts" burst forth at a heady pace, in business, media, entrepreneurship, philanthropy, education, law, commerce, sports, science, space, medicine, civil service, government, and politics. Gloria Steinem served as a role model for many. First as cofounder of *New York* magazine in 1968 and *Ms.* magazine in 1971, Steinem's lifelong career as a social activist continues to inspire and educate. As a co-convener of the 1971 National Women's Political Caucus and one of the founders of the Ms. Foundation in 1972, an organization that funds the empowerment of girls and women, she set the benchmark as a change agent for women of all ages. The firsts continue, leading up to the milestones in 2008 of a woman Speaker of the House and both a woman presidential candidate, an early boomer, and a vice-presidential candidate, a late boomer. August 2009 and another first, Sonia Sotomayor becomes the first Hispanic and third woman to serve on the Supreme Court. Led by such women as Sandra Day O'Connor, the first woman to sit on the U.S. Supreme Court, and Senator Margaret Chase Smith, the first woman to serve in both houses of

Congress, a cadre of decisive, assertive, and caring women are lighting new beacon fires for other women to use as they travel ever further, creating new milestones and contributing new legacies.

The Right Moment—for Many Reasons

Our own nation is polarized, politically, socially, and economically, and the boomer generation bears some responsibility for this. Nowhere on the recent map of time is there a point that tells us exactly when America's moral compass stopped pointing true north. However, historians agree it began verging slightly off course in the early 1960s, as an increasing number of "hot-button" issues, such as abortion, gun control, homosexuality, and separation of church and state, began to divide American politics and culture. Today we see the manifestations of the last 40 years in the frustration and anger that surrounds us in everyday life: defiant attitudes, lack of traditional manners and lifestyles, abusive language, and ever-growing violence. Today a majority of people say that civility in America has declined, and four of every five adults claim that we are a nation in moral and spiritual decline.

Yet this kind of tension and turmoil has happened several times before in our nation's history. The supposedly uncivil times we are living through are part of a recurring pattern of profound cultural transformation that each time in the past reunites people and brings new order out of the old. Social historians William Strauss and Neil Howe elaborate on this interpretation of American history. Beginning with the seventeenth century, they identify a recurring 80- to 100-year cyclical pattern of history. This cycle, the Saeculum is the length of time approximately equal to the lifetime of a person. The saeculum is divided into four sections, childhood, young adult, midlife and elderhood (see Exhibit 1.1). Each section in the cycle has a distinct characteristic social mood and turns into the next, with new periods appearing in a predetermined order. The (1) high period gives way to (2) awakening, followed by (3) unraveling, and finally (4) crisis.[20]

The four sections neatly correspond with the four seasons, beginning with spring as high and moving to winter as crisis. According to Strauss and Howe, the spring of the current cycle started in 1946 with America's euphoric mood at the conclusion of World War II and the baby boom that produced us. And for the boomer generation, the four seasons correspond directly with their four life stages: childhood in spring, young adulthood in summer, midlife in fall, and elderhood in winter. Now six decades later, our crisis season—"the winter of our discontent"—coincides with the transition of the boomer generation from midlife to elderhood and with the rising dominance within our generation of the righteous self. Together the nation and this generational cohort reach their "winter of discontent," with a mandate to define the new spirit in America, a new spring. Concurrently, the nation and an age group set out a new course for the return of values and virtues for a caring and more egalitarian society and seek the forces to draw America's moral compass back to true north.

Season of Time

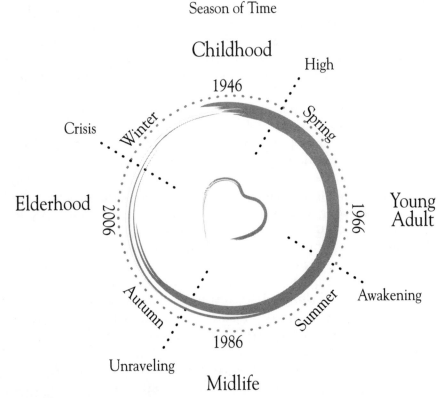

Exhibit 1.1 Millennial Saeculum

Women's New Contributions

In this winter season, the fourth turning, there is a new development: Women are more fully engaged in the fourth turning, and
that alone is history making, with huge potential for change.
Women also continue to be the pace setters in the philanthropic
sector, a leadership tradition rich in the history established by Jane
Addams and women social reformers during the Progressive Era in
the late 1890s It is as if the yang of the present is dissolving into
the yin of the past as opposites complement each other to create a
new consciousness and yet return to the fundamental virtues and
values that made America strong and philanthropically unique, as
chronicled by Alexis de Tocqueville in his historic saga *Democracy in
America.*[21] And there is a bonus: Biologically, women bring an extra
ka-pow! to the process, because we face our own mortality as we
move to the other side of the defining fiftieth birthday. While many
boomers still consider themselves middle aged at age 60, at age 50
we know our physical demise is inescapable. As we age, the sense of
time remaining to us and the need to use that time well becomes
paramount.

As women, we begin to peel away the facade and look inward
to a rebirth of spirituality, of purpose, of life's abundant meaning. We rely more on what we think and feel as individuals rather
than accept what others believe we should. Classic Greek philoso-
phers call this process the quest for *eudaimonia,* a well-being of the
soul.[22]

For centuries, scholars, theologians, and prophets have debated
how best to achieve such well-being and what the true characteristics of a virtuous person are. According to Aristotle in his
Nicomachean Ethics, the good life is achieved through *arête,* or living in excellence and virtue. He divides the virtues into intellectual
and moral. The moral virtues are prudence (common sense and
good judgment), justice (fairness, honesty, and truthfulness), fortitude (moral and physical courage), and temperance (moderation
of action, feeling, and thought). Virtue, by Aristotle's definition, is
the mean between two vices—one of excess, the other of defect—
neither too much nor too little being in the best interest of a moral
and reasonable society. What Aristotle is talking about is balance:
courage but not recklessness, effort but not burnout.[23]

Analects of Confucius tells us that "perfect virtue" is created in the practice of "gravity, generosity of soul, sincerity, earnestness and kindness." In the New Testament, Paul agrees, telling us in Colossians 3:12: "Therefore, as God's chosen people, holy and dearly loved, clothe yourselves with compassion, kindness, humility, gentleness and patience." Common to all philosophy and scripture is an underlying principle that to achieve *eudaimonia,* a person must live daily life by a set of values that leads to moral decisions.

One of the critical issues for boom-generation women is how to direct the quest for such a life when classic virtues come under siege or become incongruous with contemporary social culture and customs; not only how but what venue to use to facilitate this quest. According to Robert L. Payton, former director of the Center on Philanthropy at Indiana University, philanthropy is that venue. "The only basis for a claim of special consideration for philanthropy," says Payton, "is that it is the principal means by which our ethics and values shape the society in which we live."[24] Boom-generation women arrive at the perilous gates of America's winter of discontent steadfast in conviction, courage, and compassion to create a more benevolent and beneficent world, just when our nation's uncivil times and the world's deep need for rejuvenation reach critical mass and search for a virtuous resolution to a values revolution.

A Recent Trigger for Change

As boom-generation women began to arrive at their rite of passage, a significant set of events occurred, underlining the fact that a life is finite. We identify this as the tipping point when women began to unite in their philanthropic mandate for a better world. In 2006, three major icons in women's history died the same week. Pulitzer Prize–winning playwright Wendy Wasserstein and civil rights activist Coretta Scott King both died on January 30. The visionary and often combative feminist Betty Friedan died a few days later, on February 4. These women whom we had seen make history were now a part of eternal history, and while a generation of women paid final tribute to their mentors, it was also time to reassess and consider our own individual roles as torchbearers.

The memorials that took place in February 2006 for three tenacious, witty, and gracious mentors gave a resounding wakeup call. For other women, different reminders of mortality are sending the same message: It is time to recover lost idealism and lofty dreams and to fulfill them with the power driven by the riches of time, talent, and treasure. The quest for a virtuous legacy, for where and how to give, begins with a question: Who am I really?

Reading the New Thinking

Three contemporary philosophical and economic scenarios provide insight and direction to help women define their identity and destiny for giving more strategically and more powerfully of their wealth and time, and in the forming of partnerships.

Benevolent Economics

Riane Eisler, in her book *The Real Wealth of Nations*, speaks from her heart in offering a compelling vision of a system that goes beyond conventional economic models to support "caring for ourselves, others, and Mother Earth." Her theories make a case for including human capital and the core component of households, care giving and caring, as a measure of the true state of the world economy. Eisler's theory builds into the existing economic model several new categories, beginning with the household, the core inner sector, as a unit not of consumption but of production.

Her second sector, the unpaid community economy, includes volunteers working for charitable and other venues in civil society. Such a bold and dramatic change of perspective, giving visibility and value to the social aspects of the work of care and caregiving, could encourage a shift in the prevailing mind-set away from greed and materialism and toward creativity and generous giving. As part of her theory, Eisler exposes the "hidden system of valuations in which women, and the work of caring and care giving stereotypically associated with women, is devalued." For Eisler, a critical component in creating a caring economics is the shift away from a hierarchal leadership style, authoritarian in nature and subordinate of women and femininity, to a more democratic and equitable model with mutual respect and trust for males and females.

She identifies the former structure as the "Domination System" and the replacement model, the "Partnership System." The new paradigm has four core components: "a democratic and egalitarian family and social structure, a low level of abuse and violence, equal partnership between the male and female halves of humanity, and beliefs and stories that support relations based on mutual benefit, accountability, and caring." Although Eisler's focus is on economics, the idea is to shift to a system in which the economy includes both monetary *and* nonmonetary values.[25]

Egalitarian issues of a different sort, but equally crucial in women's giving, include the desire to better understand who we are and our relationship to our environment, our ecosystem. Nobel Prize–winning author Robert William Fogel defines this as "self-realization: the fullest development of the virtuous aspects of one's nature." In his book *The Fourth Great Awakening and the Future of Egalitarianism,* he presents several spiritual resources that need to be possessed in moderation in the quest to achieve the greatest degree of self-realization in society.[26] This list includes those that relate most specifically to creating a virtuous legacy:

- Sense of purpose
- Sense of the mainstream of work and life
- Strong family ethic
- Sense of community
- Capacity to engage with diverse groups
- Ethic of benevolence
- Sense of discipline
- Thirst for knowledge

For many of the boomer women we surveyed, this list has become a way of life, a part of how they perceive their core values and how they strive to be in the world as natural citizens.

The New Spirituality

Leading-edge research in spirituality has recently reemerged as a full-fledged discipline with organizations from the Metanexus Institute and scholars Raymond F. Palontzian and Robert A. Emmons lending more credibility to the field with their studies that interface with several areas of psychology, opening up a greater consciousness for the many ways we interconnect with every living being. This awareness clearly has the potential for enormous impact on the design of a giving plan. Meditation, quiet time, and journaling can bring into focus deeper meaning to philanthropic work. Such reflection can open up previously unconsidered paths to highly satisfying and effective philanthropic initiatives for the greater good.

Much of the cutting-edge work in expanding consciousness and worldview is found in the extensive research of the Institute of Noetic Sciences, founded by astronaut Edgar Mitchell. *Noetic* is a Greek word with an emphasis on the intellectual search for inner knowing or intuitive consciousness as a direct access to knowledge beyond what is available to our normal senses or power of reason. This research can alter the view of reality, with dramatic impact on how to live and give and connect worldwide.

No doubt the writings and work of Eckhart Tolle, Deepak Chopra, and the Dalai Lama over the past few years have become a major influence, bringing millions of people to a greater understanding of the transformation of consciousness and how it can bring forth compassion, passion for world peace, and sustainability of the planet. For boomer women, this philosophy is a natural outgrowth of the practices of the 1970s, when so many were finding new venues of expression in women's studies on liberal college campuses, in consciousness-raising groups and spiritual practices, and sometimes through the practice of Transcendental Meditation.

The rebirth of spirituality has also brought a renewed focus on the mythology of the "Divine Female" and her feminine qualities as a nurturing and sustaining influence in the universe. This image comes to us from traditions in the East, West, and Native cultures, among others, dating from approximately 40,000 BCE to 5,000 BCE. In recent years, focus on the Divine Feminine has made a resurgence as both men and women search for better partnerships and women accept a more central role in decision making for society. "Wholeness is possible," writes Jean Shinoda Bolen, in *Urgent Message from Mother*, "when human qualities, now usually designated as masculine or feminine, are seen as part of the spectrum for everyone."[27]

As part of the divine feminine movement, new programs are evolving to reconnect money to its sacred origins, to show how money takes on the energy and personality of the giver. According to Barbara Wilder, author of *Money Is Love*:

> Money is energy that has been directed by human thought and consciousness for thousands of years. That is, throughout history, humanity as a collective intelligence has created what money is and how it moves through society. Up until now this has been an unconscious activity.[28]

Today we are becoming more aware and thoughtful in numerous innovative ways about the use and power of money. Women are infusing the yin temperament into the energy and power of money, not for power and might but for altruism and caring. Bolen believes this is the time for "a call from the Sacred Feminine to bring the feminine principle into consciousness. . . . Look! Women have qualities that men have not developed, and these talents are needed right now."[29]

The Enlightened Corporate Conscious

"Conscious Capitalism" is the term author Patricia Aburdene uses to describe the trend toward enlightened self-interest in the corporate boardroom.[30] More companies are finding that sensitivity to making the work environment a more harmonious place can result in more creative productivity and sharing of ideas. This is self-interest in the largest sense, that of acting on one's highest values. The author sees such social-economic-spiritual trends as transforming free enterprise. Many companies, such as Starbucks, have integrated corporate social responsibility standards into their daily business life. Starbucks' policies include substantial health care benefits, stock options, tuition reimbursement, and retirement savings. These CSR goals and Starbucks way of doing business has raised its employee satisfaction scores to 82%, one of the highest for any business today. Some organizations, such as Salesforce.com are not only creating opportunities for employees' self-expression on the job but crediting volunteer hours for work done in the community. Salesforce.com offers its employees six paid days off a year to devote to volunteer projects of their choice. Some companies actually are providing counseling in the workplace; Marketplace Chaplains USA, founded in Dallas, Texas, in 1984, has over 2,400 chaplains in 44 states and 750 cities serving employees and family members. Aburdene's findings point to a greater spirituality in business, an emphasis on the nonmaterial: inner peace, meditation, mission, life purpose.

In this community atmosphere and with the maturity of individual experience, more and more women are making new journeys inward and are searching heart and soul for meaningful ways to give back to society and their community. Yet today's society still brings many challenges. Many of us are troubled by the injustices we see, and at times what appear to be almost insurmountable challenges in society and the economy freezes us in our tracks and paralyzes our hearts to a point where despair rather than hope sets in. Members of the boomer generation question if they made a difference and if one person actually can. It is sustaining to know that we are part of a greater universe of women with the same questions and the same resolve to make a better world for the future—and to know that we each have power. Women are well situated for becoming powerful values-based donors, each making a distinct imprint on the world.

And while we may not think of our lives as a legacy, we are off track if we do not. In the self-transforming process, boomer women, most especially those over 50, begin to move toward creating a virtuous legacy. This new paradigm of self-expressive giving has evolved over the past four decades. Women, rebelling against patriarchal order and conventional stereotypes, strove to achieve financial acumen and educational and economic parity. More than in any other venue, the achievement of financial independence, the freedom to decide the use of money, has made women equal partners in the decisions to save this world. The "power of the purse" is the power to rewrite the rules for a caring society, not only through its use in philanthropic endeavors but also in how money is invested in the financial and business institutions that control our capitalist system. The power of the purse has an exponential advantage as women unite, network, and agree on the importance of particular causes.

As women reach the sagacious stage of life, bringing with them decades of personal, economic, political, and social life experiences, they become more certain of the need to act and more aware of the urgency of time. As agents of change, we create a new vision fueled by spiritual resolve, moral purpose, and righteous principles. Red Hat soirees and menopause musical satires aside, the collective strength of 43 million women can fix a lot of what is broken. In communities throughout our nation, women are bonding and banding together in creative ways that transcend political, social, and economic barriers. "For what is done or learned by one class of women," according to suffragist Elizabeth Blackwell, "becomes by virtue of their common womanhood, the property of all women."[31]

Over the past 40 years, while boom-generation women climbed the corporate ladder, raised blended families, and achieved financial independence, dreamtime lost out. It was goal time, not soul time: Do what you have to do to get what you want to have—and to meet your obligations. Women who willingly gave up or delayed their own personal dreams for those of others now start to ask: Where is my *eudaimonia*? Isn't it time to follow some of my dreams and talents? In the movie *Out of Africa*, Karen Blixen, the heroine, ponders a haunting thought that is worth reflecting on: "My biggest fear was that I would come to the end of my life and discover that I had lived someone else's dream."[32] This is not a place where boomer women want to be. This is a generation whose members do not want to question themselves with: Who was I before I put myself last?

Yes, it is time.

Donna Hall, one of our interviewees, who is really helping other women in a big way, gives us her perspective on how she lives her dream. Donna is president and chief executive of the Women Donors Network (WDN), with a membership of women who each are giving at least $25,000 annually to charities of their choice.

Profile

You know, I went through Stanford Business School when only 20% of my class were women, and women were afraid to speak up. With money and job experience and growing self-confidence over the last 10 to 15 years, the boomer generation is really changing that paradigm. Increasing numbers of women who previously gave anonymously are now coming out of the closet about their money.

You see more women now saying: I'm proud of contributing. More have made the money themselves. And those who have inherited their wealth have learned how to manage it and make it do what they want. The ones who have married into wealth frequently have more egalitarian marriages than once was the case: They have some say over the giving, and all that has brought about a sea change in how women are looking at money and power. And it's an accomplishment, because boomer women, in my opinion, had to work harder than young women do now to overcome their cultural past.

What I think all this is going to mean is a lot more money pouring into the sorts of social, environmental, and justice issues that women are concerned about—and into work that affects women and girls. Contributing to the arts will continue, but it's likely to be funneled more to less conventional artists: perhaps rather than the New York City Ballet, to Bill T. Jones, an African American New Yorker who choreographs dance on social justice themes. What I expect we'll see less of is paying for bricks and mortar at traditional choices like churches and alma maters.

Our overall purpose at WDN is to be a safe community for women of wealth who are progressive and who want to become ever more powerful as individuals and as a voice at the progressive table. We're a membership right now of about 165. If you add up everything our members give away individually, plus all they give through WDN, these women give, I would guess, anywhere from $125 to $200 million a year.

We do a fair amount of mentoring. When we get new members, they're each assigned a buddy. And there's a lot of sharing in the organization. It's a very tight-knit community, so if somebody has a question or an issue, personal or professional, we have a number of mechanisms they can use to reach out to each other and get the support and answers they need. The bulk of our membership falls into the boomer generation. My goal is to have all of them feel powerful as leaders and change agents. We don't want to grow beyond 300 members; we want to maintain the intimate community we have.

(Continued)

It's a very diverse group, from all over the country, including women in their 20s and in their 70s. We have women who are married, who are not married, who are divorced, single, never married, who have children, who don't have children, who have interesting different living arrangements. We have a very significant number of lesbian women. The members have different levels of wealth and different lifestyles in terms of how they use their wealth; some have multiple homes and jets, others live in one-bedroom apartments because they want to give all their money away. These women come together around a table. The differences in lifestyles don't really matter.

The passion that drives me, besides being in this incredibly wonderful community, is empowering women to come into their roles as leaders. I might see a woman who has inherited $25 million and her eyes are bugging out and she's embarrassed about it and doesn't know what to do and seems like a little mouse because she's afraid of her own shadow. And within a year or two, I hear her speaking in public about what she's doing and getting involved with boards of directors, I see her emerging as a leader.

One of the things we do is to help people recognize that philanthropy starts with $4 or $5 or $100 or $200 and builds from there. We've begun to partner with some international organizations; one is in Mexico, called Semillas, which means "Seeds." They are building a women's philanthropic movement in Mexico based on the concept that when you start to give, you begin to understand the value of giving and the power of giving and you change your life and it changes you.

We need to work as a movement, but we also need to pay a lot of attention to individual women, in meeting them where they are and helping them build community, and so supporting us all.[33]

As Marilyn Wechter, one of our interviewees, a Clayton, Missouri–based wealth counselor and psychotherapist, and a boomer herself, tells us: "We are experiencing a paradigm shift that may well change our lives forever. This new world has us moving from consumption to collaboration and we're starting to realize what's really important—and recognize how little it takes to make us feel valued."[34]

Reflection on Your Life

1. Think about how you want to live your legacy.
   a. Write down three happy endings you want to see happen in your life.
      1. _____
      2. _____
      3. _____
         _____
         _____

   b. What is one action you can take to make each happen?

2. Riches are more than money. Describe five riches in your life.

   a. _____

   b. _____

   c. _____

   d. _____

   e. _____

3. We all have angels and heroes in our lives. Who are some of yours, and how have they made a difference in your life?
   a. Childhood
      _____
      _____
      _____

   b. Pre–rite of passage (Before "post-menopausal zest")
      _____
      _____
      _____

   c. Post–rite of passage
      _____
      _____
      _____

4. Ask a friend how she makes a difference in your community. Share with her what you do.

5. Identify and take one action step to reengage a suspended dream.

2

Kitchen Table Values from Childhood

To keep a lamp burning we have to keep putting oil into it.
—Mother Teresa (1928–2004)

Our core values are our soul, the beliefs that influence how we behave. It is our values that serve as our guideline for how we conduct our lives, the decisions we make and . . . how we make them. Values are the beliefs and ideals that are shared by a culture about what is good and desirable or not.

In *Kitchen Table Wisdom,* author Rachel Naomi Remen, M.D., reminds us: "Everybody is a story. When I was a child, people sat around the kitchen table and told their stories. . . . It is the way wisdom gets passed along. Despite the awesome power of technology, many of us still do not live very well. We may need to listen to each others stories once again."[1]

When we were children, we sat around the table and watched Mom cook, and if we were not running wild all over the neighborhood, we sometimes joined in. By and large, for the early boomers, Mom was a stay-at-home mom. She was there when we came home from school, and our importance was emphasized by milk and cookies and her interest in how school activities had gone. We had her attention until Dad came home at 6 PM for dinner. Then we all ate around the kitchen table, and ideas were discussed. This is how we absorbed our moral compass. We learned our values from these times together and from observing our parents and other family members. Whether we grew up in urban or suburban working-class or middle-class homes or in economically poor communities where large extended families looked out for each other, there existed a "cultural sense of belonging." Psychologist Barbara Jensen defines this "belonging" as "paying attention to and being part of the world around us."[2] And by "paying attention," our values were shaped.

Values as a Bond of Commonality

As women from a multitude of economic and social environments began collaborating on an agenda for a more relationship-centered society, they searched for a foundation of commonality. They found it in their childhood experiences; experiences they could identify with as building blocks of values and virtues that would frame their lifelong destiny as a generation dedicated to an agenda of social change. These values are the building blocks that women in midlife, with a quest to leave a legacy for a better world, can leverage with their significant economic and financial resources.

Many women agree that early in life they embraced family experiences and traditions through observation and practices that led to the development of intrinsic and invincible sets of principles. Here was a generation raised with kitchen table values assimilated from family members as they carried out respectful acts of kindness, generosity, and courage, at home, at work, and in the community. As children, they grew up in a family culture that daily put into practice the classic virtues of prudence, fortitude, justice, and temperance. Unknowingly, Aristotle's philosophy was part of day-to-day living and the doing of good deeds, evidenced by living the Golden Rule and amplifying the three theological virtues of faith, hope, and love. It was common to set an extra plate for dinner, lend a few dollars to help a less fortunate neighbor till payday, tag along with Mom to sell cookies at the July 4 picnic, or have a vote in the family gathering on how monies were allocated. Indeed, in the nuclear family, the Golden Rule became the benchmark for resolution of contemporary life problems discussed at the kitchen table.

Betty Lahti, mother of two boomer daughters, considers the time she spent with her children during their early formative years "significant in shaping who they have become today as mothers and caring and concerned community leaders."[3] Known in her Florida Treasure Coast community as a wonderful example of how one individual can make a real difference, she lives her favorite James M. Barrie quote: "Those who bring sunshine into the lives of others cannot keep it from themselves." As her daughter boomer Pat Stryker, named by Colorado *Biz Magazine* in 2004 as the state's most powerful person, tells us, it was her childhood experiences that motivate how she uses her wealth to affect public policy and get people into government who can fend for the underserved and people who are suffering. Pat tells us:

> My parents led by example with the things they did for their community. I grew up with: it doesn't matter what you say, it's what you do. So watching them volunteer and be civic minded and having other people tell me or one of the other kids what they, my parents, did for others, those were the kind of things that made me go, "Oh, this is the way you're supposed to behave." Nobody ever sat down and said, "Now give your money to charity." It probably wouldn't have worked any way. Values . . . It was more of what they showed me. You have to look at yourself in the mirror at the end of the day. You have to live with yourself. I look at people who don't have the kind of wealth I do and I guess I want to help those people. It's not so much a hand out as a hand up, to where they can become self-sufficient. And I want smart people in office; who know what needs to be done. So helping good politicians get into office is a really big thing for me.

Pat is also a leader in getting her fellow citizens involved in the care and improvement of her community through the grants made to local nonprofit organizations from her Bohemian Foundation and the Pharos Fund.

Like many boomer women, Pat sees a lot of organizations "that really help women find their voice. "I tell you what," she says, "It's one of the best feelings in the world to see you've done something to make the world a better place."[4] Her feelings are echoed by San Francisco boomer Patricia Fripp. A native of England, Patricia came to this country to make her fortune as a hairdresser and she succeeded, not only as a hairdresser but eventually as one of the top, most sought after professional speakers in the country. Well respected for her business expertise, she brings a heart as big as California to her giving. She says, "My parents told me you give enough till it hurts a little," and she does. Her parent's kitchen table values influenced her and her brother, the well-known musician Robert Fripp, because of what they did, not what they said. Patty and Robert grew up in a household that clearly valued the idea that you cannot be too kind or too generous. Patricia, a former president of the National Speakers Association, is fond of quoting a peer, Nido Quebein, also a former president of that same organization and a philanthropist himself, who believes: "Always make as much money as you possibly can, so you can be even more generous."[5]

Boomers were brought up expecting the world to be theirs, and it was. They were groomed to think bigger and better and that success was their birthright. Most especially for the boomer woman, this first decade of the twenty-first century is a defining time. As older boomers grow into their retirement years and the younger wave hits their middle years, each is going through a rite of passage, whether it is the zest we mentioned or an appreciation of the reality that there are only so many years left to us. Boomers are questioning whether this is all there is and whether they really made a difference. "I don't want to be a drop in the bucket," declares Pat Stryker, "I want to make an impact!"

What is new today is an entire generation of women who for the first time in history have assets of time and/or money and the experience and desire to reshape the world through their carefully focused use and stewardship of these talents and treasures. We were brought up believing we had the power to design the change we wanted to see in the world, and we did to some extent. Women who came of age in the 1960s and 1970s wrote their own road maps for life's journey and laid the stones for their younger sisters to step on with more confidence and empowerment.

The tumultuous history of the 1960s served women well as a springboard for traveling uncharted paths to search for their new identity. Leading-edge boomers transitioned from adolescence to young adulthood at the same time as Woodstock, Vietnam, civil rights demonstrations, man's first steps on the moon, and the feminist movement. All of these events converged in a decade that served as a wake-up call for a nation experiencing a euphoric post-war boom economy. Granted, not all fully participated in the events of the time; nevertheless, they were still affected by the action of their peers who sought and demonstrated their desire to experience the prevalent spirit of freedom and self-expression. Seventy-eight million people born from 1943 to 1964 each shares part of the collective voice making up the chorus of attitudes, beliefs, and values, along with expected outcomes that define a generational cohort during their formative years, and that travels with them throughout their life stages.

On college campuses, in city streets, and in public institutions; boomers who were charged with energy for self-fulfillment and abundance swiftly replaced their parents' attitude of self-sacrifice and scarcity. Authors J. Walter Smith and Ann Clurman state that "with few exceptions the protest of the 1960s was about guaranteeing the bright promise of that era, not about rejecting the American Dream." As idealists in search of a destiny, they point out, "The rule-breaking endemic to that era was about overturning barriers to the self, not about overthrowing the system."[6] This point of view—that the purpose of the boomers' intensity was to set right the system rather than take it hostage—calls into question the validity of a more popular view expressed by many, including historians William Strauss and Neil Howe, who label the actions of the me generation the work of "narcissistic young-crusaders."[7] If anything, their idealistic actions may well have been their impetuosity living within a noble self. There is no doubt that this generation, shared passionate beliefs as well as erratic and exuberant behavior patterns as they grew up in tumultuous times, the Awakening era of the Millennial Saeculum. Anything and everything was possible then—and still is today as boomers transition into their next life phase with an urgent resolve to revive moral and virtuous ways of living life while confronting their own mortality.

Values as Our Roots

In the 1960s, we knew we could not trust anyone over 30, yet as the flower children who had issued that warning found careers, got married, and raised children or chose alternate lifestyles, we assimilated into the very system we had rebelled against. The earlier boomers were groomed to superhood and the expectation of having it all. Women boasted of their capability, not only buying the bacon, but cooking it and serving it with panache without even breaking a sweat. We knew we could change our universe and that we had the God-given mandate to do so. And there was no doubt that we had the power and the vision to craft our personal destinies.

First: we were born into a rich tradition. We stood on the shoulders of leaders of earlier years who paved the way for us to grow. We now recognize that those women sacrificed greatly to overcome hardship, discrimination, and ridicule to earn a voice for justice and equality. The aspirations, challenges, and triumphs of Elizabeth Cady Stanton, Lucretia Mott, Margaret Sanger, Margaret Mead, Eleanor Roosevelt, Betty Freidan, and many other pioneers place us in a more powerful position than any other collective group that came before us. We took their legacy and those of our mothers as our birthright.

The early boomers were profoundly influenced by the social and political events of the 1960s and 1970s, and those impressions helped craft our values. As Landon Y. Jones says:

> The older half of the generation was the most idealistic and the most easily disappointed. The second half (born after 1957) had diminished expectations. They were more realistic. They looked ahead and saw the world was crowded. They didn't think life would be handed to them on a silver platter. As for their cultural experiences, the older half was more euphoric. They were the youth society, the protestors. They had the sense that youth could take on the world, that rock and roll would bind us. The younger half had no such charge.[8]

Early boomers, who truly believed they could make major changes in the world, did. They felt they mattered, that values and morals mattered. This was the group that had better treatment and more attention from teachers, and had better education and college and job choices.

Alexander W. Austin, a former professor at the University of California at the Los Angeles School of Education, has tracked baby boomer attitudes since 1966. Periodically he sends a survey to approximately 300,000 college freshmen all over the country in which he asks what is most important to them. In 1967, just over 40% of the students stated they wanted to be well off financially. By 1984, the percentage was at 70%. Developing a meaningful philosophy of life dropped from 80% in 1967 to under 40% by 1984. The altruistic values of the early boomers gave way to the more ambitious financially oriented ones of the younger.[9]

For some, this relationship to money is a core value. In *The Soul of Money*, author Lynne Twist tells us of the experience of a native Achuar (an Amazonian indigenous group) named Chumpi. In 1995, several years after meeting Twist, Chumpi came to live with her and her family to study and learn more of our American culture. Twist says that "everywhere Chumpi went, he noticed the language of money filled the air, from billboards and advertisements and commercials…in conversations with other students he learned about their hopes, dreams, and prospects for as they put it, life in the real world, the money world." He began to see "that in America virtually everything in our lives and every choice we make . . . everything is influenced by this thing called money."[10] Yet even though "everything" in our lives is influenced by money, seldom do we talk openly or honestly about the power of money and how the fear of its lack affects how we make important decisions in our daily lives, including those about giving.

With 78 million boomers squarely in midlife and with 4.3 million having turned 50 in 2007, in a challenging economy, the milestone of age 50 has special significance. It truly calls into question the value structure set up by boomers themselves. Assets dwindled overnight, and many recognized that retirement might never be. And for a generation brought up to meditate, contemplate, and dream, that milestone brought new angst. It has stimulated a laser look at where and what has been accomplished, what is still needed to be done, and whether there is any real hope for the future.

For this idealistic yet materialistic group, midlife may well trigger a reexamination of unfinished business and a close look at values and the nostalgia that stimulates new change and new dreams. A study of nearly 3,000 boomers conducted for *Money* magazine shows that boomers are forming a new agenda, a reinvention of the American dream that emphasizes values other than just making money. It shows a leaning toward having fun, not just working hard, and making a difference in the community and the world.[11]

The study highlights that boomers want what they do to mean something to themselves and to others. Yet whether boomers will be able to achieve this great American Dream remains to be seen. First they have to be physically up to the challenge. Just money and materialistic goals are no longer the draw they once were for boomers; boomers have not been particularly diligent about saving for their later years. Less than half of those surveyed, 45%, said they probably would not be able to maintain their current standard of living in retirement. Our well-documented pattern of consumption and appetite for cars, houses, and goodies has certainly impacted this.

Still, boomers are avid dreamers. Their optimism has not dimmed, regardless of the slow job growth in the 1970s and the recessions of the 1980s and 2008. Boomers still have their youthful optimism and want the good life they have self-indulgently pursued. Because of their past work ethic, more boomers than not want to continue working even if they do not have to, and today many now have to. The meaning and direction work offers is still a major driving force in their lives.

The 1960s ideals of the early boomers have not disappeared. Boomers want to help others and to make a difference. When asked to define success, 37% of those in the study conducted by *Money* magazine said, "My contributions to my community." In fact, and good news for volunteer organizations, 4 out of 10 boomers believe volunteering is important. Boomers already account for the largest number of volunteers in our communities, with most of these women. Even more good news: They want their volunteering at retirement to be a significant part of their lives. James V. Gambone, author of *ReFirement: A Boomer's Guide to Life after 50,* reports: "They have tremendous built-in capabilities they want to lend to nonprofits. In their lifelong search for meaning, some boomers are already leading the way by creating Peace Corp Encore and Coming of Age, which recruits seniors for leadership roles in nonprofits."[12]

Values as Teachers

The values of doing good by changing the world that so characterize boomers may well be the midlife and aging boomers' most significant contribution. As Landon Jones, author of *Great Expectations,* says: "At this point maybe you realize that it wasn't all about your kid getting into Harvard or your status in the workplace. The big question is, What is my life about?"[13]

Author Thomas J. Stanley, in his book *Millionaire Women Next Door,* shares the story of Christy, a successful business owner who reflects on her early childhood learnings about the values of giving and saving:

> We [the entire family—Mom and Dad, sisters and brothers] would sit down the first Sunday afternoon of each month . . . . . . We would always take a look at Daddy's [monthly] paycheck and then start doing our homework [financial planning and income allocation]. I had two strong, fabulous parents. . . . I knew how hard it was for them to save for us to go to college. And we would all look at these staggering amounts . . . a whole lot of digits. Dad, he would look up and smile . . . and mother too . . . while the checks were being written [for the college funds]. I had tears in my eyes. . . . It made my heart break with joy. . . . It was not easy for them. But each time Dad would write a check [for the college fund], he would smile and say . . . I love writing checks that will pay these bills for tuition . . . you can do this for your kids someday.

Stanley tells us that Christy is now doing the same nurturing of kitchen table financial and giving values with her children. Although she and her family are financially more secure than her mom and dad, she teaches her children the same values she learned when she was a child.[14]

On numerous occasions during the research and collaboration of this work, both of us were reminded of how we each absorbed our own kitchen table values that form the foundation of a lifetime, generation by generation. Niki remembers an incident that occurred recently, as she was helping one of her grandchildren apply for a People to People grant. They came to a section on volunteering that constituted a hefty percentage of how the application would be evaluated. Concerned that there would be little to put into this section, other than the proverbial saving a stray, for instance, Niki listened in amazement as her sixth-grade grand-daughter listed over a dozen major contributions, from donating her beautiful curls every other year to the Children's Leukemia Association, to serving free Thanksgiving dinners at her family's res-taurant in Northern California wine country to itinerant field work-ers who would not have had the wherewithal for such a meal, to, at her own birthday parties, asking her friends to forgo birthday gifts and donate the money they would have spent to the leukemia cause she held dear.

Her initial and pleased surprise reminded Niki that this is what she had learned around her mother's kitchen table and what she had passed on to her own children. The memory brought back a fairly recent event that occurred when she was visiting her mother. As the two women were leaving one morning to run errands and visit with other family members, her mother asked Niki to pick up a stack of neighborhood weekly papers that were near the mailbox. While Niki drove, her mother folded the newspapers and placed them inside the plastic bags." Mom," she asked, "is this a new job you've taken on for some spare change?" Her mother laughed. "No, no, when we get back I'll put them on the doorknobs of the old people who wouldn't otherwise get one because they get picked up so quickly by others." Her mother, then a young 84, did not consider herself one of those same old people. Her mother, an active volunteer throughout her life, had passed on those kitchen table values. Niki was seeing the evidence in her granddaughter's contributions.

For many women, the nurturing of their passion and purpose in how they give time and money during midlife and beyond is tied directly to their childhood experiences. Although certainly the times are more complex, the concept of the nuclear and extended family as an inclusive definition of community and the personal need to express kitchen table values in giving have never been greater. Compassionate giving of the self, expressed through wealth and service, satisfies our greatest psychological needs: a sense of belonging and a sense of purpose. Abraham Maslow, the father of humanistic psychology, refers to the fulfillment of these needs as "self-actualization." The concept is most often associated with Maslow, although he credits the term itself to Kurt Goldstein (in *A Theory of Human Motivation*, written in 1943). "This tendency," writes Maslow, "might be phrased as the desire to become more and more what one is, to become everything that one is capable of being."[15] This desire to reach one's full potential through the giving of wealth and talent, to realize profound moments of the harmony of one's values and vision, is what it means to actualize the virtuous legacy we talk about during one's own lifetime. And from the actualization of "becoming everything that one is capable of becoming" rises the power to accept and embrace ownership for a mission to define a better world. The quest to find one's true self, one's *authentic voice,* is the transformative process that shines light into the dark depth of the soul from which springs forth wisdom and courage. This is a process with the capacity to ignite a creative sustenance and energy for the sacred work of the rebirth of a sustainable and just world. What has become a paramount destiny for women in this century is how their wealth and giving opens up the pathways to achieve this quest. And in doing so, women can identify and use the most efficient and effective channels through which both intangible wealth (values) and tangible wealth (assets) flow forward in the world and to the next generation. Psychologist Erik Erikson identifies this quest as humans' stage of "generativity," a time of self-generation concerned with future identity and development.[16]

Today as women from a multitude of economic and social environments reflect on generativity, they are drawn together by a common purpose to set an agenda for a more egalitarian and relationship-centered society. For many, those childhood experiences about values pertaining to money and giving serve as a unifying bond. Lucille Griffo, chief executive officer of the Tanasi Tennessee Girl Scouts Council, says: "The gift of giving got in my blood by osmosis; it was kind of a way of life, what you did by going along with your mom and dad when they helped out a neighbor, nothing fancy, just doing what was right."[17] And that spirit of "doing what was right" is still with her in her work, that of teaching girls how their gifts of time and service transfer into gifts of wealth as they mature and more resources are available to them. Often it is only when women share their childhood memories about family members and the many ways they carried out respectful acts of kindness, generosity, and courage at home, at work, and in the community that they realize how much of their own strength of character, leadership, and courage is a direct result of those observations. In many cases, those experiences serve as building blocks, not only to create their own strategic giving plan but also to empower them to carry out their mission as members of a generation whose destiny it is to fulfill an agenda of social change.

Boom-generation women grew up at the time of America's rise as a global superpower. The decade following World War II brought optimism, prosperity, and opportunity to a nation exuberant with a new American spirit. It was also a time "when rules changed as women entered adolescence and young adulthood," as documented by Susan B. Evans and Joan P. Avis in their book *The Women Who Broke All the Rules*.[18] And perhaps it is this tenacity to survive and thrive that has given boomer women the self-authority and aspiration to take the reins of leadership and use their intellect, intuition, and courage to co-create a more compassionate world. In their young adulthood, they forged ahead from conformity and convention through chaos, often living life on the cusp of social, political, sexual, and economic challenges that tested and validated their values. Taking different roads yet unified by their willingness to remain risk takers in search of solutions, leading-edge boomers continue to write the rules and valiantly question stereotypical categories that limit their will or isolate their power.

How Values Form

Values are personal and unique to each individual. They are convictions that serve as one's foundation for the ethos and morality that guide one's decisions. Values accumulate from childhood based on observation of parents, teachers, and other influential people. And many core beliefs come from personal religious training and doctrine. As we now know, a person's generational values programming happens during the first 21 years of life. Sociologist Morris Massey tells us, "What a generation is like later in life is closely related to what they are like when they were values programmed."[19] How values are expressed becomes the autobiography of life in word and deed. In wealth and giving, values drive the creative energy that opens the mind and heart to unlimited potential for growth and fulfillment of purpose. When people's values are in alignment with their actions, decisions are easier, vision and goals are clearer, and the resultant life is congruent. For boomers, moral causes and principles continue to direct their vision and increase the clarity of a righteous voice for ethical empowerment as they address their midlife crisis and beyond.

Values programming for women, according to psychologist Carol Gilligan, occurs during adolescence as their socialization takes on a more caring, connective, and compassionate personality. If allowed to mature through adulthood and later, this personality is their more authentic voice. Gilligan's work has spawned an ethics-of-care movement, asserting that women during adolescence cultivate moral and psychological tendencies that emphasize solidarity, community, and a caring about special relationships. According to Gilligan, the reason this movement has not been better assimilated up to this time in history is mainly due to prevailing social conventions requiring that girls must disassociate from their "authentic voice"[20] as they aspire to leadership roles in a patriarchal society. As society recognizes and responds openly to the current paradigm shift in leadership styles, expanding from the entrenched hierarchal modality to more holistic models and styles, the ethics-of-care movement finally may become a normative application in co-creative leadership processes inclusive of both men and women.

Five factors are converging to create a receptive environment for the ethics-of-care movement to gain validity in the philanthropic community.

1. More women are advancing to leadership roles; according to the Council on Foundations, today women head more than 50% of this country's foundations and hold 70% of funding development officer positions. This trend will continue as donors and executives arrive at a time in their life when they have the capacity and desire to find more meaning in their life and in their work—their *eudaimonia*, well-being, and happiness.

2. The nonprofit sector is becoming more viable and visible, as a first responder to social needs in alternative and creative ways that are simply not practical or efficient for the business or political sectors of society. Hybrid and blended styles of venture philanthropy and innovative collaboration between nonprofit and for-profit entities are synthesizing into a radical

and dynamic philanthropic culture for donors and organizations. Katherine Fulton and Andrew Blau conclude in their 2005 Monitor Group study: "Change flows through philanthropy when new ideas are adapted by key actors in a position to influence others, and philanthropy today is pulsing with new actors filled with energy, passion, and ideas."[21] Women will be leading as change agents—or, as some say, "hyper-agents"—in establishing a new paradigm for philanthropy.

3. The patriarchal legacy on which the industrialization of our nation was predicated is acknowledged as being less effective as the Information Age and globalization era continue to mature and open up alternative points of view and leadership mandates. The acceptance of co-creative leadership recognizing the value of complementary yin and yang qualities is becoming more mainstream in society. There is an ever-increasing acceptance that conscious capitalism, corporate social responsibility (CSR), and caring economics, the system of including human capital as an economic measurement, creates opportunity for change.

4. Currently women control the power of the purse and own 51.3% of all personal wealth in the country. By 2010, it is predicted that this number will increase to 60%. Women's life expectancy exceeds that of men by five years, and according to the National Center for Women and Retirement Research, 80 to 90% of women will be individually responsible for their finances as some point in their lifetime.

5. Women baby boomers are in their peak earning years, and women-owned businesses are the fastest-growing sector in the U.S. economy, representing 10.1 million firms, employing more than 13 million people and generating $1.9 trillion in sales as of 2008.[22]

What kind of "oil" do we women need to keep putting in the lamp to continue to shed light on the pathways to becoming more strategic and thoughtful givers of time, talent, and treasure in the second half of our lives? Some 40 years have elapsed since the late 1960s. There may be closets to clean out, dreams to dust off, and spirits to rekindle. The freedoms women won and the goals they achieved in the external world of career and family have led to this retrospective time in life when post menopausal zest kicks into high gear. How do we get in touch with our human spirit, and what would be some of the benefits of shifting perception from the materialist age of conspicuous consumption to a meaningful age of conspicuous compassion? How does such a shift support the quest to find *eudaimonia?*

The three key principles are passion, purpose, and power.

1. Giving with passion enriches integrity in life.

    This is a way to identify in our heart the greatest desires for the use of our time, talent, and treasure that we are blessed to control while we are on this earth and to remember to engage them in the spirit of justice, prudence, and moderation. Jung notes that later in life, individuals have the opportunity to look deeper into themselves and recover renewed vitality and zest.[23] Life at times can become confusing and complicated. Having the ability to center thoughts and deeds on conspicuous compassion can simplify life and free the mind and the soul to be attentive to seeing the needs of others and being open to creative solutions. It brings clarity of focus to what's important in life, and it can reprioritize values to complement vision and redirect wealth to bring more meaning into life and to the work we do.

2. Giving with purpose illuminates wisdom in life.

    This is the technique to focus on generativity—giving back, reaching out, cultivating strength in the next generation, and bridging the past and the future. It reflects the essence of our identity. Finding purpose in life can guide our spirit as we interact with individuals in thoughtful, caring ways as an influence for good. Sharing kindness and compassion creates a ripple effect as it radiates from one person to another, from one generation to another. It directs the flow of faith, hope, and love into the future. It is Maslow's self -actualization in action, "becoming everything one is capable of becoming." It enhances self-knowledge of who we are and how we want to interact with others as we live our life.

3. Giving with power releases freedom in life.

This is the method to take responsibility for decisions and take ownership of the outcome. It reflects the strength and courage to garner all possible resources to fulfill a mission and publicly acknowledge our values. Taking responsibility is empowering and makes us an enthusiastic participant in all of life's abundance. With freedom comes the confidence to build on experience and remain steadfast in principle. With freedom also comes the self-power to transfer the giving of time to the giving of money, not as a replacement but rather as a reinforcement and amplification of who we are and what is important in life. It provides the frame for choosing how we want wealth and giving to impact society.

Source of the Three Ps

The search for *eudaimonia* takes people inward to the soul and spirit to discover where their real values dwell. Quite often this reflective process involves meditation and writing about feelings and memories of significant experiences in life, the circumstances and the people involved, the outcome and what was learned. In most cases, given sufficient time to reflect on the episode, it becomes clear that certain intrinsic values guide specific behavior. This is not to say that situations are completely controlled by such values but that values do play a prominent role in determining relevant action. And the extent to which women know and regularly practice and live by their core values greatly determines their capacity to live in the fullness of life with purpose, passion, and power. When exploring how childhood experiences and kitchen table values impact current wealth and giving decisions, the values pyramid (see Exhibit 2.1) helps women center and focus as they map out their strategic giving plan. Self-knowledge of the evolution from childhood on of personal values in the context of generational issues allows for a more dynamic perspective of what brings meaning to women who want their values to live through their wealth. With self-knowledge comes an inner confidence from the soul to make and validate tough choices for the allocation of resources, especially when there is so much need in the world.

Path to Your Virtuous Legacy

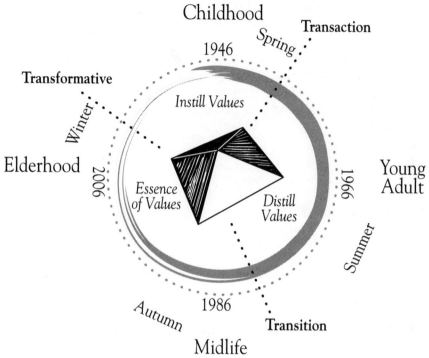

Exhibit 2.1 Values Pyramid
Illustrations by Elizabeth Huggins-Thompson.

The three stages to the values pyramid are:

Stage 1. Values are instilled.
    Transaction: How values are received in childhood are through the ways you:
    • Communicate
    • Observe
    • Act

Stage 2. Values begin to distill.

Transition: How values are processed from youth through midlife are by experiences in which you:
- Engage
- Challenge
- Adapt

Stage 3. Values reach essence.

Transformative: How values are transferred at the beginning of elderhood and beyond are through actions by which you:
- Impart
- Self-actualize
- Focus on generativity

Values Pyramid

"I find that as we move through each stage our core values intensify and refine," says Margaret, "quite like the slow aging of a vintage wine or the artistic creation of an elegant perfume. We appreciate and cherish the essence."

Use of the values pyramid as a reflective technique allows people to step back from their current giving plan and evaluate if and how it is in alignment with their core values. It provides the framework to assess if what is currently being done is the most efficient and effective use of available philanthropic money. It is a tool to prioritize values that serve as the cornerstone of an articulate, strategic, and decisive wealth-giving plan. Such a cornerstone can provide a point of reference when seeking out like-minded donors or evaluating a giving opportunity. Or it may provide the structure to reaffirm what values are most important to living a meaningful life. The ability for women to capture their vision for a better world through greater alignment with their values is one of the greatest hopes this world has of finding solutions to a dying ecosystem, the threat of nuclear annihilation, and worldwide disrespect of human rights. The virtuous legacy of a generation of women who stand at the crossroads of a season in life and a time in history may well be to fulfill the destiny of their birthright as "righteous self" leading a nation to find ethical and moral ways for a more compassionate and civil world.

The Muse Speaks

When Margaret developed the values pyramid technique for her clients, she first used it in her own life to examine her own values. She tells us:

Profile

One of the precious and lasting memories from my childhood centers around the performance and appreciation of classical music in our home. Like many other girls growing up in the 1950s, my mother insisted I take the piano lessons that she never did. We had an old upright and lived in a first-floor apartment of a three-story house with very understanding neighbors. My mom had a beautiful soprano voice, and she loved to sing in the church choir with me. She also sang with my grandmother in the local German Club Ladies Chorus. While I was not the best piano student, I did practice enough to accompany the German chorus, and when I was a teenager, at times when they went to a competition I took the train ride with them up and down the Hudson River Valley. To this day I still like to ride trains, and one of my fondest memories was a trip I took with my mom when she was 89. We spent three days "catching up on life" while riding on the rails from West Palm Beach, Florida, to Los Angeles, California, precious moments, indeed.

While I enjoyed playing the piano, the flute became my real love. I started with public school lessons when I was 10. Mom always reminds me that I first came home with a trumpet and asked her to sign the rental slip, but she decided giving the neighbors' ears a rest was more important. We rented a flute instead. Throughout high school years in Albany, New York, I was blessed by having a great band instructor, Luke Matthews, who encouraged my musical ability and helped me settle on a career in music. I was fortunate to receive a work scholarship to Boston University, School of Music, when tuition was $900 a semester. I got a job in the residence hall to pay for room and board. I did graduate and teach music education in a small New England town for one year, but like most young women of my generation, my life and career took other paths. I packed away my Haynes flute, bought in 1961, by my folks with a loan from Dad's life insurance policy, and went on with life in nonprofit management and fundraising. Twenty years later, I moved to Florida, with my old flute and new husband. Several years later, during the Thanksgiving holiday season, Dad, who had been quite ill for

(Continued)

many years, died and I found myself getting divorced. But I still owned my flute. Over the years, I would take it out of the case when I was down and play my favorite tunes to console my soul. Sporadically I played for church services and weddings (of course not my own). I now live in a town with a pretty good size community band, so a few years ago I sent my 40-year-old Haynes flute back to Boston for an overhaul to remove the dents and replace the pads. When I got it back all shiny and new, I practiced a bit more and went down to the community center to audition for a seat. I got in. The band rehearses on Monday night. When I am not traveling, I am in my chair with flute in hand. What does all this have to do with the values pyramid? It was while I was designing the pyramid for my clients that I realized where my values and love for harmony, beauty, classical music, creativity, education, persistence, and trains came from—bingo! My childhood! And while I did not fully pursue a music career, music was there always as part of my life. It helped me through adversity, the loss of loved ones, changing economic situations, and life-altering situations.

How does this relate to wealth and giving? Recently I revised my will and estate planning documents and set up a charitable remainder trust with a scholarship for a female flute student to Boston University and a bequest to Sigma Alpha Iota International Music Fraternity (SAI). So by getting in touch with my values, I have become more strategic in my giving, and feel more joy in my life knowing I can help a student start on her musical path, just as a scholarship got me started on my life journey, and also leave a legacy for SAI. No matter if it's mini-money or megabucks, funding a flute scholarship or leading a cause to stop global warming, the values pyramid works to help each of us get in touch with the childhood values that give shape and insight to our current and future wealth allocation and giving decisions.

What Is Your Story?

In your life timeline, divide your life span into three time periods. Identify core values that have become more meaningful in your life as you travel on the journey toward your virtuous legacy.

Birth To Age 21 instill Values (What and Who)

1. _____
2. _____
3. _____

Age 22 To 59   Distill Values (How and Why)

1. _____
2. _____
3. _____

Age 60+:   Essence of Values (Action and Legacy)

If you have not reached this stage, look back at the first two stages and see how they may be leading you to many of the decisions you now make about the use of your time, talent, and treasure. This reflection can point you in new directions or confirm the path you have chosen.

1. _____
2. _____
3. _____

Build Your Legacy Life Circle

The legacy you leave is the life you live. Your legacy will be the sum total of the experiences that make up the sections of your Legacy Life Circle (see Exhibit 2.2). The exercises below are tools to help you get a richer and more colorful snapshot of each part of your life and the experiences which form your values and give you the memories you cheish. In this fast-moving world, it is easy to forget the moments that cause us to be and act as we are today. Completing each "slice of life" can rekindle the past. Find a photo of yourself from each life stage to put in the appropriate frame. Choose a quiet time, a sacred space, and give yourself permission to reflect and reminisce. For the most benefit we suggest that you make a separate time to complete each "slice of life," and work in sequence: childhood (see Exhibit 2.3), young adulthood and midlife (see Exhibit 2.4), and elderhood (see Exhibit 2.5). As you complete each section you may find certain recollections spark other remembrances.

Life Circle

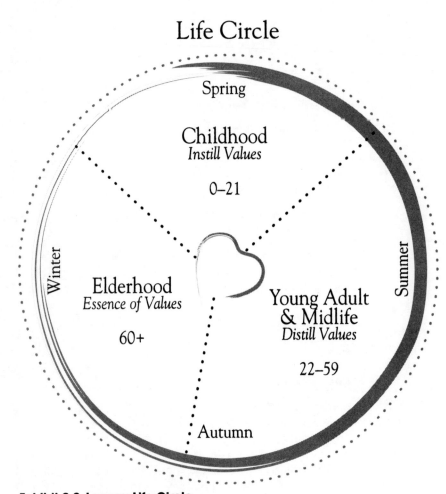

Exhibit 2.2 Legacy Life Circle
Illustrations by Elizabeth Huggins-Thompson.

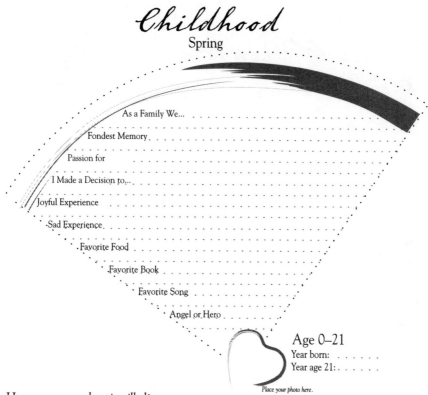

Childhood
Spring

As a Family We...

Fondest Memory

Passion for

I Made a Decision to,...

Joyful Experience

Sad Experience

Favorite Food

Favorite Book

Favorite Song

Angel or Hero

Age 0–21
Year born:
Year age 21:

Place your photo here.

How were my values instilled?

Exhibit 2.3 Childhood Slice of Life
Illustrations by Elizabeth Huggins-Thompson.

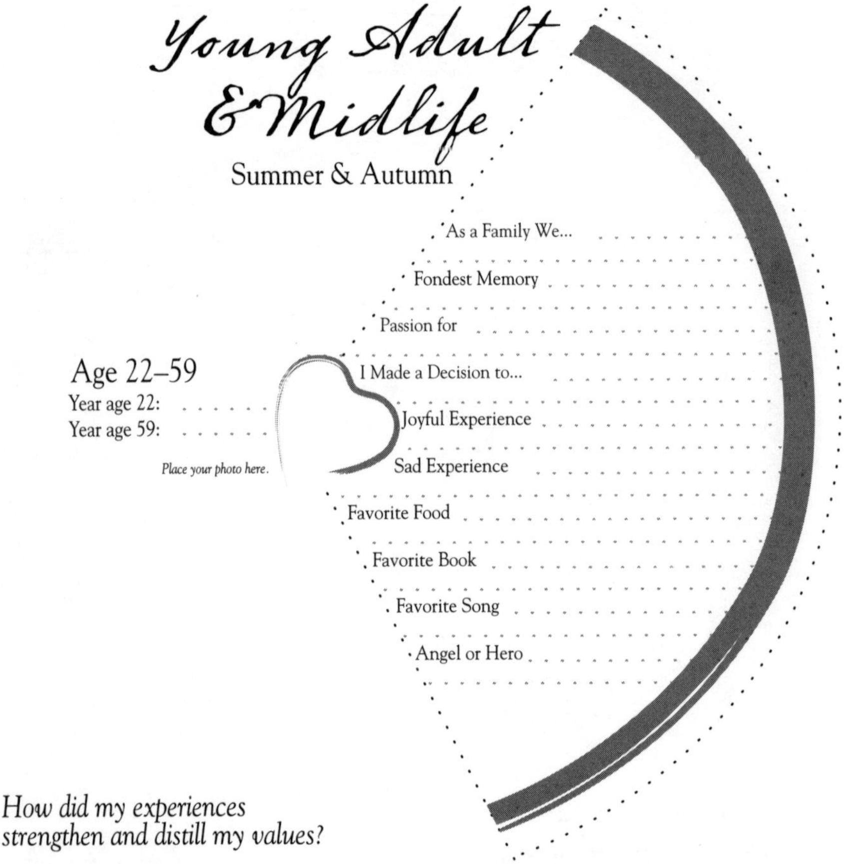

Young Adult & Midlife

Summer & Autumn

As a Family We...

Fondest Memory

Passion for

Age 22–59

Year age 22:

Year age 59:

I Made a Decision to...

Joyful Experience

Place your photo here.

Sad Experience

Favorite Food

Favorite Book

Favorite Song

Angel or Hero

How did my experiences strengthen and distill my values?

Exhibit 2.4 Young Adult and Midlife Slice of Life

Illustrations by Elizabeth Huggins-Thompson.

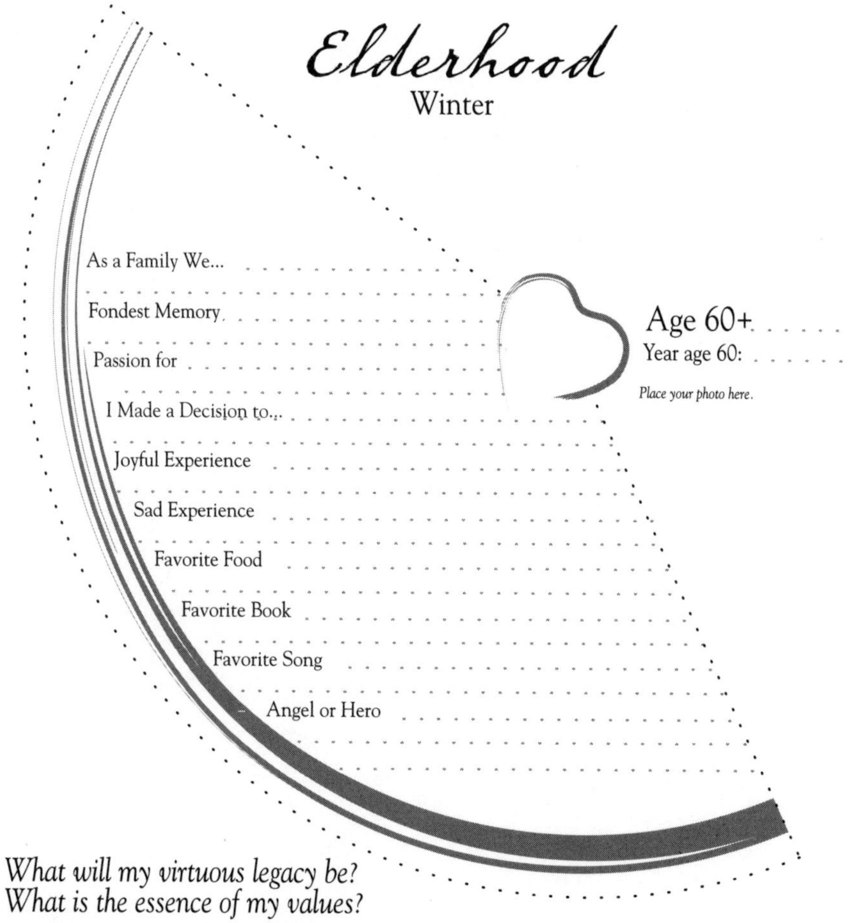

Elderhood
Winter

As a Family We...

Fondest Memory

Passion for

I Made a Decision to...

Joyful Experience

Sad Experience

Favorite Food

Favorite Book

Favorite Song

Angel or Hero

Age 60+

Year age 60:

Place your photo here.

What will my virtuous legacy be?
What is the essence of my values?

Exhibit 2.5 Elderhood Slice of Life

Illustrations by Elizabeth Huggins-Thompson.

3

Affluence, Influence, and Altruism

The good we secure for ourselves is precarious and uncertain until it is secured for all of us and incorporated into our common life.
—Jane Addams (1860–1935)

For women, the first decade of the twenty-first century is an exciting time: euphoric for some, burdensome to many, and challenging for all. As the undercurrent of uncertainty shifts in all aspects of women's lives, our ability to impact with our giving opens up opportunities for a generation that still has an uncompleted agenda. It is a generation that still wants to make a difference and leave a legacy that is not associated with the narcissism they were known for.

A sizable group of women are "waking up to the fact that we have the voice, power, and money to bring to the table," says Jennifer Buffett, daughter-in-law of billionaire investor Warren Buffett.[1] Part of the legacy of boom-generation women may well be as alchemists for altruism in today's society, by using the most obvious channel women have to effect positive change: their pocketbooks. The synergy among affluence, women's wealth, and their altruism is beginning to converge into a heady mixture as women look for ways to influence. More and more women are starting to realize they have the power that comes with controlling 60% of the nation's wealth. Many recognize it is time to seize the "gold ring," get off the merry-go-round, and truly get on with a purposeful life. "Philanthropy gives women a platform and a place of leadership in a world," says philanthropist and Inspired Legacies founder Tracy Gary, "that still largely has not permitted women to fully lead, especially behind the doors where a great deal of money or power still is stored."[2]

Many of us can relate to the feelings expressed by fashion designer Sigrid Olsen, in a recent *New York Times* interview: "Being a child of the 1960s, I still have that idealist in me, that I think I can pull it all together and give people an uplifting positive message and still be an entrepreneur and a capitalist at the same time."[3] Yet pulling it all together is what many women in this first decade of the twenty-first century who are standing at the crossroads facing major shifts in the economy, their lifestyle, and their family responsibilities have imposed on themselves. Many women of this generation have decided very deliberately to pull it all together, when their generation is caught up in an urgent search for a moralistic rebirth in society.

Marilyn Wechter, one of our interviewees, is a wealth counselor and psychotherapist from Clayton, Missouri, who believes we are in a major societal paradigm shift. The economy and our values are shifting us from the idea of consumption to collaboration. Says Wechter:

> We need to start defining ourselves as citizens as opposed to consumers, as people who are interconnected and right now we are all in the same boat. If we come out of this and just repeat what we have done before—then "shame" on us. We need to redefine our entire system, of sustainability of the environment and for other people with a sense of interconnectedness and with a responsibility for one another. Women are charged with connection. Our sense of ourselves is defined by our sameness to one another, compared to the male identity which is formed by its difference from the other. As women we want by nature to connect and times of extreme anxiety make this need even stronger. Women have a tendency to work cooperatively, and harnessing that kind of energy can make an enormous difference, especially in challenging times. For women of our generation philanthropy underscores even more the importance of funding things we feel passionate about. We're learning it's not about things. Things don't define us, leaving a legacy does.[4]

Consumption to Collaboration

Connect, collaborate, and change are three of the six Cs that authors Sondra Shaw-Hardy and Martha Taylor first identified in their 1995 book, *Reinventing Fundraising: Realizing the Potential of Women's Philanthropy*. In their extensive research into identifiable character traits that define how women's giving style is distinguishable from men's, the authors find that women want to join with others in identifying a need and consult with a variety of experts as they seek practical solutions for issues that they are passionate about changing for the greater good.[5] Colleen Willoughby, cofounder and for many years the president of the Washington Women's Foundation, was among the vanguard of women who championed the giving circle model in the mid-1990s to "address the growing new donor group of women emerging in the new millennium." Willoughby's model was based on the desire to "create a multiplier effect by giving together; allowing each individual dollar to be leveraged for greater impact than if it was given alone."[6]

Marilyn reminds us that today it is even more important to fund those things we feel passionate about. "It's important to feel empowered by having something to offer. So maybe if I can give $5 a month to some organization that can then feed a family, that feels pretty darn good. It reminds me of how we're all connected, how we as women are connected, and today that is empowering." Her sentiments were echoed recently by another boomer, television personality and philanthropist Oprah Winfrey, speaking at a college commencement, when she said: "Success is not about having a jet, though that's nice. It's about making a difference by being of value to someone's life; it's about contribution to our world."[7]

Scarcity

Women have begun to find their authentic voice and use their capacity to connect, to leverage their abundance, and to use their influence to reinvent themselves as agents of change. However, even as studies show that this is a time of affluence for women, many are concerned that there still is not enough. A fear creeps into some women's thinking about their money and how to handle it. Wechter and others call it the "bag lady syndrome." She reminds us:

> This is a fear that means we are alone and unloved. We're so afraid of being without and a big part of that is that we are taught we're someone because of what we have, what we own, what we look like. We had so much, we were coddled and anything and everything we wanted was ours—is it [Malcolm] Forbes who said, he who has the most toys wins? Well, we're learning it's not about the toys. Being able to part with things means that one is relatively secure and the fact is more will flow again. Giving implies generativity. That it's cyclical and it is constantly replenishable.

Wechter argues against a world of scarcity:

> Contrary to what economists would have us believe, we live in a world of sufficiency. There's enough, it's just how we allocate it and I think it's one of the things that we have been whipped into a frenzy about, that there's not enough. Not enough love, not enough money, not enough resources. This is part of what I mean when I talk about a paradigm shift. I'm not saying that people who work hard are not entitled to good things and material comfort, but if we define ourselves by our material comforts there will never be enough. Is it important that the pants we wore last season aren't wide enough for this year's fashions? Is a $1000 handbag really going to define our happiness?
>
> I think that if women of our generation were able to see this money-scarcity fear and get over it—we're talking about smart capable women who have a bag lady fear—a not enough fear, smart capable women who have the capacity to know better. What we don't want is to make women feel ashamed that they don't get it, that they haven't gotten it. What you want to be able to say is you can learn, you can change this, you can think about this differently. Getting smart and unhooked about money and the conflicts about it is a right of passage and a transformational experience. Women can't afford to be ambivalent about money.

Fifty years ago, Simone de Beauvoir said that women will always be the *Second Sex* until they take financial responsibility for their own lives.[8]

Wechter agrees.

When women take care of their financial health and their psychological relation to it they will live life on their own terms. If, however, they avoid taking responsibility for this important area they relinquish their power to forces outside themselves. Money is power and it's neither masculine nor feminine to seek one's effective power source. It's merely human. Money is a tool. It can be used for all sorts of things. It can control people, intimidate them, buy freedom, all sorts of things. It depends on what you want it to do.

If there were anything I could say to women as it relates to how they think, feel, and act about their money it would be that first they see themselves as a source of agency. Having agency is the ability to make things that are important in one's life happen. It's about exerting power over one's life. When we feel a sense of agency, which is the very opposite of powerlessness, then we have more power to control or direct our lives in the direction we want it to go. For many women, our power has come from whom we're with. And until we start seeing ourselves as our own power source, we will limit our capacity to make the difference we so desire to and to give to what's important to us.[9]

In the past, many economists have conditioned us to believe in a mind-set of scarcity, often brought about by prevailing economic systems that use fear and competition to control and exploit the resources necessary to maintain power. This scarcity thinking is often at the expense of emulating and embracing the spirit of love and collaboration necessary to create more abundance and equality. Emotions can play a central role to keeping us in that mind-set and perpetuating the scarcity myth. This is especially true for women who are more familiar and comfortable with the traditional giving of their time rather than using their money as power and as a forceful commodity to bring lasting change to the economic, political, and social agendas in their community and around the world. For many women, the emotional paralysis of the heart keeps the pocketbook locked even as the spirit of abundance dances all around it. It is only when we recognize scarcity as a myth and confront our fears and the destructive and limiting nature such a mind-set has on our abilities to be as effective as possible in the use of our resources that we come to terms with scarcity and realize its defective logic. And by coming to terms with the myth of scarcity, women more quickly move on with confidence not only to write larger checks but also to invest more of their financial assets into programs and organizations working for a better and more just world.

What is the scarcity myth? Lynne Twist, in her book *The Soul of Money*, describes it this way:

> In the conversation for scarcity we judge, compare and criticize; we label winners and losers. We celebrate increasing quantity and excess. We center ourselves in yearning, expectation, and dissatisfaction. We define ourselves as better-than or worse-than. We let money define us, rather than defining ourselves in a deeper way and expressing that quality through money.

In her experience with the Hunger Project, Twist believes, "The words we say create our thoughts and our experiences and even our world."[10] Thoughts driven by scarcity keep us from leveraging "the power of the purse" to achieve goals, live purposeful lives, and use affluence to do what we know we can do to make a difference in society.

Abundance

There are signs that the age-old myth of scarcity is being replaced by a more abundant or "sufficiency" mind-set as boom-generation women define a new giving culture for themselves and the use of their newly acquired affluence. The power dynamics and conversations around money are undergoing transformative meaning as women gain confidence in their ability to manage and direct greater sums of money for good. As part of their effort to crash the glass ceiling, they have also cashed in, setting a new tone for how their generation would participate in "money talk." It is no longer taboo to discuss inherited or earned money and how the power of money can change the world for the better. For many women, their intense desire and enthusiasm to support causes with their wealth greatly overshadows the more outdated conventional cultural norms about gender and money talk. Conversations cut through convention. A new mind-set evolves around what money can do, not just what money is worth.

This ripple effect is growing from a trickle to a torrent; the more women talk about what the power of their money to do good can do, the more this becomes the "right thing" to do. And talk leads to action and the realization that there is not a scarcity of wealth but an abundance that is created by putting money into flow in society. And putting money into flow, according to author Deepak Chopra, is good for the spirit and the world. "When you practice generosity, it relaxes the spirit, provides a sense of well being and facilitates the flow of money in and through life; ultimately it makes your world a better place."[11] As Marilyn Wechter called it, "this generativity," this paradigm shift, is worth noting; those boomer women's values direct the use of money and drive this conversation from just talk to action and sufficiency. In her book, *The Soul of Money,* Twist says, "In the conversation for sufficiency, we acknowledge what is, appreciate its value, and envision how to make a difference with it. We recognize, affirm, and embrace. We celebrate quality over quantity. We center ourselves in integrity, possibility, and resourcefulness. We define our money with our energy and intention."[12]

As our generation matures in age and further develops its network of like-minded individuals who are comfortable and confident in leveraging their financial power, so will its ability and determination to garner energy and reengage civility, morality, and ethics in the community for its vision for a better world. "Enlightened capitalism" is how University of South Carolina business school benefactor Darla Moore calls using money to improve the world. In 1988, she donated $25 million to the USC business school, which was then renamed the Moore School of Business. In 2002, she founded the Palmetto Institute, an independent nonprofit agency dedicated to increase the wealth of every South Carolina citizen. In 2005, Moore contributed an additional $45 million to expand the business school named after her.[13]

For the next 30 years, women and men of the boom generation will be the dominant economic, political, and social power in our nation. Like Darla Moore, women are writing new rules for virtuous philanthropy and backing them up with the power of the purse.

The stage is set for leading-edge boom-generation women to fund and champion a new community of voluntary philanthropic, educational, and service agencies designed and supported by a vibrant tapestry of affluence, influence, and altruism. Examples are being set by women such as former president and chief executive officer (CEO) of eBay, Inc., Meg Whitman, who recently made a gift of $30 million toward the construction of a new residential college at her alma mater, Princeton University. The new college, to be named Whitman College, will enable the school to expand its undergraduate programs. "The university inspired me to think in ways that have guided me throughout my life," said Whitman. "I'm pleased that my gift will benefit the institution for generations to come."[11]

The presence of women in the workforce in leadership positions, as entrepreneurs and business owners, lends itself to a new interconnectivity with a larger circle of decision makers helping to reshape and revitalize our "social capital." Civic engagement, community activities, grassroots organizations, and a plethora of active and dedicated volunteers are benchmarks of a healthy and vibrant community rich in social capital. Political scientist Robert Putnam, in his book *Bowling Alone: The Collapse and Revival of American Community*, maintains that our nation stands at a crossroads challenged to restore the civic engagement that now is decaying.[15] In this globalized world, a sense of community takes on more significant meaning and need, not for geographical definition but rather for cultural definition. It is in this environment that women, the nurturers, gatherers, and keepers of "society's sacred torch," stand ready to find solutions as part of their unfulfilled agenda to leave a legacy. Idealistic boomer women are eager to restore social capital. Leading-edge boomers accept their charge to define a culture community rich in diversity and united in spirit. As de Tocqueville observed on his tour of early America, "It is women who make mores."

Influence

Empowered by their newly acquired money, their ability to influence, and the abundance to do so, women are gaining momentum to effect the transformation of a community by first shifting the consciousness of their own soul. Many women who have achieved success in the workplace have decided it is time to take a look back at their family roots and reconnect, according to psychologist Barbara Jensen, with their "cultural sense of belonging."[16] Regardless of where we were raised or the size of our current paycheck, many midlife women still remember growing up in a neighborhood where everyone looked out for each other, where the neighborhood kids walked to school, could roller skate on the sidewalk and count on a neighbor to offer a glass of Kool-Aid on a hot summer day. There was a sense of community, of belonging, safety, and caring for one another. As midlife women reconnect to their culture of belonging, it helps set up models for envisioning a more compassionate and sustainable world. In her book *The Promise*, written with Caille Miller, Oral Lee Brown tells the inspirational story of how in 2003 her dream to make a difference in the lives of 19 first-grade students at a local elementary school came true. In 1987, Brown, a sharecropper's daughter with an annual income of $45,000, promised each of the 19 students that if they finished high school, she would fund their college education. With great sacrifice and determination, she saved, invested her money, created the Oral Lee Brown Foundation, and for the next 12 years deposited $10,000 annually into the trust. In 2003, that money enabled the first student to graduate from college, the first in her family to do so. Brown continues to adopt a new classroom every four years and proves that as more and more boom-generation women reflect on ways to give back and share their concerns and dreams, a collective voice is quickly being put into motion.[17] And it is this concerned and compassionate voice of community that allows for social capital to flourish, personalized by one's beliefs and values. This voice shares a commonality in every area, economic, social, and political that needs change, and at an opportune time when our nation is looking for a new direction to weather our winter of our discontent.

Altruism

In these challenging economic times, as women identify with a more purposeful life, a realignment of spending habits seems to be reinforcing the new consciousness of the soul. More thought is being given to putting assets toward building a better world rather than just consuming. Author Thomas J. Stanley, in the *Millionaire*

Women Next Door, finds a direct and significant correlation between women's ability to increase their altruism for the issues they care about and the values they apply to their lifestyle. How women spend and invest money mirrors who they are and what they believe is important in life. When he compared the rate at which net worth increased over time for businesswomen similar in age and income, the increase in net worth was greater for those who gave away 10% of their annual income than for those who gave away 1% or less. Women who gave a greater percentage of their income to charity also allocated and invested more of their money to long-term assets that increased in value; those who gave less allocated and spent more of their income for short- term products that depreciated rapidly. And those women who gave 10%, according to the research, "seem to get greater satisfaction from giving rather than consuming more and more."[18]

Psychotherapist Marilyn Wechter believes that moving away from boomer narcissism is important to our mental health, not just to our net worth. From her perspective, altruism is about exercising one's own self-interests. In her interview she says:

> I think women need to learn that it's not bad to have self-inter-ests of their own. I'm just asking us all to rethink what that is and to recognize that exercising our self interest is taking care of the planet and our sisters. It's going outside and beyond our immediate world.

This alignment of vision and values is strengthened as women find reassurance and confidence in knowing who they are, and reflect on their life blessings and realize that achieving something with their gifts is better than spending on a consumer-driven life-style. It is about recognizing that it is not only self-interest to use one's resources for the common good but that it is also altruis-tic and fulfilling to express what is in one's heart through one's pocketbook.

At a recent conference one of us attended, a woman delegate started her talk by saying "I'm having fun with my money. I'm giving now so I can have the pleasure of watching it make a difference." In 2005, when University of Kansas (KU) graduate Sally Hare- Schriner heard Tracy Gary speak at a Women Philanthropists for KU event, she remembers thinking how wonderful it would be if she could give money away in her lifetime and see it grow and multiply and be part of this. "I was sitting there, thinking 'I don't need this money to live on so why not? Why wait until I die? Just do it!' and so I did."[19] Schriner's experience is part of the new spirit and culture that is open to the first generation with the passion, power, and purpose to just do it, if you have the means. And part of being able to have meaningful "fun" with money is because this generation has the capacity and motivation to break free of the century-old consumerism stigma that sociologist Thorstein Veblen labeled as American society's insatiable "conscious consumption," our never-ending appetite for more and more opulent "stuff." According to Veblen, consumption is a waste if it "does not serve human life or human-well being on the whole."[20] The term first appeared in 1899 in Veblen's book *Theory of the Leisure Class*, but it still remains appropriate to describe the materialism and consumerism that perpetuates the myth that self-worth is defined by buying power. In truth, this never-ending cycle of consumption is what has hastened our arrival at the winter of our discontent. As Wechter asks, "How much is enough?"

We are bombarded by thousands of messages thrown at us by modern-day media—from TV to radio and encroaching ever further in elevators and at the gas pump—to buy. Insidious marketing messages insist that happiness can be found in a package, a product, and a new pair of designer shoes or a flashy red convertible. Increasingly, the studies being conducted on happiness say the opposite. In *The How of Happiness*, prize-winning psychologist and researcher Dr. Sonja Lyubormirsky tells us:

> One of the reasons for the failure of materialism to make us happier may be that even when people finally attain their monetary goals, the achievement does not translate into an increase in happiness. In fact[,] materialism may distract people from relatively more meaningful and joyful aspects of their lives, such as nurturing their relationships with family and friends, enjoying the present, and contributing to their communities. Finally, materialistic people have been found to hold unrealistically high expectations of what material things can do for them.[21]

Lyubormirsky talks about hedonic adaptation—which means some "thing," a purchase—may make us happier for a while, then we quickly become adjusted to it and it is part of the ordinary, not something that continues to imbue happiness. So it is not money, not things, not changes in jobs, homes, or people that make us permanently happy. We have to keep adding and changing—more stuff, and it is all temporary anyway.

It seems that more midlife women finally understand this and are turning a deaf ear to the Madison Avenue public relations hype. Women are jumping off the glitzy merry-go-round to experience the merits and happiness of how their heart can sing through strategic, compassionate giving. They are empowering themselves by looking inward to find meaning in their lives by their actions and deeds, not outwardly through things. As women succeed in their quest of virtuous philanthropy, a new optimism is unleashed that a cohort of women so great in number, so powerful in affluence or influence, may, for the first time in our nation's history, set a new course away from materialism toward a more just, spiritual, and transformational existence for humankind. And in setting a new course, they are torchbearers for generations to follow. They are truly blazing new paths away from conspicuous computation toward conspicuous compassion and in doing so have begun to restyle the rules of philanthropy.

Our interviews continually show that living virtuously—meaning connected to the community, engaging social capital, and giving back in meaningful ways—as opposed to the "old" boomer values of consumption and narcissism brings out the goodness in people and rewards both the giver and the receiver. It brings joy to man- and womankind on both the giving and the receiving end. Doing virtuous deeds and being recognized as a community citizen brings balance to altruism and egotism and moderation to life. It allows each of us to define and enjoy our *eudaimonia*.

Characteristics of Virtuous Philanthropists

In our research, we have found that women, who knowingly choose the path to make a difference in their own unique style through their giving of time, talent, and treasure, consistently identify five character traits that guide them on the way to their authentic social and personal legacy.

Practicing Inconspicuous Consumption

Each day they tell others—by their actions, spoken or not—what their priorities are. Their lifestyles reflect the values they believe are important to support with their resources. Many have found that collaborating with others through inconspicuous consumption and working to meet community needs has brought profound harmony to their life and has elevated their wealth of self.

Abused and neglected children had virtually nowhere to go in Martin County, Florida, 20 years ago. But in 1985, LaVaughn Tilton-Drysdale, using the principles of collaboration and inconspicuous consumption with the help of a few caring people who knew a few more caring people, changed all that. The idea originally came to Tilton-Drysdale while she was watching a training video in order to work with parents suspected of child abuse and neglect. "Immediately my interest turned to the children," she said. "What happens to one of these children if their home is unsafe for living?" She managed to rally the community to the idea, raising money and in-kind donations from builders and landowners. In 1989, Hibiscus House, a safe place to send children removed from their homes, opened its doors. Today it has expanded to a multimillion-dollar 36-bed facility. When asked about her leadership role, Tilton-Drysdale says, "I may have made the decision that something needed to be done, but I didn't do it alone, the community did it."[22]

Confident in Their Decisions

Every day, virtuous philanthropists reinforce their commitment to the issues and concerns they support by not allowing adversity to drag them down. These perennial optimists lead others through uncharted territory in search of lasting solutions to systemic problems confronting the well-being of their world. They remain restless until their goal is met and exceeded. They remain responsible for their actions yet open to working with others, and are both leaders and followers for the same cause, knowing and respecting all diversity of thought and individualism.

Such an example of a confident, virtuous philanthropist is Margaret Smith, CEO of Dormus, one of the San Francisco Bay area's largest independently owned kitchen and home accessories stores. In 2000, she was honored by the Women's Hall of Fame, which recognized her work as a past president of the National

Association of Women Business Owners (NAWBO) and for her work in 1995–1996 negotiating a $1 billion loan program for entrepreneurs with Wells Fargo Bank. Smith is the immediate past chair of the Center for Women's Business Research. As an entrepreneur, she herself has been generous with her time and talent and money for over 30 years. Much of her volunteer leadership work is for the benefit of entrepreneurs worldwide. "My volunteerism at the center is more cause-based. I really believe in the causes of women entrepreneurs and in the validation of the social, economic, and political impact they are making on the world and the world economy."[23]

One of the concerns Smith has championed for several years is how to build positive messages and focus on solutions built on what is right, not on what is wrong, in our world.

> People still want to make a difference, they still want to volunteer, and they still want to adjust or address social issues. We're just focusing on what is wrong rather than celebrating what is right and moving forward with it. Women entrepreneurship, that is right. There's a whole culture of financially independent, thinking people who have inculcated special values into the workforce. It's a $4 trillion business. That's what's right. So let's encourage this right and move forward.

Consistent in Their Values

The investments that virtuous philanthropists make through their wealth, wisdom, and work reflect personal beliefs as well as values they feel strongly will create a more just and humane community. The entries in their checkbook registers reflect the issues they support. The money in their investment portfolios is allocated to corporate and social institutions that practice responsible corporate citizenship in their conduct of business. Volunteer time is specific and focused on the causes that they have identified as important and that reinforce their shared family and community values and the giving of their other resources of money and talent.

Business owner and entrepreneur Jody Potts Bond gives us another example of how she puts the principles to work on a daily basis. Bond tells us that she has been blessed with a wonderful family. It is always a joy to visit her jewelry store, Just Gold in Stuart,

Florida, where on many occasions a contented grandchild sits happily in a playpen while mother and grandmother attend to customers. As a community activist, Bond believes in family values and in the economic vitality of a community fostered by a good education system. A former school board member and past president of the Soroptimist International of Stuart, Florida, she grew up in a loving family where "we always looked out for each other, worked hard, and encouraged each other to do our best at home and in school." For Bond, family, education, and community were and still are her most cherished values.

"I prefer that my money help families. I think more than anything about family issues, whether they are domestic problems or children's issues, that's where my first allegiance lies," she says. "These are values I hope my daughters and grandchildren will inherit from me as we work side by side in the business. I want them to take an active part in making the business decisions of where we volunteer our time or give financial support in the community." When it comes to her philanthropy, Bond is very focused and direct and purposeful.

> If I think there's a real need out there, I research it; I go over it; and I decide what I want to do about it. Do I want to give it my time? Do I want to write them a check? Do I want to give them material goods? I have to determine if there's a real value, a real need. I primarily only give to local charities, because I want to make sure those dollars go to the individuals or the entity that needs it. And I am the first to recognize that when you do it, you feel good about yourself, you feel good that you can share with another person, that you can help someone that needs help.[24]

Belief in Their Dreams

Virtuous philanthropists have an unshakable faith in their ability and in the capacity of others to achieve and sustain the goals they want their philanthropy to achieve. Their vision is long term, and considers that what is started by one generation may need to be completed by another. They see their life story as an inspiration for others and a legacy of significance for family, friends, and the community.

These women bring harmony and balance to their lives and to the lives of others, one person at a time.

Beverly Holmes, former senior vice president for Retirement Services at MassMutual Financial Group, now chair of the Center for Women's Business Research and a member of the Massachusetts Board of Elementary and Secondary Education, not only believes in her dreams, she has seen them come true during her life. At a very early age she made a conscious decision that philanthropy would be part of her life. "I wanted to save women and children from all of the atrocities going on in the world that negatively affect their lives, and I still believe I can make a difference," says Holmes. Soon after graduating from college and finding that employment opportunities in the nonprofit sector were great but the pay was not, she turned instead to pursue a career in the financial service industry, since her undergraduate degree was in human resources with a special interest in finance. That was 30 years ago. From then to now, as Holmes has been a successful leader adding billions in assets, and new revenue, and profits to her company, she always held very dear her focus and attention on the nonprofit and education sectors, especially areas that impact women and children. Says Holmes:

> It was a conscious decision on my part that giving back was something that I would do the rest of my life, once I met my financial goals. From my perspective, I knew I had to be financially secure to spend the kind of time that I wanted to spend helping people nationally and internationally. I knew I could make my dream come true.

Holmes established a scholarship for young women at Bay Path College in Longmeadow, Massachusetts, specifically for women who have little in the way of money to obtain a college education. "I was particular to emphasize the field of study would be in finance and at the same time have a human service element." "For me to know, Holmes says, "that this scholarship will live on after I am gone gives me a wonderful feeling of joy. I am hopeful that it will have tremendous impact in the lives of the women who get to complete their degree and that they too will go on to give back to their community and make a difference in the world."[25]

Living Their Passion

Each day you find virtuous philanthropists advocating for their causes and inviting others to join them in the experience. There is enthusiasm and determination in their attitude and aptitude to find creative ways to inspire others to follow their lead. They are nurturing to others and disciplined in carrying out the mission of their philanthropic biography. Their positive energy is like a magnet, attracting others to give gratitude for blessings received and the quality of life they work to sustain. They bring vision and virtue to each decision, which is reflected in their actions for a more compassionate world.

When Florida Cultural Alliance president Sherron Long talks about philanthropy, she means living her entire life working for and supporting her passion for the transformative power of the arts and art education experiences on individual lives, communities, and schools. Her goal in high school was to study marine biology because she loved the ocean and wanted to sail the seas with Jacques Cousteau. But in 1967, she went on a humanities trip to New York City with her Duval Country, Florida, senior class where they saw the musical *Man of La Mancha.* She remembers how moving the production was and watching her classmates at the end of the performance crying and be deeply touched by what they experienced in the theater. She thought to herself, if something can move people that much, in that short a period of time, that's what I want to major in.

Long went on to get an undergraduate degree in theater, went back to get her MFA in theater directing, and taught in high school and college. Eventually she went to work for the Florida Department of State Division of Cultural Affairs, where she got involved with the political process and learned how important government partnerships were to sustain cultural organizations and artists. She realized how critical advocacy was to the arts and worked to ensure that not only did the arts have a voice in state government but that government understands its role to help sustain policies and funding for the continued development of diverse and quality arts, arts education, and cultural resources throughout the state. By creating stronger partnerships with both the public and private sectors to sustain and advance cultural resources, greater access to the arts and cultural experiences are possible not only for children but for everyone. Says Long:

> Those of us who work in the not-for-profit world certainly understand the importance and appreciate the philanthropic monetary gifts of others to help sustain the vital work our organizations do. Many of us would like to be in stronger financial positions to also turn around and make major monetary contributions to organizations and causes we believe are critical; however, many of us earn modest amounts and can only make modest monetary contributions to the causes we believe in. I can, however, give enthusiastically of my knowledge and time and devote my entire professional life in ways I know are going to help support a creative industry that enriches people's lives and connects them in meaningful ways through arts and cultural experiences. It is my way of giving back to the community.[26]

The stories of our virtuous philanthropists share a common thread, a bond that weaves their lives together even though they may not know each other. That bond is echoed by the late Dame Anita Roddick, founder of the Body Shop. When asked to comment on her decision to sell $150 million of the company's stock and give the proceeds to charity, she said, "They thought that eccentric of me. But you can't take it with you and you're a long time dead."[27] Dame Roddick died in 2007, at age of 64, from a cerebral hemorrhage, after a long battle with hepatitis C from a blood transfusion, which had gone undiagnosed for several years. She fulfilled her promise to leave her estate to charities on the same moral grounds that she gave to her life as an active campaigner for environmental and social issues, including helping disadvantaged children in Europe and Asia through Children on Edge, an organization she founded in 1990. A truly virtuous philanthropist, the late Dame Roddick saw it as her responsibility to fulfill her legacy in the way she conducted her business, clearly outlined in the company culture and mission and in her quest to promote ethical consumerism.

Here in the United States, that same ethical consumerism and social capital of community and philanthropy is exemplified in fashion designer Sigrid Olsen's confidence that she can pull it all together, and by philanthropist Tracy Gary, who, on inheriting $1 million at age 21, proceeded to give it all away.. Gary wanted to see that money go places and accomplish things, and she has, with her organization Inspired Legacies, These and other women like them personify the qualities of many women boomers who are innovative, responsible, compassionate change agents These are women who don't bury their gold in the ground (see Exhibit 3.1). As Marilyn Wechter reminds us, "We need to create community, and that's one of the things that philanthropy does. It creates a community of like-minded people who come together for a cause they champion, for something they believe in, because they envision the world a better place."

And with the work of our boomers, it will be.

Recognize and Honor Your Virtuous Philanthropist Characteristics

1. I practice inconspicuous consumption by:
   1. _____
   2. _____

2. Two confident decisions I have made and carried out in spite of adversity are:
   1. _____
   2. _____

3. Examples of how my philanthropic actions are consistent with my values are:
   1. Time (work) _____
   2. Talent (wisdom) _____
   3. Treasure (wealth) _____

4. Two dreams that I believe I can fulfill in my life are:
   1. What _____ How _____
   2. What _____ How _____

5. What I do in life to live my passion:
   1. With my time _____
   2. With my talent _____
   3. With my treasure _____
   4. With my friends _____
   5. With my family _____

Aesop's Fable

The Miser

A miser sold everything he had and melted down his hoard of gold into a single lump, which he buried secretly in a field. Every day he went back to look at it, and would sometimes spend long hours gloating over his treasure. One of his men noticed his frequent visits to the spot, and one day watched him and discovered the secret. Waiting for his opportunity, he went one night and dug up the gold and stole it. Next day the miser visited the place as usual and, finding his treasure gone, fell to tearing his hair and groaning over his loss. In this condition, he was seen by one of his neighbors, who asked him what his trouble was. The miser told him of his misfortune, but the other replied, "Don't take it so much to heart, my friend: Put a brick into the hole, and take a look at it every day. You won't be any worse off than before, for even when you had your gold, it was of no earthly use to you."

Exhibit 3.1 Aesop Fable

Source: Reprint permission from Barnes & Noble, Inc., Aesop. *Aesop's Fables*, ed. D. L. Ashliman, "The Miser," New York, 2003, p 229.

CHAPTER 4

Women Philanthropists . . .
Dispelling the Myths

*Whatever you can do, or think you can do, begin it. Boldness has
genius, power and magic.*
Johann Wolfgang von Goethe (1749–1832)

The new frontier for boomer women is philanthropy, which gives
them a forum in which to truly make a difference. More and more
women are using their strengths—those of collaboration and connection—to impact their community with new energy and vigor.
Kathleen D. McCarthy, in her study *Women and Philanthropy in the
United States, 1790–1900,* says: "Philanthropy has long provided
women in the United States and elsewhere with the means to leave
an imprint on legislations and institutions. . . . Today women are
shaping the future direction of the political, social, and economic
arena, and perhaps, the shape of philanthropy itself."[1]

Traditionally women are generous to causes that touch their
hearts. Yet we are seeing a new frontier in that issues that matter to
their families and the well-being of the community at large are also
benefiting from the boomer philanthropic need to change the
world. Yes, while women have been at the forefront of charitable
giving, establishing many of the institutions that serve humankind,
they are finally realizing their real potential to apply their dollars to

shaping the future of society. This is an exciting frontier, and it is the boomer woman who is its pioneer.

Our studies show that although a significant number of women agree with Dallas boomer Brenda Pejovich that "It's our checks that influence, and it's never been more important to open our handbags and give,"[2] these same women have a challenge accepting the fact that they are philanthropists. Although boomer women very much want to be involved and are opening their checkbooks more generously than ever, they push back when called philanthropic. Many are quick to note that they want to make change happen yet do not consider what they do as philanthropic but rather as affecting change. "These women not only want to affect change," according to former CARE fundraiser Suzanne Horstman, "they also want to support their values."[3] The women we talked with want to make change happen and they have the wealth to do it, yet there is still a lingering mind-set, the myth that "I do not have enough money to be a philanthropist." Others who have the time and talent to make change happen are burdened by the myth "There is no way I can make a difference."

Exposing the Myths

Let us take a brief look at why both these myths have little reality and no substance for twenty-first-century boomer women.

The first common myth: "I do not have enough money to be a philanthropist." Really? If you have bought Girl Scout cookies, dropped money into the Salvation Army kettle, had a payroll deduction taken out of your paycheck for the United Way, or supported a "Save the Whales" or other cause dear to your heart, you are a philanthropist. Yes, you are a philanthropist because you chose to give money to a cause you believe in. Whether you choose to donate $1 million to build an animal shelter or give $5 to save a stray, philanthropy is about keeping the energy and flow of money doing good work in society.

The second common myth: "There is no way I can make a difference."

Oh—have you ever volunteered? You make a difference if what you do makes someone's life easier and you bring a smile or good feeling to someone else. Whether you travel 3,000 miles on a mission trip to Africa or three miles to volunteer at a playhouse or food shelter, your action makes a difference to those you meet. Whether it is the staff member who is shorthanded or the client you served, making a difference with your time brings happiness and ease to someone else and is very definitely philanthropy.

One of the most powerful arguments to dispel these myths is the work by psychologist Janet Surrey of the Stone Center at Wellesley College. According to Surrey, "Our conception of the self-in-relation involves the recognition that, for women, the primary experience of self is relational; that is, the self is organized and developed in the context of important relationships."[4] Boomer women understand they have the power to solve problems and make a better environment for future generations by forming partnerships with other philanthropists and other nonprofit organizations and using that collective voice to shape philanthropy and society. "I feel like I have a voice for women who don't have the power to speak," says Ronda Stryker, one of our interviewees and a member of the Michigan Women's Commission. "It seems like everyone's got a voice, but not everyone has a box to stand on and speak. I feel maybe that's what I'm doing, building that base to give someone a voice."[5] This collective voice through collaboration and connection with like-minded women and not-for-profit organizations reinforces their role as philanthropists who can and do make a difference. In short, they are using their relationships to forge stronger futures for themselves and others. In doing so, they empower themselves and others to be philanthropists. This reflects the new "caring economics" that Riane Eisler writes about in her book, *The Real Wealth of Nations.* Eisler sees this as a movement toward the realization of a new "partnership" leadership model, which she envisions as *the* equitable model in our future, a model where there is mutual trust and respect for all persons and the world's natural resources.[6]

These myths we've mentioned are no longer valid. Boom-generation women are entering midlife at a time when a greater segment of society recognizes and accepts the intrinsic virtues of the feminine perspective and its primary function in setting a new agenda for compassionate and creative interdependence in the world. Women are changing careers in order to put their time and money behind efforts they think will make a difference. According to Melissa Morriss-Olson, dean, of the graduate school and professor of Nonprofit Management and Philanthropy at Massachusetts Bay Path College:

> I've got a lot of women in my classes who are in their early to mid-50s, who've been in corporate life and who now want to make a change. Some of them want to become fundraisers for organizations they have a commitment to or that they have been volunteering for. Others want to become nonprofit administrators. That's one of the most significant things I've noticed in the last seven or eight years I've been teaching the subject.[7]

Anne McCormick, executive director of the Boys and Girls Club of Martin County, Florida, started out as a volunteer for the organization several years before she left her career as vice president of operations for Yeager International in North America, to head up the nonprofit organization. "Sure I had to change my lifestyle to go along with the pay cut," says McCormick, "but it was nice to simplify, and I don't think there was any downside to it at all. I've become more spiritual and reflective and just more in tune with what my true values are. This is work, but it's rewarding beyond my wildest dreams."[8]

Education of the Abundant Heart

The twentieth-century high-tech legacy is unprecedented access to information. The twenty-first-century legacy may well be unprecedented access to the "good heart." Although the recent surge of creative technology provides us with gadgets to "educate the mind," it short-circuits the "education of the heart."

Boom-generation women recognize this and are already shifting the paradigm from matters of the mind to matters of the heart. "We need to follow our hearts more and not worry about what other people think. If we could do more without worrying what everyone else was imagining, I reason we would be a lot better off," declares interviewee Ronda Stryker.

It is as if society has become all too left-brained. The technological revolution "is dominated by a form of thinking and an approach to life that is narrowly reductive and deeply analytical," writes

Daniel H. Pink in his book, *A Whole New Mind.*[9] Neuroscientists identify the left hemisphere of the brain with logical and sequential thinking while the right hemisphere engages intuitive and holistic thinking. In the last century, left-brain thinking garnered center stage in our society.

But now, according to Pink, right-brain thinking, "exemplified by creators and caregivers, is becoming more dominant—and more necessary as our society searches for meaning, balance, and harmony in a world paranoid and polarized by greed, power, and terror." Right-brain thinking plays a key role in the early childhood development of woman's lifelong sense of self and how she will relate to others. As women's leadership becomes more universal, the ethics of care of the yin begin to assimilate the binary thinking of the yang to create a mind-shift toward conceptual and holistic thought. "We have to use both male and female energy," says Stryker. "I just don't think we're going to get anywhere if we have too much of either." The process of embracing the wholeness of yin and yang intensifies the education of the heart as a compelling focal point for women's philanthropy. Their actions bring to life the wisdom and words of Sir Walter Scott: "We shall never learn to feel and respect our real calling and destiny, unless we have taught ourselves to consider everything moonshine, compared to education of the heart." Boom-generation women lead their generation and the next by modeling ways to listen to their heart and live their authentic self through philanthropic deeds.

This feminine perspective also takes on a collective voice for the sense of self by articulating two key precepts, abundance and spirituality. It may seem that these concepts contradict rather than complement one another, yet both provide energy for the soul. Spirituality is the quality and grace of our actions; it is the push to make sense of our spiritual existence, however we define it, while abundance is the quantity and state of experience for our actions. An abundant person is one rich in positive values of emotional and intellectual discernment. She is rich in self-knowledge—the emotional intelligence that honors the beauty of interconnectivity and interdependence. This abundant person knows that every cause has an effect, every action a pebble dropped into a pond, radiating ripples in all directions. Abundance represents the totality of our life, the good and bad, happy, sorrow, joy, giving and receiving.

Abundance is energy in the fullness of our life. It is not those material assets we acquire that can be subject to adversity; rather, abundance is the wealth from our soul that transcends adversity. We can recognize, impart, transfer, and most of all celebrate it through philanthropic empowerment.

Dr. Sherry Buffington, author of *The Law of Abundance,* believes that the law of abundance is "a precise science that brings great clarity and predictability to every outcome; a philosophy that broadens insights and expands influence; a spirituality that can insulate you from failure; a journey that can take you anywhere you want to go." Buffington's research states that by using this law, we can "create the world we live in . . . find deep joy and contentment, and accomplish every great thing." Her studies on abundance emphasize the bountiful joyous balance it brings and that when we have abundance ourselves, we can give it back.[10] This seems to be a core belief of the boomer women we have studied who take joy in giving back, even if they do not call it philanthropy.

Lucy Crow Billingsley is one of those boomer women who takes joy in giving back. She grew up as the only daughter of the legendary Dallas developer Trammel Crow with her dad's motto: "There must always be a burn in your heart to achieve. In the quiet of your solitude, close your eyes, bow your head, grit your teeth, and clench your fists. Achieve in your heart, vow and dedicate yourself to achieve, to achieve." And true to his motto, she has. Lucy says, "All I knew was that I wanted to do something of substance. I was yearning for the grittiness in life." Her real estate projects include Austin Ranch, a 1,900-acre development, and the spectacular One Arts Plaza, a 24-story tower in the new Arts District that will house the headquarters of 7-Eleven, Inc. She told us, "I have always yearned for purpose that is for the greater good of us all. I have been hugely blessed, with so many gifts, and I not only have the opportunity to give back, it is my responsibility to give back to others." Lucy is one of the founders of the Chiapas Project, which helps alleviate poverty in Latin America through its microfinancing programs. She says:

> I meet women who make less than $1 a day. I give them a loan. With that loan, they can buy chickens or sheep to raise and sell, or start a little business that will put food on the table and educate their kids. That loan, that start gives them the opportunity

to be trusted. Someone gave me the opportunity, so I give that gift and I get purpose. Without purpose life is hollow. I am actually getting the greater gift.

Lucy exemplifies abundance. She is an example of the pioneer boomer philanthropist we are talking about, who recognizes her dollars can make a difference and has committed herself very decisively to seeing that they do. She counsels her peers:

Give, don't imagine you can't. Why do we defer to men? Why do we not make big gifts? How silly of us. When you die you want to be able to know that you gave more than you took. And the only time to deal with that is now." Her advice to women is bold. "Go as big as you can. Give it away today."[11]

What Is a Philanthropist?

Unlike Lucy Crow Billingsley, many of our women interviewees did not regard themselves as philanthropists in spite of giving large or small sums and time to charitable concerns. Instead, they hold rather stereotypical ideas about philanthropists. Some said philanthropists were wealthy individuals who fund "arts and humanities projects" or were wealthy patrons of the symphony and opera.

Some saw philanthropists as "Robber Barons"; others as social activists who need tax write-offs. Finally, they associated philanthropy with "benevolence" and people who give large amounts of money to schools and hospitals to better the world and community they live in. And while traditionally philanthropy bears this out to some degree, it also includes a broader definition that needs to be taken into consideration, especially in how philanthropic endeavors shape the ethics and values in contemporary society.

In *American Philanthropy*, Robert H. Bremner defines philanthropy in its broadest sense as "the improvement in the quality of human life. Whatever motivates individual philanthropists, the purpose of philanthropy itself is to promote the welfare, happiness and culture of mankind." Bremner says philanthropy is one of "the principal methods of social advance." We have all benefited from philanthropy, in enjoying our museums, parks, churches, schools, hospitals and music halls, among others. American philanthropy has a rich history. It is a basic way of life for Americans. Bremner also reminds us, "Americans have long thought of ourselves, immodestly so, as a nation of philanthropists."[12]

American history corroborates this idea. Since the days of Columbus, America has exhibited generosity toward others. Native Americans initially welcomed settlers and taught them how to adjust to their new living circumstances and the harsh environment. One of our first colonists, John Winthrop, said about his own people, the Puritans, "We must bear one another's burdens, we must not look only on our own things but also on the things of our brethren . . . to improve our lives to do more service to the Lord . . . and the care of the public must take precedence over all private interests."[13]

Bremner also writes about Cotton Mather, one of the founders of Yale, who proposed "that men and women, acting as individuals or as members of voluntary associations, should engage in a perpetual endeavor to do good in the world." Mather believed that philanthropy, helping the unfortunate, was "an honor, a privilege, an incomparable pleasure." He advocated doing "good" as a sound policy and an effective social control. Mather promoted the practice of philanthropy by enlisting the support of others in helping those who had less than they did. He likened good deeds to "a stone falling into a pool—one circle and service will produce another, till they extend—who can tell how far?" The original settlers' traditions of doing "good" were passed on to our founding fathers and formed the pillars of our community through the revolution and up to present times.[14]

The American tradition takes its definition of philanthropy and good works from the ancient Greek definition of philanthropy, "to love people." Kim Klein reported in *Fund Raising for Social Change* that Americans express this love "in donations of property, money, or volunteer work to worthy causes. Charity meaning 'love' . . . is expressed in unconditional loving kindness, compassion and seeking to do good." Klein suggests that corporations do not donate the most money to nonprofit causes, government does, and after government, it is individuals who are the most generous.

Klein points out that 80% of all contributions are from individual donors, with 85% of those funds coming from families with a combined income of $50,000 or less. Seven out of 10 people regularly give to charities. They give for many reasons; tax deductions, because they feel good doing so, or they believe in the cause of the organization, "because the group expresses their own ideals and enables them to reinforce their image of themselves as principled people."[15]

Philanthropy has been interpreted in different ways. In his writings in *Giving, Charity and Philanthropy in History,* Bremner makes this perfectly clear. The philosopher Thomas Hobbes defined philanthropy as "desire of good to another, benevolence, good will, charity, good nature." Yet despite these words, Hobbes had difficulty thinking anyone who was a philanthropist did so except to "enhance the esteem or 'honor' in which he was held in the community or to promote his own security and power." Thomas Browne, an English physician (1605–1662) who is credited with the expression "charity begins at home," believed that charity required both cool-headedness and humility. Browne said that being uncharitable "meant disregard of and indifference to well-being that, in one's own case, led to self-destruction."[16]

The premise taken by well-known philanthropists Andrew Carnegie, John D. Rockefeller, Ben Franklin, and others, was that philanthropy is about seeking practical, usefully social ways to dispose of surplus wealth. Until now, to a large degree that is the American model of philanthropy. Perhaps the most compelling statement of how wealth should be used was expressed by Carnegie in his 1889 essay "Wealth," which later became known as "The Gospel of Wealth":

> Thus is the problem of rich and poor to be solved. The laws of accumulation will be left free; the laws of distribution free. Individualism will continue, but the millionaire will be but a trustee for the poor; entrusted for a season with a great part of the increased wealth of the community, but administering it for the community far better than it could or would have done for itself. [17]

Just giving money to the poor or needy was not acceptable without also teaching them moral lessons. Carnegie believed philanthropy's purpose was to "stimulate the best and most inspiring of the poor . . . for efforts to further their own improvement." Rockefeller believed "the best philanthropy is not what is usually called charity." Both men considered the worst thing a millionaire could do with his money was to give it away to the "irreclaimably poor."

Women today are changing the traditional model. An example of the new, more progressive model, Tracy Gary, a volunteer fundraiser and entrepreneur, helps women live up to their philanthropic potential through her work with Inspired Legacies, an organization she founded. She believes that "You're a philanthropist if you give away time and money." Gary not only embodies philanthropy, she teaches women how they can be philanthropic and why they must be. At a recent Dallas Women's Foundation meeting, she advised the attendees to really look at their values, to examine what was important to them and what gave them joy, to be abundant and designate their gifts based on where their interests are, whether it was the environment, culture, education, or social action.[18]

Kathleen Miller, a certified financial planner, tells us:

> Women want to understand every angle, research on their own, and above all, ask questions. Women seem increasingly drawn to nontraditional charities. Powerful women are fully aware that they can leverage their philanthropy by serving as role models and mentors for other aspiring business women who may be less fortunate.

Miller states: "One of the driving forces behind women's newfound financial power, and philanthropic mind-set is entrepreneurial. Women are making more giving decisions."[19] She believes that a key benefit is the sense of service and connection to the community philanthropy brings to the participant. Another key benefit, according to former Ms. Foundation President Marie C. Wilson, founder and president of the White House Project, is that

> the boom generation is starting to realize it is leadership that you fund. We've been raising awareness in politics, business and media. You get them to see that if you want to make change in anybody's leadership, you have to put money behind changes that show more women as leaders, more women in power and politics and more women in business. You have to make those kinds of connections.[20]

And while women are taking more risks in moving individual philanthropy, family philanthropy and community foundations in a positive direction, they are also finding ways to work together to have power to make more of the philanthropic decisions. "We haven't always loved and trusted each other but we've worked together because we wouldn't have any power if we didn't," says Wilson. In her work to get a critical mass of women into leadership, she sees boom-generation women beginning to realize that more grassroots women in leadership across the country really "lift all boats."

Our research suggests that women traditionally gave for a number of reasons. According to Kathleen D. McCarthy, director of the Center for the Study of Philanthropy for City University of New York, *noblesse oblige* formed a strong motive for women's traditional giving. For women as agents of community spirit, who could well afford their generosity of time and money, giving was important. Altruism, social prestige, sometimes the guilt of having more than others less fortunate, the desire to make a difference and the cachet philanthropy brings to a certain level of society drove their generosity. Wealthy women may not have "owned" their wealth—it belonged to their husbands—yet they often used their power and influence for a variety of causes. McCarthy observes: "Americans are some of the more generous people in the world, freely giving of their time and money. Women, especially, have played a pivotal role in philanthropy, then and now."

McCarthy extensively documents the contributions women have made to every area of society, working with their churches and personally being involved in missionary work. Women volunteered at schools, shelters, and hospitals, and established associations that helped the poor, children, and other women in need. These women started many of the charitable associations that form the foundation of our current charitable organizations, from the Red Cross to Planned Parenthood. Women have been pivotal at initiating societal reform, contributing generously with time and money to change society. McCarthy notes that "middle-class women have historically comprised the bulk of the nation's volunteers" but expressed concerns that, as more women now work, their ability to volunteer is dramatically reduced.[21]

Our evidence shows that as women boomers mature and become more affluent, they are even more generous and are not following the lead of their male family members which was to give when asked by a colleague because they in turn would be asking the same colleague to fund their favorite cause. Women donors did not so much give to fulfill a political tit for tat, but rather gave to causes dear to their values. And while Abbie J. von Schlegell and Joan M. Fisher, authors of *Women as Donors, Women as Philanthropists,* wrote in 1993, "women are in increasingly good positions to be major contributors to charities . . . but there is still a dearth of clear empirical data about why women contribute to charity,"[22] we are finding more evidence that boomer women are poised to change the landscape of philanthropy. Fifteen years after von Schlegell and Fisher published their book, the November 2008 symposium on women's philanthropy at the Center on Philanthropy at Indiana University, validates with research what these trend-setting authors predicted. According to the symposium report, "Across the board, women's deepening engagement in philanthropy is having an impact on social policy, the choice of grant awards, program development, nonprofit management, fund-raising and even grantor-grantee relationships. That adds up to unparalleled potential as more and more women eye their legacies."[23] Cam Kelley, former director of Campaign and Gift Planning at Smith College and currently assistant vice president for the Principal Gifts Programs at Duke University, defines boomer women as "a generation of women who don't have to ask anyone's permission to make philanthropic decisions."[24] And we are getting a clearer picture of why they contribute to charity, as well.

Jennifer Kahlow, then development professional at the College of St. Benedict's, in 1996 said, "The demographics of wealth are changing. The world is changing. Women are assuming more of a leadership role. They're in careers they weren't in before, they're volunteering where they haven't before and they're giving their financial resources as they never have before. It's now about more choices."[25] Little did she know how much stronger this trend would grow, taking on a life of its own. Our research suggests, as hers did, that as women earn larger sums and achieve significant success the potential exists for them to make a far-reaching impact on the face of philanthropy.

Anne Mosle, vice president for programs at the W. K. Kellogg Foundation said, "This is a historic shift moment . . . in the next five to ten years, anything is possible. For every Oprah Winfrey there are a hundred other women like her [boomers] we don't yet know about."[26] Demographer Harold Hodgkinson predicted the future when he said: "74 million baby boomers...will be writing an enormous number of wills in the next decade, and they will have an extraordinarily small number of children. That translates into a lot of dollars to philanthropy."[27]

Giving Influenced by Husband's Wealth and Interest

In the past, women's philanthropic activities and social status have been tied to their husband's wealth. Men of means often gave substantial amounts of money to their alma mater or their favorite charities; however, unless a woman earned her own salary, she felt she had no real say in where gifts should go. Women might give from their cash flow or allowances, but that resulted in smaller gifts than men's. The wealth and social status of their husband often determined the amount of time women could devote to charity, benevolent acts, and doing good in society. If their families could afford it, women gave back by helping the poor, other women and children, involving themselves with education, health-related causes, slavery, and other social concerns.

Although women have traditionally deferred to male family members, as they control a larger and growing share of the nation's wealth, they are becoming more independent and much less influenced by the males in their family. Today women are making their own decisions as to where and to whom their checks should go, and for how much they should be. Still, as Lucy Crow laments, "Why do we still defer to men?"

Giving Time Instead of Money

Philanthropy has changed as women's independence has grown. In the early years of this country, women were agents of community spirit and health, establishing institutions to care for the ill and incapable. They often risked their lives to serve. Over the years, women's philanthropy evolved and focused on the arts, culture, and education. In the nineteenth and early twentieth century, charitable work was sometimes what wealthy women "dabbled in," between lunches and events. Without women's philanthropy America would be a very different place. "From American's earliest days," according to Gretchen Kreuter, "women have given their energy, intelligence, time and money. Women were in a sense 'natural housekeepers' able to clean up American cities just as they attacked dirt and grime at home."[28] As Gigi Fourre Schumacher (senior development officer at St. Benedict's College, St. Joseph, Minnesota) said, "Women are more accustomed to giving time than money, women will bake brownies, they'll volunteer, but they're not used to giving money."[29] Women have a long history of giving what they could of their time and money; stories abound of women like Carrie Chapman Catt, who sold her sapphire jewelry to start the League of Women Voters. Yet, for most women, giving to a cause typically meant bake sales, auctions, or other forms of volunteering. Sociologists describe this as their "opportunity structures," patterns of easier access to some positions than others, and social forces that contribute to the pattern of social relationships and behaviors at that time.

The Wealthier the Woman, the Greater the Voluntary Commitment

Although the paradigm that the wealthier the woman, the greater the voluntary commitment is no longer absolute, at one time, charity was the work of the privileged, with white middle-class women bridging the gap to transcend class differences between themselves and the poor. Many historians refer to women's social reform activism in the decades between 1889 and 1920 as the foundation of contemporary women's philanthropic culture, as well as the first wave of feminism in our country. Working within their network of civic organizations and clubs and using the "opportunity structures" available to them as moral guardians of home, family, and community, women effected positive social change, first in their community and then nationwide. Their social reforms embraced education, healthcare, children's welfare, wage and working conditions for women, the environment, public health services, and political reform. Culminating with the passage in 1920 of the Nineteenth Amendment, which gave some, but not all, women the right to vote, women used their vast club and organizational networks to further the causes for lasting social justice reform and greater equality. Women have long played a role in nation building and shaping American civil society. And this role is growing. Even without having access to many of the resources men had, women effected change with what they did have, in time and money. And as a woman's wealth increases, studies and our research show that she commits even more of her time and dollars.

In the future, women will contribute more financial resources and continue to volunteer their time and talent. The studies conducted by the Center for Women in Philanthropy quote Donna E. Shalala, former secretary of the U.S. Department of Health and Human Services, as saying: "In the coming century women are going to contribute even more significantly, not just to industry and government, but to social activism. . . . The new presence of women in philanthropy is not just expanding its profile, it is changing that profile."[30] Boomer women of achievement are clear about how much and to whom they give. As Andrea Kaminski, a former Executive Director of the Women's Philanthropy Institute summarized in our interview:

> All across North America women have begun to see their potential through philanthropy, to help solve problems and create a better environment for future generations. . . . [W]omen see that by forming valuable partnerships with not-for-profit organizations and other philanthropists, they can have a greater voice in shaping the future of society. The main thing is to make their financial giving and volunteer leadership count.[31]

In our interviews, we asked women what social benefit they hope to accomplish as a result of their philanthropic involvement. Consistently we heard that the social benefits of giving were seen as an opportunity to do good and to "really make a difference." Some saw it as a real, tangible way to help their community and perhaps even "discover a cure." Smith Class of 1968—the class that changed the world and is still trying—graduate Phyllis Rappaport is a founding member and major funder, along with her husband, Jerome, of the Cure Alzheimer Fund, in Wellesley, Massachusetts. Said Rappaport:

> I quickly realized that my baby boomer generation—the biggest to ever hit this world—plays a central role in the Alzheimer

equation. As we age, our Alzheimer's and the care we demand is going to bankrupt Medicare and Medicaid and drain state and national treasuries. I don't want this to be our legacy. I coined and trademarked these words: "Curing Alzheimer's Gene by Gene, It's My Future."

Rappaport hopes to bring attention to the Alzheimer crisis by working with jeans manufacturing and marketing companies to "brand " her trademark so that a double entendre (jean by jean) will "lead to some retail marketing play," to raise money to find a cure.[32]

A highly developed sense of personal responsibility character-ized our interviewees' responses to the question about personal motivation for giving. One said, "Giving is part of my life, we were taught it." Another put it more emphatically: "We have no choice, we exist, and therefore, we have an obligation to give back." Others said: "I want to make a difference," and "We can all impact society, and we must."

By and large, the women we interviewed are not expecting to see any tangible rewards or significant personal recognition for their giving, although to a degree we are seeing a shift here. Boomer women do believe that if, by example, they can inspire oth-ers to live their true values through philanthropy, they are more willing to talk publicly about their work. On average, however, they saw their giving in humanistic terms. "I want to see the world a better, caring more concerned place," said one. Another wants "to wake up every morning and know I've made a difference." Still another wants to make a personal difference because, as she said, "It's cold out there."

Our research showed some changes in boomer women's chari-table interests during the last decade. There was a definite trend to more discernment and researching a charitable organization more thoroughly than earlier. The women said that they look for "well-run" organizations. Boomer women, especially those in the business world, are not easily influenced, are more selective in their giving, and make sure their dollars have social and political signifi-cance. They give because they can give and want to have an impact. And they have the time and success to change society and their community.

These women share a strong sense of being able to make a better world through their donations and volunteering. One said, "We are human and must make this world better so I am making sure I count and my money counts." Another said, "We could change the world if we wanted to—so I make sure I'm doing the right thing." The style and motivation of how they give was important to each. "I give to what my heart says is important," wrote one more mature boomer, while another said, "I reach out with loving kindness." One called her way of giving "gracious and formidable. I get people involved." For our boomer women, as many reach a mature stage of success in their careers, giving has become "a way of life."

The boomer women we interviewed also saw a clear difference in the way the men in their lives give and their own giving. They suggested that they gave more sincerely and from the heart while their male counterparts care more for panache, being seen, and who's who. Like men, they might still want some recognition, but they are more willing to give to causes that are not "popular" if the cause touches their heart. Women boomers are keenly aware of their position as role models. "Every culture that you come to, educate a woman and you educate a generation," says Suzanne Horstman, former CARE fundraiser and now Martin County, Florida, Library Foundation director. "That's in Africa, South America, China, and around the world. Women clearly care about the next generation. I wonder if men do? I wonder if that makes a difference? What do men fund—buildings—which, interestingly enough, are a testimony to themselves."[33]

The free-ranging conversations we had spoke to participants' need for involvement in their community and their need to give to a particular cause. Most of the women emphasize the importance of helping others, particularly women and children fulfill their potential. The women spoke of a desire to be role models for their female children and other women. Several were emphatic on the desire for recognition, as it serves to inspire other women to stretch in their own giving and involvement. Comments that women often expressed included: "I had it tough; I'd like others to have better choices than I did," and, "We need more powerful women in business; I intend to help women grow, any way I can." Not only community recognition but media recognition is important, "because the way you get permanent change," Marie C. Wilson told us, "is to show women in the media and make it normal to see women as leaders, and to trust women."

As boomer women move from economic dependence to using their financial strength, they support what they believe in, and less quietly at that. Maya Thornell-Sandifor, senior communications director of the Women's Foundation of California, notes that today's women philanthropists are giving to "programs that strive for systemic change, rather than ones that provide just direct services to a specific number of people."[34] Women are looking for a cause or an organization with an aspect of social change to it. Yet they have clear intentions about how much and to whom they give to. Once they believe in the cause, they support the organization for the long term and consider their gifts as investments, for the organization and for their local and global community. Community is relationship with people who share their passion for that particular cause. Personal involvement is a critical component of their generosity.

Women's traditional patterns of giving are shifting. Women make more of the giving decisions and one of the driving forces behind women's new financial power and the philanthropic mindset are boomers' social values. Women are drawn to nontraditional charities, and many are taking a serious look at community and women's foundations as the vehicle of choice to help them choose to what and to whom their dollars go to. Boomer women invest time in programs that impact the community, their way of life as well as the rest of the planet's citizen's. There is a decided global sense of giving.

In 1902, Jane Addams of Hull House said, "The most effective form of giving is for work that leads to justice." Today that value shows up even more in the causes women are aligning themselves with. It is part of the return to virtue and the respect for values. What Donna E. Shalala said in 1993 has come true. "[W]omen are recognizing their resources are theirs to give. Women cannot be assumed to want to give to the same sort of projects as men."[35] And in fact, they are not. Women are definitely contributing more strategically. Our studies show that the majority, over 50%, cite a feeling of social responsibility as their primary reason for giving. Women want to see change, they want a greater voice. "Shaping the future of society" is something we have heard over and over. Women are eager to make sure their giving and volunteer leadership count and are recognizing that their dollars can indeed do so.

With that said, it is the foundations and organizations that understand women's growing generosity, social activism, and commitment to change and that develop new ways to reach and cultivate women entrepreneur donors that will succeed in this new arena of giving. The paradigm shift is from success to significance for midlife women who realize the urgency to achieve their destiny, to fulfill suspended dreams, to leave a lasting legacy. Anna Lloyd, a former director of the Committee of 200, defined significance "as the work of making a life. Significance means doing work that you are called to do, not just work that you enjoy, or that merely pays well."[36] The women we interviewed deliberately chose to govern their own lives and make them significant, through their own philanthropic efforts and generosity, way beyond the work they did. In some cases, the women's work constituted a calling, and that calling was used to give back.

The term "from success to significance" was used in several of the interviews and conversations for this study. For many of the women interviewed, this theme was a central core of their lives. Making money was not nearly enough. Helping the world around them and leaving that world a better place because they actively contributed to that betterment was an essential goal. Philanthropic giving, doing something significant with their money, was very much part of this legacy.

"Success to significance" embodies the theory of Abraham Maslow's hierarchy of needs. Maslow studied successful people, and felt that people are basically trustworthy, self protective, and self-governing. They tend toward growth and love. Maslow believed that general types of needs must be satisfied before an individual can act unselfishly: physiological, safety, love, and esteem. He believed that each of these types of needs must be met before a person goes on to the next level. Once physiological, safety, belongingness, and esteem needs have been met, a person can move on to self-actualization (a growth need). Maslow divided self-actualization into two areas: the cognitive and the aesthetic. He defined self-actualization as self-fulfillment and the realizing of one's potential, as well as self-transcendence, connecting to something beyond one's own ego and helping others find self-fulfillment and realize their own potential.[37]

The women interviewed tell us they have experienced all the levels Maslow cites, and especially continue to strive for "the highest natural faculty or element of the human soul or moral sense." Philanthropy has been a basis for women's contribution since time immemorial, and several of these accomplishments are identified in the mini-quiz, "Know the Women Who Shaped Our Destiny" (see Exhibit 4.1). Women boomers are motivated to give because they feel it is the right thing to do. They are interested in solving and impacting a specific cause or concern and very much want to give back to their community. As they move from satisfying their basic needs to self-fulfillment, they are motivated to give back, self-actualization. As Detroit attorney Shirley A. Kaiglor says, "I believe, as you are moving forward, you have to have your hand reaching back to someone else."[38]

Dispel the Myths

1. Give two examples of how you are a philanthropist. What are you doing to dispel the myths?
   a._____
   b._____

2. Who is a role model for your abundance? Why?
   Who are you a role model for?
   How does that make you feel?

3. How do you volunteer?
   Do you focus on one group, or do you share your time among several causes? What connection or commonality is there with your values in the volunteer work you do?

4. How do the organizations you support fulfill your aesthetic self-actualization? If not, what will you change?

5. What are three things you do to "educate your heart"?
   a._____
   b._____
   c._____

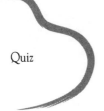

Know the Women Who
Shaped Our Destiny

Quiz

Before women won the right to vote in 1920, they earned their "Badge of Citizenship" by championing social, political, educational, and cultural reforms in our country. Choose your answer from the list of names. Place the letter in the heart next to the question. *(The answers are below.)*

A. Jane Addams
B. Mary McLeod Bethune
C. Betty Friedan
D. Margaret Fuller
E. Julia Ward Howe

F. Margaret Mead
G. Abby Greene Aldrich Rockefeller
H. Margaret Olivia Slocum Sage
I. Elizabeth Cady Stanton
J. Victoria Clafin Woodhull

1. Suffragist; president, National Women Suffrage Association (1869–1892)

2. Social reformer, founder of Hull House (1887), awarded Nobel Peace Prize (1931)

3. Educator, founder of National Council of Negro Women (1935)

4. Writer, social reformer, pioneer feminist author of *Women of the 19th Century* (1845)

5. Spiritualist, publisher, reformer, first woman to be nominated to run for President (1872)

6. Anthropologist, curator of the American Museum of Natural History (1964–1969)

7. Philanthropist, endowed Russell Sage Foundation with $10 million (1907)

8. Writer, social reformer, founder of NOW (1966), author of *The Feminine Mystique*

9. Writer, author of the *Battle Hymn of the Republic* (1908)

10. Philanthropist, leading patron to establish the New York City Museum of Modern Art (1929)

(Answers: 1. I, 2. A, 3. B, 4. D, 5. J, 6. F, 7. H, 8. C, 9. E, 10. G)

Exhibit 4.1 Quiz
Illustrations by Elizabeth Huggins-Thompson.

CHAPTER 5

Empowerment

All life is an expression of a single spiritual unity. We can no longer afford false divisions between work and community, between ethics and economics. But how can we change from a system which values endless increasing profit and materialism, to one in which the core values are community, caring for the environment, creating, and growing things and personal development?
The answer: We empower people.
—Dame Anita Roddick (1942–2007)

Give Yourself Power

Empowerment is something you give yourself, not something you get from someone else. And it is not a zero-sum process, where one person's gain is balanced by another person's loss. Rather, it is the dynamism and intensity that a woman uses to bring focus and clarity to how her values connect to the philanthropic issues she defines as important in her life. It is a process by which she chooses how to direct her energy to find creative solutions for those critical issues. She must take an active role in finding ways to leverage her energy with that of others also in pursuit of creative solutions to their social concerns. A woman empowers herself by her ability to establish goals, monitor progress, and evaluate the impact of her philanthropic agenda as it relates both to individual progress and community betterment. It is a process that provides a structure for her philanthropic journey and brings purpose into her life.

Some have called empowerment the force that keeps all the dots connected. Some call it the force that gives the courage and fortitude to transcend doubt and distrust in one's ability to transform dreams into reality, while others say it is the force that leads them to collaborate with other like-minded individuals and community members. Empowerment shifts the consciousness of a woman's mind-set from what *has been* to what *can be*, through the synthesis of her creative thought in meaningful association with other community members who are also charged by an energy grounded in the integrity of purpose, the wisdom of passion, and the freedom that comes with power.

Empowerment is visioning. It is taking responsibility for your actions and controlling your future. Empowerment allows you to draw on your knowledge, combine it with your experience and your values, and act from an internal locus of motivation, acting with strength and taking initiative. It traditionally has not been the strength of women, who too often turned over their power to others. As activist Petra Kelly reminds us, "We must work from our own values and elevate their influence to those of men. There is a saying, 'where power is, women are not.' Women must be willing to be powerful. Because we bear scars from the ways men have used their power . . . women often want no part of power."[1] We believe it is the patriarchic definition of power as authority and control that women want no part of rather than power itself. Women do see power as a way to achieve their goals, and part of the destiny for boom-generation women is to redefine power using their values, which include nurturing and egalitarianism.

The foundation for empowerment is abundance, the wealth we recognize from within our soul as the energy we celebrate by our words, actions, and deeds. Daniel H. Pink in his book, *A Whole New Mind*, says, "Abundance has brought beautiful things to our lives, but that bevy of material goods has not necessarily made us much happier. That's why more people—liberated by prosperity, but not fulfilled by it—are resolving the paradox by searching for meaning." Pink reminds us that "as more of us lead lives of abundance we'll have a greater opportunity to pursue lives of meaning."[2] Hundreds of millions of people all over the world no longer have to struggle for survival. As Nobel Prize–winning economist Robert William Fogel writes, this has "made it possible to extend the quest for self-realization from a minute fraction to almost the whole of it."[3]

Most especially for boomer women, as they empower themselves and others to fully realize their vision for a better world, the acquisition of material abundance accelerates their need and heightens their desire for self-realization and meaning in their life. In a recent management certification class one of us attended, counselor and career coach, Dr. Sherry Buffington, author of *The Law of Abundance* emphasized, "Ultimately, it is happiness, contentment, and a deep sense of satisfaction that are the true measures of abundance."[4] And unless we own the responsibility of empowerment for ourselves and fulfill it through meaning, philanthropy and our virtuous legacy for our communities suffer.

The model for empowerment is found in the Three Principles of Abundance.™

Principles

1. Every woman has a legacy.
2. Every woman is a philanthropist.
3. Every woman makes a difference.

These principles are designed to create a mind-set for future thinking in this new convergence of boom-generation women's leadership and their economic power, at a precarious cycle in America's history. These principles and our studies provide alternative ways to say "good riddance" to the old stereotypical myths we carry around with us. What is gaining momentum today is a society that boomer women have helped form and that uses their unique strengths. As Pink points out:

> What is emerging today is a new economy and society, built more on people's right brain. It is an age animated by a different form of thinking and new approach to life—one that prizes aptitudes that I call "high concept" and "high touch." High concept involves the capacity to detect patterns and opportunities, to create artistic and emotional beauty, to craft a satisfying narrative, and to combine seemingly unrelated ideas into something new. High touch involves the ability to empathize

with others, to understand the subtleties of human interaction, to find joy in one's self and to elicit it in others, and to stretch beyond the quotidian in pursuit of purpose and meaning.[5]

The boomer woman's legacy is in fact gaining ground and being sanctioned as the new model. Part of this model includes the trend Margaret identifies as "speak female," where our words paint pictures of results, not needs. When you focus on the results, envision the outcome, and paint verbal pictures, it sends out words from the heart that engage the listener's heart. It encourages active listening and facilitates holistic thinking.

Principle One: Every Woman Has a Legacy

A legacy has two forms. The more familiar one deals with tangible assets, valuables that we pass on through legal documents, trusts, and wills. The less familiar one deals with intangible assets, values that we pass on through our words and deeds. It is the abundance in the story of our life that tells others who we are, what we believe in, and how we want to be remembered—the story about how our inner wealth, our core beliefs, values, and virtues guide our decisions in daily life. It is the engine of our soul that drives our actions and directs how we live our lives, not what we have in our life. And finding ways to preserve and pass on our story takes on an added significance as the pace of the modern world quickens and more and more emphasis gets put on material things.

Finding ways to express our gratitude, advice, and blessings for lessons learned from our experiences becomes more urgent as we pass through midlife and begin to realize that if we do not tell our own story, it may not get told at all. It is how we live our "dash," our time on earth that Linda Ellis writes about in her poem *The Dash*.[6] And what a wonderful and unique story each one of us has to tell! It is a precious gift and the greatest treasure we can give to those we love, as a lasting message to nurture, guide, and inspire them when we are gone. There is no other gift in the world we can share with others that has the essence of our compassion, our love, our courage, our caring, and our reason for being than a legacy. And when other material assets are consumed, damaged, lost, or forgotten, it will be our history, our story, our legacy, and the words from our hearts that remain imprinted for eternity in the hearts of those we love.

Throughout history, stories have been used to pass on values, beliefs, traditions, and meaningful lessons in life from generation to generation. These are the "ties that bind" humanity, a universal message of how we fulfilled the purpose of our life. Think back to your childhood: What memories make you laugh, cry, bring a smile or cause a sigh? What values and beliefs do you hold dear today that came from those ancestral stories passed on from family member to family member? Don't you wish you could know what each felt in their heart—what they cared about and how they wanted to be remembered? Don't you wish those old faded photographs would come to life and tell you the story from the hearts and mouths of the person depicted?

For many boom-generation women, telling their story also provides clarity of purpose in their lives at a time when they need and seek new direction and meaning. Sometimes the death of a loved one, a life-altering event, loss of a job or family member, a divorce, or an unexpected inheritance is the jolt needed to stir our souls into meditation and reflection. In other cases, it may be the urgency to preserve our parents' legacies of meaningful stories that inspire us to pass them on. In all cases, it is a time to take inventory of where we have been and what we have done and what still remains to be accomplished with our time, talent, and treasure.

Our stories, our legacies in the making . . . become the blueprint for our action, the recipe for our significance, and the elixir for the well-being of our soul. It is a time to reflect on our personal place in the cycle of history. It is the dynamics of a moment, that one page in our life that unites who we are now with our future self, with our hopes, fears, dreams, and desires, as we realize the profound dimension our story has and will continue to have in the cosmic realities of creating a better world. We are compelled to act, not only to share our story but also to become more resourceful in how we will live the story of the rest of our life. We honor our unique story, we respect our zest for life, and as torchbearers we become that beacon of light so others may follow.

As women, who tend to process information more through the right brain hemisphere, telling, writing, and reflecting on our life experiences is the creative process that brings focus to our vision and inspires us to imagine. It is asking the question: Looking back 5 years from now, 10 years from now, a lifetime from now, what would cause me to feel good about my life, and that I acted on my values and beliefs in a positive way as a torchbearer of virtuous philanthropy? And not only feel good about what I did, but also how I inspired others to have courage and conviction to take the next step. What kind of role model can I be through my deeds and work? How does my story reflect who I am and who I want to become with the time, talent, and treasure I have been blessed with during my life? How do I empower others to live and act on their legacy?

Your legacy is your story, your lifelong experiences, your learning, your yearning. Your legacy is how you interconnect with and relate, past and present, to others in your quest to live a good life and leave the world a little better for the future. Your story, as Margaret Mead said, is how you are part of "a small group of thoughtful committed citizens that can change the world, indeed, it's the only thing that ever has." As Niki puts it, "It's making a dent in the universe." What a wonderful time to be alive. Just imagine the energy that can travel around the world if you tell your story and you inspire others to tell their story and they inspire others to tell their story. Each person and each story is a "rolling stone," creating a positive surge of energy in the consciousness of the universe and receiving back the compassion, love, inspiration, and courage to find meaningful solutions for a sustainable and interconnected world. You are living the pebble-in-the-pond metaphor.

Why Your Story Is Important

Let us talk about one of women's greatest gifts, our ability to bond as communicators. One of our special talents is our ability to communicate holistically. By and large, we are good talkers, active listeners; we can see others' point of view, empathize with them, and yet, not lose our core essence, our own point of view. We can share and at the same time still care. Deborah Tannen identifies this gender-specific communication in her book *You Just Don't Understand: Women and Men in Conversation* as "rapport- talk."[7]

These personality traits are distinct to women, and it is time for us to use and fine-tune them to their fullest capacity for the benefit of a better world, to truly make a dent. It is time to use our communicative strengths for two reasons: to inspire and to attract. To inspire others who may just need that extra "nudge" of confidence to say, "Yes, I can do that too!" And to attract others to join together and find common threads of passion, caring, and talent that provide support and strength in numbers to write a new chapter for a better world. To use the synergy of life experiences that build trust and belief in our ability to make every action in our daily life bring us closer to living in a kinder, gentler world. To find and speak with an authentic voice as torchbearers for virtuous philanthropy, using our stories as a magnet, and that draws and unites all living generations of men and women around the world in harmonious thought and deed. "I think we need to embrace all these differences," says Ronda Stryker, a member of the Michigan Women's Commission. "Men and women think differently. But we all live on this planet together."[8] Philanthropy is a viable platform for creating and carrying out a vision for a more just, understanding, compassionate, and forgiving world, respectful of all and judgmental of none.

How to Tell Your Story

How do you begin to tell your story, especially those of us, boom-generation women now in midlife, looking forward with urgency and a calling to find the ultimate purpose and meaning in our life? Where do we find the time, the courage, and the direction? We need to look first at some of the recurring motifs we identify as our core values. For many of us, it will be some if not all of the seven virtues, the four cardinal ones—prudence, fortitude, justice, and temperance—and the three theological ones—faith, hope, and love. These are the themes on which to build your story. These are the virtues that lead us to the values we cherish in our life, such as beauty, equality, excellence, education, family, harmony, healing, opportunity, and traditions, and to the causes and concerns that are most important for us to support, such as children, education, healthcare, environment, art, theater, music, and religion. Think of experiences you have had that relate to your specific values—how you felt, who was involved, what were the circumstances, why it made a difference, and what there is still left to do by using your time, talent, and treasure to fulfill your hopes and dreams.

There are several techniques to help organize your thoughts and provide a structure for telling and preserving your story; some are included in this chapter. Use whatever is most appropriate for your situation, be creative, and enjoy the journey. You may prefer to work in a group, or you may prefer to work alone. It is the message, not the medium, which is important; it is in sharing your words from your heart that you will inspire others and yourself and realize how each woman's story, although unique in content, is alike in purpose and passion.

If you approach the organization of your thought from a visual perspective, storyboard and scrapbooking techniques work well. They are not only flexible but fun and a wonderful way to relive many of the experiences and memories that form the foundation for the values and beliefs that shape our present and future actions. Storyboarding is a useful and flexible way to set down and construct the large footprint of your legacy story. It can be done on the computer, but most often it works best with a cork board, pushpins, and Post-it notes. Scrapbooking is a creative way to give personality to your legacy since you have the freedom to choose the photographs, memorabilia (e.g., newspaper clippings), and letters and design how you want to display them. In addition to keeping the family memories alive in a creative way, scrapbooking in a group or club meeting sets the tone for building social capital in the community, as well. And modern technology makes it easy to preserve the artifacts in digital form when appropriate. Specific information and resources on storyboarding and scrapbooking can be found in the Resources section of this book.

If you are more inclined to organize your thoughts by writing, consider writing a letter, joining a writing circle, or composing an ethical will. Margaret created the Heart-O-Gram™ as a starting thought point (see Exhibit 5.1). It provides a road map for the journey of your thought where you decide the destination—a good way to "prime the pump," as her grandmother would say. A starting thought point is: "From my grandmother I learned that" and the destination point is your answer. Your response can be as short or long as you wish, and your answer leads you to write other meaningful Heart-O-Grams. For example: "I care about _____, and if I had all the money in the world I would ____." In this way, a

Words from the
Heart-O-Gram ♡™

Voice,
Values, &
Vision

I make a difference in my community by . . . .
. . . .
. . . .
. . . .
. . . .
. . . .

I want to be remembered as a person who . . . .
. . . .
. . . .
. . . .
. . . .
. . . .

I receive joy from giving because . . . .
. . . .
. . . .
. . . .
. . . .
. . . .

Something that I am grateful for that has changed my life is . . . .
. . . .
. . . .
. . . .
. . . .
. . . .

If I had a million dollars I would change the world by . . . .
. . . .
. . . .
. . . .
. . . .

Exhibit 5.1 Words from the Heart-O-Gram™
Illustrations by Elizabeth Huggins-Thompson.

legacy *value* (caring) uses a legacy *valuable* (money) to connect to an authentic heartfelt issue in need of attention. And even though you might not have "all the money in the world," you may find that your answer leads you to other resourceful ways to support your cause and honor your legacy. The Heart-O-Grams are useful guides as you write your personal legacy statement. Some refer to their legacy statement as an ethical will. The origin of the ethical will dates back to early religious and spiritual teachings. First as an oral tradition and later as a written directive, an ethical will provides a way to convey moral directives, future blessings, and advice of an ethical nature, "bidding them [the readers] to go forward and lead full, principled, and virtuous lives," writes Barry K. Baines in his book *Ethical Wills,* a step-by-step manual on how to write, use, and archive this powerful document.[9] Author Rachael Freed in her book *Women's Lives: Women's Legacies* notes that the ethical will "remains, in many ways, a Jewish patriarchal tradition. . . . And yet, legacy writing seems a natural undertaking for many women today. We are the weavers, the storytellers, the memory vessels who gather, build, and sustain our communities." Freed has renamed the ethical will written by women as a "spiritual-ethical will, because "writing about our deepest values is courageous, spiritual work," and it "allows your work to resonate with [your] own sense of sacred."[10]

If you prefer to use technology to preserve and transmit your life story, a growing number of professionals will work with you to produce a customized biographical video or DVD. All these techniques and mediums serve one ultimate goal: to enable you to affirm who you are, articulate what you believe, and share your story in a meaningful way.

Writing your story provides a way for you to:

1. Articulate your legacy of unique talents and abilities.
2. Spark your passion to engage in projects with others that make your heart sing.
3. Give energy and meaning to your values, voice, and vision for a better world.
4. Engage you heart and head in creative thinking for a sustainable community.
5. Live with peace, joy, and happiness in your soul.

Principle Two: Every Woman Is a Philanthropist

Every woman is a philanthropist who gives her time, talent, and treasure to the best of her ability. As we have heard over and over again, it is not a requirement to have great wealth to be a philanthropist, only to have a desire to make a difference and leave the world a better place than you found it. Practicing philanthropy is living the values you believe through the authentic use and direction of your resources. It is not an act of doing but rather a way of living, of intrinsically being your values. Throughout the annals of history, women's courage, compassion, and caring spirit is well documented. Their universal deeds in strengthening the fabric of society carry forward the true meaning of the secular dimensions of the Greek word *philanthropos,* the love of humankind. Philanthropy is how we integrate and express spirituality and abundance by the freedom we have to choose how we give our time, talent, and treasure.

With the freedom to choose how we distribute our gifts, however, comes the responsibility of being either a voluntary or an involuntary philanthropist. If our action is outer driven, we respond or react only to outside influences and requests for our gifts, such as peer pressure or quid pro quo appeals. Our energy gets pushed and pulled in several directions, our values and our valuables scatter, and we are involuntary philanthropists. We have limited accountability for our action. We have very little rationale for why we say yes or no to a specific project, and we lack empowerment. If our action is inner directed, we respond proactively to requests by first deciding if they align with our values. If we then consciously direct our energy to strategic alliances that provide us with measurable ways to account for our actions, we are voluntary philanthropists. We have a framework from which to leverage our gifts and develop meaningful and trustful relationships with the community we serve and support. We build an environment for open dialogue and creative thinking among like-minded individuals in search of long-term solutions by the prudent use of time and talent. And the prudent use of these resources reflects ultimately in how we choose to allocate our money.

"Money is congealed energy," writes mythologist Joseph Campbell, "and releasing it releases life's possibilities."[11] How we direct our energy gives money its meaning. Money is the emotional currency through which we express our values, our dreams, our hopes and aspirations. We give cold cash its warm heart when we use and direct the flow of energy to fund and support the projects that we believe will make the world a better place. "Material wealth," says Jean Shinoda Bolen, M.D., in her book *Urgent Message from Mother*, "is like good health, good genes, and natural talent—it is part of our personal, spiritual, and psychological journey to use or waste."[12] It is the same with time and talent; we can be either a voluntary or an involuntary philanthropist with our money. Again, it is a matter of choice and having our actions align with our values as to where and how we release the congealed energy. How we use our money reflects our beliefs and priorities in life. For many boom-generation women, living a meaningful life is no longer about buying more and more "stuff." It is time to clean out the closets, unburden ourselves of years of accumulated must-haves, and reflect on where our money can do the most good in society. We realize and accept media hype for the short-term euphoria that it promises, turn a deaf ear, and listen instead to our authentic inner voice. That inner voice coaches and directs us in how to invest our money for solutions to bring more harmony, compassion, and equality into our community and into the global world to which we are all interconnected as one family. We listen and learn from each other's ways to invest our money in purposeful ways rather than spend it on perishable goods. Our mind-set turns from living a life of conspicuous consumption to living a life of contagious compassion. And we have the courage to say enough is enough.

A voluntary philanthropist directs her money; an involuntary philanthropist allows money to direct her. One is empowered, the other is disenfranchised. A voluntary philanthropist seeks guidance from financial and legal professionals to assess the benefits of using our tax system to direct her money while alive and through her estate planning at death, to ensure that her story lives on in her legacy for her family and for her community. A voluntary philanthropist has the necessary clarity of purpose, passion, and power, and her wealth mirrors her values.

Being a voluntary philanthropist requires making choices that align living your values with the giving of your valuables. In her book *Inspired Philanthropy*, Tracy Gary offers a technique

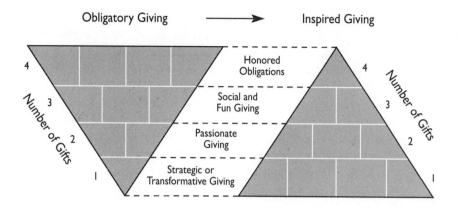

Obligatory Giving   ⟶   Inspired Giving

Honored Obligations

Social and Fun Giving

Passionate Giving

Strategic or Transformative Giving

American households, on average, give $1,900 per year to charity, spread among 10 donations. Most of these gifts fall into the "obligatory" sphere. You can turn your current giving upside-down with inspired philanthropy.

Exhibit 5.2 Inspired Philanthropy Paradigm

Reprinted with permission of John Wiley & Sons, Inc. First published in Inspired Legacies, third edition by Tracy Gary with Nancy Adess, Jossey-Bass, A Wiley Imprint, San Francisco 2008

(see Exhibit 5.2) to focus your gifts so that they reflect your passion and help you to engage the Three Principles of Abundance. Although you may be giving the same total amount of money, you will have repositioned your individual gifts and moved from "obligatory giving to inspired giving."[13]

Principle Three: Every Woman Makes a Difference

How do you know you truly make a difference? How do you know if you do not? Neither question requires an answer, because if you are living your legacy as a voluntary philanthropist, you *are* making a difference. It is only human to question and want to see results from the voluntary gifts of our time, talent, and treasure. But by what standards can or should we measure whether we make a difference or not? If you believe in your values and your work, you lead by example, and if you listen to your heart, you know the world would be less but for the kindness of your actions, your thoughts, and your love. "We ourselves feel that what we are doing is just a drop in the ocean," Mother Teresa says, "But the ocean would be less because of that missing drop."

Carolyn Eychaner and her daughter, Alisa, who live in the Augusta, Georgia, area, listened to their heart while on a two-week medical mission trip to Honduras. They served on an eye team, going to two villages with no electricity or running water and taking with them 10, 000 pair of glasses donated by the Lions Club. "There were some very touching moments," Carolyn recalls.

> We set up our equipment in a school yard and worked from sunup to sundown giving eye exams and coming up with readings for their glasses, and then finding the closest match in the glasses we had with us. When we fit one elderly man, who probably had not seen well in years, we could not find a perfect match and the glasses' frames were not the best, but what a smile he had on his face, because he could see! The love in that place was so wonderful. You actually felt it.

As she and her daughter reflected on the trip, they both agreed that their most important memory from the experience was that

> We don't really have to do much to make a difference. We just have to have a willing heart and listen for when God calls us to do something in His name. And it made us truly know what it means to "count our blessings" and appreciate them, because we have seen how little some have and how grateful they are for a smile or a hug or a pat on the head, and a pair of eyeglasses.[14]

Empowerment Cycle

How the Cycle Works

For many women, empowerment is not simple but it is intuitive. To bring clarity to the process, we have identified four distinct steps that create a cycle that helps a woman design, optimize, and empower her life as a torchbearer for virtuous philanthropy. We call this process the Empowerment Cycle™ (see Exhibit 5.3).

Here are the four steps of the cycle:

1. Affirm and discover your core values.
2. Align to causes.

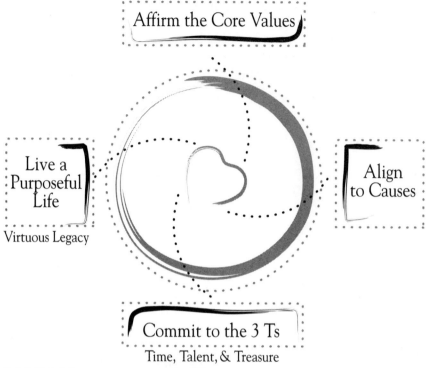

Exhibit 5.3 Empowerment Cycle™
Illustrations by Elizabeth Huggins-Thompson.

3. Commit to the three Ts: time, talent, and treasure.
4. Live a purposeful life.

Each step leads to the next. Each step strengthens awareness and purpose. It illuminates truth and beauty while building trust, confidence, and respect. The Empowerment Cycle is designed to bring a woman closer to a celebration of her life story, to define her part as a weaver of the invisible web for a sustainable worldview of universal harmony.

The process is paradoxical in that you become more myopic in your view yet you also become more mystic in your vision. The more clearly you see the truth of who you are, the more freedom you have to imagine and dream of what you can accomplish. And as with most cycles, once the process is put in motion, it will continue to spiral, bringing new consciousness and greater empowerment to all your endeavors.

As you begin to work with this empowerment cycle, it is useful to use the next quartet of questions (which spells out the acronym REAL) as a reference and litmus guide to how you construct your personal cycle. Doing so will keep you focused and a voluntary philanthropist.

REAL Questions

Is it *relevant* to how I live my life?
Can it *engage* my passion?
Will it compel me to take *action*?
How does it inspire my *legacy*?

When Sally Hare-Schriner first sat down with her financial planner to set up her charitable remainder trust, her alma mater, the University of Kansas in Lawrence, was just establishing its United Early Childhood Program. This program, in the School of Education, trains teachers to work with young children. Sally's advisor from her graduate-school days was the development director for the program. Here is an example of how REAL actually can work and did:

Relevant. Sally's undergraduate degree was in Human and Child Development and her graduate degree was in Early Childhood Special Education. She now teaches in the afternoons, five days a week, at a small rural public school where a program for at-risk four-year-olds is now in its thirteenth year. "We work with students who are on the low socioeconomic scale, are being raised by a single parent, or have some sort of developmental delay, but not serious enough for special education services," says Sally. "And statistically these kids are at risk for failure in school. We work with them to help them become strong and confident so they're ready to start kindergarten and hit the ground running." As Sally found out when talking to her advisor, the United Early Childhood Program was underfunded, and the school had to limit the number of students in the program.

Engage. "They were limiting the number of students they could bring into a program that has always been a passion of mine," recalls Sally. "I was thinking, this is not right, I'm going to give this money to them now so they've got some money and the program can go forward and expand.

Action. Sally explains: "After I made the decision to give to the program now, I didn't realize that it solidified the program because this money is earmarked only for the United Early Childhood Program. The program can't be disbanded because the fund could not be spent for any other program within the School of Education. And that was the icing on the cake for me."

Legacy. The Sally Hare-Schriner Educational Fund.[15]

Creating Your Empowerment Cycle

Step 1: Affirm and Discover Core Values. The values developed in youth serve as a foundation for what we honor and believe as adults. Values are what we believe, what we cherish, what guides our decisions, and what impact how we think and act. And while values form in early childhood through association and experience, and from our role models, they tend to remain elusive unless we make a conscious effort to take the time to reflect and engage both the heart and the mind to find answers to what is important and why it is important. Go back to Chapter 2 to review your values pyramid to confirm your decisions.

Validating the qualities and feelings that we intuitively know direct the way to live life and make choices is a formal process. Think of those admirable and honorable qualities that impact your life: creativity, knowledge, freedom, justice, harmony, and excellence. What qualities give you happiness and joy when they are present in your life and bring you sadness and discomfort when they are not? These provide the first set of clues for understanding what you are truly passionate about and where you can make a difference in the world. For instance, if you value the beauty, harmony, and knowledge of classical music, you may support the local community orchestra, music education in local schools, or even create a perpetual scholarship for a talented student at the local conservatory or university. These values are relevant to the REAL you.

Answer these questions to help affirm and discover your core values:

1. What did my parents and grandparents find important, and how did they influence my values?

2. Who were the three or so most influential people in my child-hood, and how did they influence my values?
3. What are some of the most important family traditions that guide my actions and thoughts?
4. Identify a difficult life experience and describe how your values shaped the decisions you had to make.
5. What are three values you feel are important and want to instill in the lives of your loved ones?

Step 2: Align to Causes. Perhaps now you have a better idea of your core values. But you must align these beliefs to a cause in order to focus your legacy and truly make a difference. In this instant-information age of the Internet, something as simple as a using a search engine, like Google, can be an efficient technique to keep focus and intent on what brings purpose and passion in our lives. Yet even that can seem like too much work sometimes. Constant multitasking often leads to the fragmentation of our time and compromise of our ability to enjoy quality moments with our family, our friends, and in our community activities. Boom-generation women must expand their worldview so their hearts can stay open to see more and more ways to be of service. Yes, we are the first to admit, it can be overwhelming. The realities of the needs we see far exceed our resources and abilities, and without boundaries, disillusionment might well deter even the most dedicated from completing a task. How do you validate the choices you made for the use of your time, talent, and treasure? How do you foster deeper connections with organizations and causes that you believe in your heart can best make use of your resources? How do you gain the self-knowledge that your actions do indeed reinforce your values and beliefs? A conscious alignment of values with the causes we support is one of the most reliable and ethical filters designed to set recognizable and responsible boundaries for philanthropic work.

"To thine own self be true!" This maxim resonates with great authenticity and purpose, builds natural boundaries, and provides direction for our empowerment. You may care about parks and recreational facilities in your community, and you may value equality for all children so they all have access to well-equipped facilities. If so, you can sit on the community advisory board to leave a legacy of service for a cause that is dear to your heart. It engages the REAL you.

Consider these questions to help align your values with your causes:

1. What would make your community a better place?
2. Name at least one current initiative you know of that speaks to your values.
3. Identify three community organizations that reflect your values, and describe the projects that you would undertake to make the world a little better for the next generation.
4. What do you appreciate most about the opportunity to support a cause you know will make a difference in your community? Write down your feelings.
5. What roadblocks can you identify, if any, that stand in the way of achieving your goals? What resources can you identify to help you get past the roadblocks?

Step 3: Commit to the Three Ts: Time, Talent, and Treasure. Time, talent, and treasure are the tangible attributes used to connect our important values and issues that are a reflection of the truth in our lives. The process of empowerment brings with it a critical assessment of where and how to appropriate the three Ts. It is an evaluation to see if your current situation meets the REAL criteria from Steps 1 and 2. And be REAL indeed! This is the time to be factual. To leave a legacy, you have to know what you are willing to give up and understand where you are in life. You must balance your lifestyle with your selfless passion in order to become an effective and efficient part of a cause. You will need to make a commitment. This is a matter of holding yourself accountable. If your Ts do not honestly reflect your desire and determination to allocate precious resources, there will not be a great societal impact in tandem with your fundamental values. The critical questions regarding how much time and money and the talent and skills available demand forthright attention, not only in what you can give but also what you can get others to give. How vast is your network? For many boom-generation women, this may be a first-time assessment. For others, it may be a review of current strategies, either of a simplistic or sophisticated nature, triggered by a life-altering event. Some of the more common of these events include death of a loved one, unexpected inheritance, a divorce settlement, a pending planned retirement (bringing with it extra time to volunteer), or even the completion of a financial analysis heralding news that you probably will never outlive your assets or income stream, resulting in significant discretionary income. Perhaps you have recently completed drafting estate planning documents—from simple bequests to complex family foundations and trusts, depending on your situation, that adequately reflect your values and valuables. Step 3 is an ongoing process as new experiences, opportunities, and challenges appear on the horizon and demand critical assessment of current strategies. It compels you to take REAL action.

Consider these questions when determining how and where to commit your time, talent, and treasure:

1. Whom do I know with similar values and who can complement my resources so that together we can maximize our time, talent, and treasure for our own mutual benefit and that of the organization. How might we create extended networks with like-minded individuals and organizations?
2. What are the creative ways in which I may use my skills to facilitate a higher visibility for the issues I care about in the community? What civic or social clubs do I belong to where I can recruit volunteers?
3. How can I maximize my current gifts, especially money, so that I can participate in the important work of making a difference and be able to carry out my values while I am alive? Would a challenge or a matching grant be effective?
4. What are some of the legal documents I can use to teach my grandchildren and children how to be good stewards of philanthropy, and how can I do this while I am still alive?
5. When I think about my legacy, how would I like to be remembered in my obituary? How did I spend my "dash"?

Step 4: Live a Purposeful Life. The act of empowerment manifests itself in a purposeful life. Confidence replaces doubt. Choice replaces chance. With less effort, more gets accomplished. The energy and conviction of purpose in actions becomes a magnet that attracts others to leadership and mission. In meaningful ways, you can help others in their journey. New solutions to old problems appear on the horizon and lead to a more sustainable neighborhood, a new playground and a safe house for children, a medical break-through for Alzheimer's disease, or perhaps a midlife career change transitioning to the nonprofit sector. Empowerment gives you the freedom to believe in the beauty of your dreams. It confirms your REAL life.

To live a purposeful life, it is helpful to create your own mission statement. This statement will serve as your philanthropic "mantra." It is your calling card to inform the world of your virtuous philanthropy, and in doing so, it can inspire others to be more strategic about their mission. It is a statement to center your current giving strategy and build a deeper relationship with the people and the institutions you support. It tells the reason you give your money, time, and talent. It may take a few drafts to get it down to one or two sentences, but keep at it. Build on your insight from the empowerment cycle. Most statements are two to three sentences and paint a vivid picture of what your belief or passion is, what you do about it, and how you do it. They are brief, positive, joyful, and full of energy. Your statement is your authentic voice shouting to the world, "This is my purpose. This is my passion. These are my values. I can connect my bank book with my soul bank."

Here are four examples:

1. I believe that education is the door to opportunity for young children. Therefore, I give $500 or more each year to the library fund specifically to buy books for children ages five to seven.
2. I believe every child deserves a safe and loving environment. I volunteer on the facilities committee at the local safe-haven shelter for young women, and I ask my friends to donate their furniture, clothes, and money.
3. My purpose in life is to bring dignity and respect to elders in my community. I serve on the fundraising committee to raise the money to build a new million-dollar wing for the Senior Citizens' Day Care Center and volunteer to play the guitar once a week.
4. I want to make the environment safe and sustainable for future generations. My purpose is to educate and inform as many people as possible as to how they can start grassroots advocacy organizations in their community, and I fund projects through my donor-advised fund set up at the community foundation.

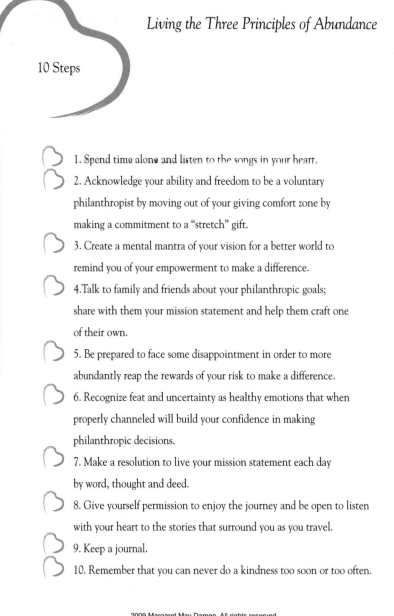

Living the Three Principles of Abundance

10 Steps

1. Spend time alone and listen to the songs in your heart.

2. Acknowledge your ability and freedom to be a voluntary philanthropist by moving out of your giving comfort zone by making a commitment to a "stretch" gift.

3. Create a mental mantra of your vision for a better world to remind you of your empowerment to make a difference.

4. Talk to family and friends about your philanthropic goals; share with them your mission statement and help them craft one of their own.

5. Be prepared to face some disappointment in order to more abundantly reap the rewards of your risk to make a difference.

6. Recognize feat and uncertainty as healthy emotions that when properly channeled will build your confidence in making philanthropic decisions.

7. Make a resolution to live your mission statement each day by word, thought and deed.

8. Give yourself permission to enjoy the journey and be open to listen with your heart to the stories that surround you as you travel.

9. Keep a journal.

10. Remember that you can never do a kindness too soon or too often.

Exhibit 5.4 Living the Three Principles of Abundance

As you continue your journey and take action on implementing your mission statement, it is important to have touchstones that remind you of your progress. It is also a source to use in times when patience and trust may be in the shadow of anxiety and doubt. This ten-step guide (see Exhibit 5.4) to Living the Three Principles of Abundance is a foundation and model to which you can add your own personal expressions and experiences.

What Is Your Mission Statement?

How Do You Define Philanthropic Empowerment?

1. This is what I empower myself to believe:
   I believe that _____

2. This is what I empower myself to do:
   Therefore, my purpose is to _____

3. This is how I empower myself to do it:
   And so I _____

4. This is why I empower myself to do it:
   Because it makes_____

5. This is where I empower myself to do it:
   As a _____ at the _____

Write your complete mission statement by hand on a postcard or in a letter; do not type your statement. Address the card or envelope to yourself, and send it by post-mail, not e-mail, the same day you write it. When you receive and open it, read it out loud to another person or family member. Then place it where you can read it daily and reflect on how your empowerment makes a difference that day.
My mission is to _____
_____
_____
_____

Ask yourself: What would you attempt to do if you knew you could not fail?
_____
_____
_____
_____
_____
_____

CHAPTER

6

Trust, Leverage, Capital

A WOMAN'S WAY

Only those who risk going too far can possibly find out how far they can go.

—T. S. Elliott (1888–1965)

When women choose to invest their energy and leadership capacity in virtuous philanthropy, they envision an energetic, diverse, and vibrant community of which they are a part. This means the human community of relationships, not cold steel buildings. In 1910, suffragist Rheta Childe Dorr, proclaimed, "Women's place is in the home, but home is not contained within the four walls of an individual home. Home is the Community."[1] The modern thinking, planning, self-governing, educated woman came into a world that is losing faith in the commercial ideal, and is endeavoring to substitute in its place a social ideal. One hundred years later, community is still home. It is the sanctuary for women, sensitive to the nuances of eclectic and nontraditional ideas, to gather and surround themselves with the free flow of information and knowledge so desperately needed to transform problems into solutions. "You live your life and you experience everything, and you learn things along the way," says Cincinnati Impact 100 founder Wendy Steele. "When you come together in a group it gives you a way to look at things in a fresh new way and find a solution for problems that

117

other women may recognize but may not fully address in the same way. The bottom line, what some may think selfish is the wonderful feeling it is to be part of the solution and to be giving back."[2]

In her book *Everyday Grace*, author Marianne Williamson expresses her concern about today's world: "We cannot escape one another, and in our right minds we wouldn't want to. Spending extraordinary resources trying to protect ourselves from our fellow human beings, rather than on efforts to build righteous relationships, is a backward model of human interaction." She reminds us: "Only by finding the love within us can we provide the love that will save the world."[3] This first decade of the twenty-first century is about loving relationships, about giving back to society and healing a world that will not survive without a reaching out from us all to make the environment, the society we have created, whole.

It is service with love that will save the world, and as boomer women, we are drawn to serve others in a holistic way. Service to others not only heals and makes us happy; it creates a trusting, transparent environment in which to maximize our leadership capability. Empowerment gives us the leverage, the tools, to use our strengths collaboratively, which, in turn, builds the social, intellectual, spiritual, and financial capital of trust, leverage, and capital (TLC)—in a woman's way. And it has never been more important to build TLC that sticks, that has teeth and can manifest itself in a virtuous legacy and the doing of good, practical, solid works that mend the world.

Trust is the first ingredient in our formula. Without it we cannot make the world function effectively. In fact, we believe it is not possible to have lasting TLC without absolute trust. It is transparency that enables us to work together side by side, and it is not a one-time act but an ongoing process. For a nonprofit, transparency is critical. It says about the organization: Hey, look at us, we have nothing to hide, our books are clean, we're proud of the way we do business, give to the community, donate our time and talent and treasure, treat our employees, clients and stakeholders. It is a process of letting people see we live in a glass house in a world where so many believe that transparency is nothing more than a buzzword. We believe transparency builds trust. It is the fabric of our lives and embraces our ethics, integrity, and values.

Mark Twain said, "If you tell the truth you don't have to remember." For boomer women, telling the truth is part of their social promise. We rebelled for truth, marched for truth, and embraced it. Standing up for our truth empowered us to be the women we are today. Our writers, both of prose and poetry; our heroes, whether male or female, Steinem or Mandela, were transparent, "open kimono,"[4] with nothing to hide. Our heroes were not about flaunting virtuous character when someone was looking; just the opposite. The actions of the heroes on which we modeled ourselves led to transparent leadership: the act of putting the needs and concerns of people first so that the whole organization (society or family) prospers. From many of our boomer filmmakers, such as Steven Spielberg and George Lucas, we saw transparency in action: Consider Oskar Schindler using TLC and taking huge risks in service to Jews in Germany, or George Lucas, with "May the force be with you,"[5] or even Spike Lee, with an honesty that made us squirm. We grew up expecting transparency; we made it a fact of life.

Yet the world today is suffering from a lack of honesty that threatens to destroy our public and private institutions. This trust—or lack thereof—guides our service to the nonprofits we give our resources to. It is becoming even more important for our nonprofits to do their due diligence. Because boomer women tend to get involved with an organization first, then contribute to it, it is critical that nonprofits establish transparency from the very beginning. Transparency is part of honoring and living by the Donor Bill of Rights, a document to assure that philanthropy merits the trust and respect of the general public, (this document is printed at the end of Chapter 7).[6] Transparency serves both the giver and the recipient. A recent Guidestar survey promoting the disclosure of financial records found that of the 1,837 nonprofits/charities surveyed, only 13% had extensive financial information posted on their Web sites, even though transparency is the key to building a community of donors.[7] In the world of giving, we expect our charities to be transparent or we vote a loud resounding no, by not contributing our dollars.

Transparency, open communication and absolute truth telling, builds trust and loyalty and is necessary for the future of business, public and private. Yet in the United States, according to a 2005

Harris poll, only 22% of us trust the media, only 8% trust political parties, 27% trust government (recent economic/political and other events may have lowered that figure), and only 12% trust big companies. British sociologist David Halpern tells us that only 34% of Americans believe other people can be trusted. And we are far from the most distrustful; the British are at a 29% trust ratio; Latin Americans, at 23%.[8]

Is it any wonder that a 2004 study of 25,000 high school students showed that 67% of the boys and 52% of the girls surveyed said: "In the real world, successful people do what they have to do to win, even if others consider it cheating."[9] According to Stephen M. R. Covey, author of *The Speed of Trust*, 75% of business students, 63% of law students, 63% of medical students, 52% of education students (our future teachers), and 43% of liberal arts students cheat to get into graduate school. Covey goes on to say that convicts in minimum security prisons score as high as do MBA students on their ethical dilemma exams. So why all the fuss? If everyone's doing it, it must be okay.[10]

Enter the Sarbanes-Oxley Act.[11] The act was passed in the early 2000s in response to the corporate havoc created by cheaters, such as the chief executive officer (CEO) of WorldCom, Bernie Ebbers, worth $1.4 billion, who in 2005 was convicted of fraud, with $3.85 billion in company accounting misstatements, and Enron's Jeff Skilling, who talked about his company's 64-page ethics manual and how ethical his company was. The Enron greed and malfeasance debacle led to one of the largest company bankruptcies in United States history. Many of its employees became financial victims losing all of their retirement savings as a result.[12] Sarbanes-Oxley requires company CEOs to certify the accuracy of their revenue reporting. Yet the cheating goes on: Witness today's financial debacle and the Ponzi scams in the world. Although Sarbanes-Oxley has had a somewhat positive effect on improving/sustaining trust in the public's eye, this has come about at a substantial price. A recent study shows that the price of implementing policies of just one section, at $35 billion, exceeds the original estimate of the Security and Exchange Commission by 28 times.[13] The compliance to the act and to the regulations involved are a tremendous cost to doing business. Consider the opposite: high trust, lower costs and time involved. We still want to do business on a handshake. When trust is there because of transparency, we are confident about working with an organization. Covey tells us when trust is low, speed goes down and costs go up.

The late Peter Drucker, management guru and long a hero in the nonprofit world, believed that organizations are built on trust. "Trust means that you know what to expect of people, it's mutual understanding. Not mutual love, not even mutual respect, but predictability. This is even more important in the nonprofit organization because it typically has to depend on the work of so many volunteers and so many people whom it does not control."[14] He and others believe that we are in a crisis of trust and that transparency is the key to building a community of donors.

Patricia Aburdene, author of *Megatrends 2010,* says: "Transcendent values like trust and integrity literally translate into revenue, profits, and prosperity."[15] What we have learned from the boomer women we interviewed is that transparency is vital to their being involved and giving of their time and monies to an organization. They have grown up in the world of *Wired* magazine, in which in a March 2007 article quoted CEO Glen Kelman of Redfin, who advocates complete transparency in his organization and says, "Fire the publicist, go off message, let your employees blab and blog. In the new world of radical transparency the path to business success is clear—clarity."[16] Don Tapscott, coauthor of *The Naked Corporation,* tells us that transparency is the future of business. He believes that information technology lays bare the internal dealings of companies and nonprofits.[17] Tapscott advocates a policy of transparency whereby organizations disclose all possible information, which he believes that by doing so boosts employee morale and performance and builds client and stakeholder trust.

Our interviews bear out the need for a charity to be more transparent. In our interviews, we asked our boomer women to identify their primary motivations for giving. We wanted to know what engaged a donor and what kept her engaged when there was so much competition for her time and money. What we discovered is the thought our interviewees put into the process. Overwhelmingly our group said they wanted to be assured the organizations they gave to were well run. This fact was almost as important to them as the cause the organization espoused. Our interviewees also wanted to feel vested in the organization. They felt a strong need for personal relationships, and they wanted to know how their contributions specifically made a difference. Both before they became involved and most especially during their involvement, they wanted and needed detailed information on the organization, from its financials to its trustees. They wanted to know how it managed its finances, the leadership's management philosophy and accountability, and the organization's ability to meet its mission. The more they understood how their contribution supported the organization's mission and how their gift was integral to its success, the more generous they were with their support.

The giving of time often served as the leading indicator of our interviewees' involvement with an organization, and the more involved they became, the more generous they then were with their money. According to a recent national survey by the Points of Light Institute, people who volunteer contribute 2.5 times more money to causes than those who do not. Each of our interviewees wanted to see the results of her giving and to know she was making a difference. Many said they gave to empower other women, and to causes near to their hearts, often involving women and children. In most cases, the gifts are up close and personal, yet they expressed an interest in sound management so the gift could be leveraged. For our interviewees, the organization's overall business acumen, professionalism, and efficiency were major elements in the decision to give.

The cause given to initially hit a hot button with our interviewees; they clearly favored making contributions that produced successful change, not to keep the status quo. They gave to make a shift in the current situation as they observed it. These women were not easily influenced. They researched, they were selective, and they made sure their dollars had social and political significance. They were the power behind the gift, not the gentle hand guiding it. They knew they had the power to solve problems and make a better environment for future generations. Many were interested in or already had formed partnerships with other women so as to have a stronger voice in shaping the future of philanthropy and of society.

In their lifetimes, boomer women have lived through and experienced major social upheaval. Their world today is very different from that of their mothers. In some cases, they personally had a hand in forming the environment we live in. That environment trusts less and asks more. Several of our interviewees had stopped giving to some organizations because of what they perceived to be the organization's lack of accountability. A donation was felt to be an investment in the future of the organization, its mission, and the community.

They are asking some serious questions that are causing non-profits to rethink and review their current policies. Nonprofits must examine many areas of concern; possibly none is more critical than the need for transparency and public accountability. Nonprofits depend on charitable contributions, which in turn depend on public trust. Without that trust, they can not raise the monies to carry out their mission. Yet many are paying little attention to proper governance, to excessive compensation and perquisites to their officers and executives, and to conflicts of interest. The many scandals relating to shoddy practices, overcompensation, ethical practices, and just poor oversight in some nonprofits brand the innocent rest.

Boomer women, who grew up with the mentality "Don't trust anyone over 30," are demanding more oversight. Nonprofits that want their time and treasure would do well to open their books and practices, and share specifically where each dollar goes. Spending too much to raise monies is frowned on, and, as one interviewee said, "There is no such thing as too much information." A major distinguishing characteristic of nonprofits is the mission to serve the public interest. If boomer women are going to continue to gift, transparency and trust is of the highest importance. We advise both the giver and the recipient to engage, to be willing to ask and answer, to know what is important to both, and to get involved. With involvement comes an understanding of how the organization is run in all areas of its mission. And knowledge is the first fundamental of transparency: the openness that leads to trust.

Leverage

The dictionary gives several meanings to the word "leverage," from a type of "dance" connection to any influence that is compounded or used to gain an advantage; to use; to take full advantage. And in charitable giving, for our purposes, we can say that leverage is in fact all of the above—truly a "dance" connection, so that the giver and the gift of resources can magnify and compound the financial outcome and influence.

In *The Greater Good*, speaking to the future of philanthropy, author Claire Gaudiani tells us:

> What we do now will define the future. . . . Despite some real pitfalls possible in generosity, there are currently a significant number of excellent ideas already moving around the country, awaiting scaling up and out. If these and other ideas succeed, history may one day say that this wealth accumulation was a world-class opportunity that Americans knew how to exploit for the common good.[18]

Yet now that what the United States had managed to achieve economically and otherwise is in question, it has never been more important to look at socioeconomic pitfalls and recognize that we may not have the same resources. This makes it even more important to understand and appreciate the fact that it is women who are changing the face of philanthropy. Among women, it is boomer women who are the most generous this society has ever seen.

It is imperative that we as a society take full advantage of generosity so that our charities can collaborate to serve the common good, a cause near and dear to boomers. Wendy Steele is passionate about collaboration and leverage. She says:

> In learning about the nonprofit world and women's involvement and empowerment and volunteering and what boards need, I sort of came up with a solution—to better leverage our resources, and that is what Impact 100 was and is. Typically if women get together and talk about how to raise money for a cause they are passionate about, they will come up with a very hand's on activity. Men, they are more likely to get on the phone and call their friends and ask them to write a check. So part of the solution is to get more women engaged in philanthropy. If they were more engaged they would want to do more and more. So Impact 100 was about women writing a check for $1,000 to join, having an equal vote as the president—me, at the time—on what we did and who we gifted. We pooled our money together and now we have a bigger impact, $100,000 rather than a $1,000. Now I can be connected to a really significant gift of a $100,000 gift to the community. And if I feel

connected to that gift in a very special way, then I'd want to give more, I'd want to stay involved, I'd want my friends to do the same—and the ripple effect would continue to grow.[19]

That is the leverage through collaboration—the "dance connection." We believe that women are reinventing the term "collaboration" for social change—their hot button—in philanthropy in dozens of ways. Through strategic alliances they are changing the face of media, politics, and educational and social institutions. In spite of the downturn in the economy in 2008, women are banding together more forcefully, and their target is the common good for social change . . . the recurring theme of boomer women, except this time around they have got the power and the dollars behind them.

In its August 2008 release of the most current data, the Internal Revenue Service reported that 43% of the nation's top 2.7 million wealth holders in 2004 were women. More than a third (35%) of the women in that group are between 50 and 65 years old.[20] In 2009, as the economy went into a downturn spiral, economists predicted that women were more likely to keep their jobs than men. And as Margaret reminds us, more women have been learning to manage financial portfolios and steward their wealth: "Women are no longer like a deer in headlights about finances. They know profit and loss, understand the balance sheet and write big checks." As the *Economist* magazine recently said, "Arguably, women are now the most powerful engine of global growth."[21]

Kimberly Davis, president of the JPMorgan Chase Foundation, speaking at a Women's Philanthropy Institute conference on women and philanthropy in November 2008, said: "I ask you to ask yourself what it will take on your part, on my part, on our part, to be able to read in ten years that women have taken the leadership role to rebuild the world communities. The power is within our control."[22] And that power is being leveraged daily through, mentoring our children and young people to step up to the plate and be the next generation of philanthropists, modeling, through giving circles, community foundations, women's funds, e-philanthropy, social venture philanthropy, and nurturing the dance of connection.

For women boomers, there comes a time when we look at ourselves in the eye and say, What's this all about? What should I be doing, what do I want to do, how can I contribute? What is my life about? What is my legacy? We wrote this book specifically with the intent to stimulate your thinking. To do so, we are discussing the myriad ways that you can contribute to our society. We encourage you to you explore each of these areas further. Next we briefly address several areas to see how we may be more effective in leveraging our resources for the greater good. Many outstanding resources discuss these in greater detail. Our purpose here it to give you an overview so that you may follow your own head and heart.

Community Foundations

A community foundation is a public foundation that receives donations from a broad base of community-minded citizens. From 1975 to 1985 there were approximately 300 such foundations in the United States; today there are over 1,000. Community foundations have increased their rate of giving faster than either individual or corporate foundations. They share a unique characteristic: their local nature. Their focus is on local people and local issues; their funding comes from former and current members of the community. A community foundation's major purpose is to improve the quality of life and economic well-being of the community. An example of the work such foundations do recently occurred in Dallas on Donor Bridge Day, in which the local community foundation pledged to match up to a certain amount of gifts. It stimulated giving that might not otherwise have occurred.

Community foundations enable donors to set up funds for designated purposes. In essence, they enable donors and corporations within a community to give money into one fund. A set committee assures that the funds are used to address the needs of a community in the way that most closely matches the intent of the donor. The pooling of resources from many allows a community foundation to leverage gifts with significant giving power. Such funds allow donors of modest or more means to make an impact in their community and maximize the tax benefits for their estate. Staff takes care of the accounting and other paperwork; donors have the satisfaction of knowing they can leverage their contribution for the benefit of the community they live, work, and belong to.

E-Philanthropy

As of June 2009, the United States claimed 251.7 million Internet users.[23] We are a connected nation, with iPhones, Twitter, Facebook, Digg; you name it—the list keeps growing. And while the Internet actually may prevent us from having real, up-close and personal conversation, it has certainly allowed for more electronic conversation about philanthropy, which gives nonprofits an effective and efficient and inexpensive way to communicate. Not only can the Internet raise dollars; it illuminates concepts of philanthropy.

For millions, the Internet is a way of life. It not only gives us the information we need for work and play, to buy products and services from movie tickets to cars, but also it allows us to maintain our social connections, from meeting our soul mates to sending personal cards. Today we spend over $100 billion online. Internet use is thriving, and women make up the larger percentage of users. Social activism is rapidly becoming a staple. The Internet allows individuals and organizations to connect to causes more easily. This Internet explosion makes it easier to attract new donors and educate them on the mission of the organization. A person can decide what charity to give money to by clicking and reading the mission and history of an organization, learning what it does, perusing its financials, and donating if the mission matches his or her interest, all without talking to one person in the charity.

E-philanthropy is a tool both giver and recipient can benefit from.

In some cases, profit-making organizations are mixing charity and offering shoppers an automatic charitable contribution when they buy one of their products. Charity Portal is a Web site (www.charityportal.org) that offers a directory of nonprofits. These portals attract traffic to sites and encourage visitors to make a donation to the charity of their choice. E-commerce commission portals encourage members to do their shopping through a portal with a percentage of the purchase going to the buyer's charity of choice.

Many sites allow charitable freedom online. Network for Good, (www.networkforgood.org) for instance, is the Internet's largest charitable resource, where individuals can donate, volunteer, and speak out on the issues they care about. Kiva (www.kiva.org) is a

Web site where donors can choose to enter into a micro-loan contract with entrepreneurs around the world. The rapid explosion of the Internet is creating exciting possibilities for women and giving and social change. From charity malls, to charity portals, e-commerce commission portals, e-grants, and others, the maze is worth exploring.

Giving and Donor Circles

Giving and donor circles have grown as new models of giving. Both involve groups of people who pool resources and make joint decisions on where their philanthropic dollars should go. Giving circles generally operate outside of institutional affiliation. The members share common interests and values and make their gifts through collective giving. A giving circle is somewhat like an investment club, with the funds invested in a nonprofit or charity. By acting collectively, the members can leverage their impact with shared giving of dollars and volunteering. Giving circles have become very popular. They encourage the sense of community for women and encourage philanthropy as something everyone can be involved in.

A donor circle is affiliated with an established giving institution for the benefit of its own grantees or programs. The funds are donated through the institution and often represent significant pools of money for specific interests or projects. Donor engagement is a benefit; donors learn more about the projects supported, and that in turn may lead to closer affiliation with a cause and even more donor generosity.

Another area that opens opportunities for gifting are donor-advised funds. This alternative to establishing your own foundation permits you to make contributions of cash and securities to an organization that acts as your fiscal manager and distributes the income or assets to a nonprofit on your behalf.

Mentoring and Modeling

At the 2008 Women in Philanthropy conference sponsored by the Women's Philanthropy Institute, Kimberly Davis advised attendees to "concentrate on mentoring in order to ensure that the next generation of women learn strong and effective leadership skills." She defined those as the ability to "manage, listen, communicate and negotiate."[24] Many of our interviewees expressed how important it is to model the behavior that will encourage their children or other women to give.

More and more they are finding that going public with their gifts inspires others to give as well, sometimes even more generously. While traditionally women have not mentored or deliberately modeled the leadership that men have, they are recognizing that the need for doing so is becoming ever more important—to stand and be counted and model the way. It is this modeling and mentoring that contributed to the unprecedented amounts women gave to the two major party presidential candidates of 2008. According to a study commissioned by the Women's Campaign Forum Foundation, women gave more than $109 million, three times the amount they had contributed eight years earlier.

Women are actively mentoring and networking and attending functions to better understand the dynamics of the mentoring role. They are joining hands to model the values of mutuality and more actively taking on the responsibility of being their sister's keeper. Cynthia Ryan, a trustee of Women for Women International, tells us, "Women with means now have the influence to be heard; finally they can create different paradigms of power."[25]

This is made apparent in the initiative started by Swanee Hunt, director of the Women and Public Policy program at Harvard University's Kennedy School of Government. Swanee often works with the United Nations and in this role was taking an assignment in Liberia. In 2005, she wanted to get her affairs in order, went over her will, and decided to leave her sister Helen $6 million to honor Helen's work with nonprofit groups and women's foundations. It occurred to her that she might outlive her sister, even though she was going to a war zone. Or that by the time Helen inherited, she might be too old to do the work. "That was the turning point. I realized I could do this right now. Why wait till I'm dead? It would be so much more fun to watch her and her young daughters and sons distribute the money to worthy women's foundations for their important community-based nonprofits."[26]

The job in Liberia did not materialize, the Hunt sisters got together, donated $10 million in seed money and partnered with the Women's Funding Network, and became the cofounders of

Women Moving Millions: Women's Funds Making History. "We are delighted, but not surprised, by the fact that against the bleak backdrop of the global recession women have stepped forward to raise the bar on giving to women and girls. They recognized that giving more, not less, is what is needed when we are in the midst of an economic crisis," said Helen LaKelly Hunt, when announcing they had surpassed the $150 million goal set for the three-year campaign. By mid-May 2009, the campaign had reached $176 million, exceeding its initial goal by 16%. Women Moving Millions has attracted a diverse range of women's wealth and power, from Jane Fonda to Jennifer Buffett. More than 50 new $1 million donors have joined the Hunts and 40 other trailblazing women in making gifts of $1 million or more to one of the 145 women's funds nationally and globally.[27]

Venture Philanthropy

Another way some have chosen to leverage their gifts is through "social" venture philanthropy. In essence, business entrepreneurs have joined together in an effort to collectively address social needs. These donors—venture philanthropists—apply the principles and practices of venture capitalism to the nonprofit world. This model includes long-term partnerships and strategic management assistance to leverage and augment financial investments. Donors consider themselves to be investors and have high investor engagement, with a long-term investment of three to six years. Investors act as managing partners who require ongoing accountability. They provide cash, expertise, and problem solving and closely monitor projects. Venture philanthropy is still new, and its practices are fairly wide ranging. Venture philanthropists refer to the nonprofit partners they have invested in as social entrepreneurs, who work to create sustainable profit models within a business environment. One of the pluses to this form of leverage is that it serves as a counter to the typical undercapitalization of infrastructure that most nonprofits have to struggle with. As most foundations tie funding to the organization's program, not to operations, nonprofits scramble for funds to actually run the operation, from salaries to databases. Venture philanthropy's focus is to assist the organization it invests in to manage itself like a business, while doing the work of the nonprofit, so its mission can be carried out effectively. Its premise is that you cannot function effectively without adequate capital to fulfill your mission.

Leverage, building trust, and collaboration are critical for the twenty-first century. All three elements form the core of a consistent and strategic communication platform that builds a stronger community because of its synergy. And women are at the center of this movement. As Anne B. Mosle, former president of the Washington Area Women's Foundation and now vice president for programs at the W.K. Kellogg Foundation, said: "Women are central not only to the future of our communities, but also to the future of philanthropy. We are a critical source of innovation, expertise, and resources. Despite the current economic climate, our experiences fuel our optimism about the future of women's role in both challenging and expanding the field of philanthropy."[28]

Social Capital

It is the synergy of TLC that is the foundation of community. And, for women, it is in community that there is an abundance of trust, the collective leverage of financial and intellectual capital, and an innovative network of social capital working to focus on ways to promulgate the love of humankind. As Dorr says, "home is the community." The conclusions from the 2003 MetLife Foundation Conference on Baby Boomers and Retirement confirmed her observations. "Indeed, for many [individuals], their physical and emotional well-being may be strongly influenced by their ability to stay connected and to connect in new ways to the community around them, especially as they disengage from work and family based-care giving."[29] Community takes on an even greater significance as women use that newly identified zest we keep referring to as the pursuit of *eudaimonia*, the well-being of the soul and their true identity of self. In addition, at a defining moment in their personal search, there is a moment when women come to realize that when they address the needs for the greater good, they also find peace, joy, and unexpected self-satisfaction. For women, their community is a microcosmic view of the world in their own backyards; to effect change somewhere else, women first need to effect change within their own community. "Where is the money going? I want it to be local," says business owner Jody Bond. "It has to be helping the communities where my family and children live. I care about this community; I care about the people, because they also have shown they care for me."[30]

Some might challenge that self-interest is the source of the decision to first effect change in your own community; after all, self-interest is the self-absorbed behavior associated with the me generation. But such an assumption is unfair for a generation whose self-interest ignited a nation in the 1960s to move forward with radical social, political, and educational reforms that today are part of mainstream and main street. For boomer women, expanding their sense of community is a continuation of defining a culture that is more inclusive of diverse social, economic, religious, and political ideology. Community then becomes a nurturing environment in which women can pursue their self-interest through values they consider paramount for the creation of a more compassionate and caring society. Indeed, their self- interest arises from a strong idealistic moral center for the good of society as a whole. In hindsight, history may well prove that boomer women were the first generation to fully implement the principle of self-interest by their legacy of virtuous philanthropy and their ability to build consensus in their reshaping of society.

The principle of self-interest is a term expounded on by Alexis de Tocqueville in his epic 1835 book, *Democracy in America*. In it he said: "Americans . . . are pleased to explain nearly all their actions in terms of self-interest properly understood. They will obligingly demonstrate how enlightened love of themselves regularly leads them to help one another out and make them ready and willing to sacrifice a portion of their time and wealth for the good of the state."[31] Tocqueville complimented and commented on our forebears' commitment to help, to nurture, to give to neighbors. He was amazed by our charitable actions and our sense of community. It is no accident that even in troubled times we continue to show caring and compassion for others. This is part of the character of who we are as a people.

It is this enlightened self-interest that drives boom-generation women's profound sense of passion for the well-being of the community. Tocqueville gives us the foundation for contemporary philanthropy by showing how we all have self-interest for our own well-being and that it is not selfish to use such self-interest to foster vibrant and energetic communities for the public good. Bruce Frohnen, senior fellow at the Russell Kirk Center for Cultural Renewal in Mecosta, Michigan, writes:

> In part, one has merely built on a commonality of interest, but more importantly, the individual has in this process come to redefine his self-interest in broader, more spiritual terms. Instead of seeking only material well-being, he now seeks to be part of a vital community, in which neighbors care for one another. Through this transforming process of the free society, the "self" in which his interest lies has been expanded to contain other selves as well.[32]

University of Kansas alumna Sally Hare-Schriner built on her commonality of interest with her KU professor and student teachers when she established the Sally Hare-Schriner Education Fund. The money supports a program to train the students to work with at-risk young children. The students who enroll in the United Early Childhood curriculum can get training by volunteering in Sally's classroom. And Sally can expand the number of young children she can work with in her small rural public school, so fewer children are at risk for failure at school when they start kindergarten. Sally is a model of what we are talking about, enlightened self-interest.

When Robert Putnam writes about community in his book, *Bowling Alone: The Collapse and Revival of American Community*, he refers to social capital as "the connections among individuals' social networks and the norms of reciprocity and trustworthiness that arise from them." Putnam makes a distinction between bonding (exclusive) and bridging (inclusive) social capital. Bonding social capital networks tend to be homogeneous groups, such as fraternal organizations. Bridging social capital networks link a variety of socioeconomic elements having a shared interest. While bonding capital is more relevant for getting by in difficult times, bridging capital is more useful for getting ahead. Putman distinguishes the two by saying, "Bonding social capital constitutes a kind of sociological superglue, whereas bridging social capital provides a sociological WD-40."[33] Both exist simultaneously in society. For example, a Women's Impact 100 giving circle may bond individuals by its funding goals and assessment of community needs for children and bridge individuals across ethnic, social, and economic classes. A 2004 Harvard School of Public Health-MetLife Foundation study reinforces the need for bonding and bridging capital with its directive: "If social capital is to build on a more inclusive sense of community, images of community service need to be reframed in a way that can more effectively expand the appeal of such activities across cultural and class lines."[34] Indeed, a great strength and an innate character of boom-generation women is their ability to collaborate and communicate using both bonding and bridging social capital models.

It is a natural instinct for women to "gather together" when adversity is at hand or when creative solutions are required to solve multidimensional problems. Jean Shinoda Bolen, M.D., in her book *Urgent Message from Mother*, reports on such findings from research at the University of California at Los Angeles. She writes: "Shelley E. Taylor, the principal investigator, and the team of women researchers found that females of many species, including humans, responded to stressful conditions with a '*tend and befriend*' response. Females protected and nurtured their young, and sought social contact and support from others, especially other females."[35]

Although there is consensus about Putnam's affirmation that "[f]or the first two-thirds of the twentieth century a powerful tide bore Americans into ever deepening engagement in the life of their communities, but a few decades ago—silently, without warning—that tide reversed and we were overtaken by a treacherous rip current."[36] There is also controversy as to the ability to quantify a nation's social capital. To have anything like "a believable census of a society's stock of social capital," according to political economist Francis Fukuyama, "is a nearly impossible task, since it involves multiplying numbers that are either subjectively estimated or simply nonexistent." Fukuyama further explains that while it may be possible for a society to have too much social capital, "it is doubtless worse to have too little. For in addition to being a source of spontaneously-organized groups, social capital is vital to the proper functioning of formal public institutions."[37] Both Putnam and Fukuyama do concur, however, that an abundant stock of social capital is presumably what produces a dense civil society, which in turn has been almost universally seen as a necessary condition for modern liberal democracy.

Democracy is a hallmark of virtuous philanthropy. It is one the key elements that makes Impact 100 giving so successful. Says Elaine Suess, the 2008 president of Cincinnati Impact 100:

> We try to make it clear to our members, that the beauty of being a donor to Impact 100 is you can be as involved as much or as little as you like or are able in the organization structure and grant making process. Each woman can choose for herself, and there is a bond of trust among the members and a mutual respect for how decisions are made. That appeals to a wide range of women who have a very broad range of circumstances, working women, mothers, and retirees. We really try to concentrate on diversity in our membership, including geographically, and culturally, and age wise—from the younger women who may not be able to afford $1,000, who can join in a group up to four, each giving $250, or an 80-year-old who is just a spark plug of energy. Each $1,000 unit gets one vote.

Elaine and her group hosted the 2008 Impact conference of chapter board members from around the country. "It boggles your mind," she says, "that most of these women have full-time jobs and those on the board end up with two full-time jobs, which is not a problem because we are so passionate about our work and feel so privileged to be part of Impact 100."[38]

In the twenty-first century, a dense civil society provides the philanthropic sector an opportunity to bring added value to corporate and political entities by its freedom from bottom-line profit or voting booth plurality. According to Peter Drucker, nonprofit organizations create citizenship. "Modern society and modern polity," writes Drucker, "have become so big and complex that citizenship—that is, responsible participation—is no longer possible. All we can do as citizens is vote once every few years and to pay taxes all the time. As a volunteer in a social-sector institution, the individual can again make a difference."[39] When Drucker made this statement in 1994, little would he realize how relevant it remains in today's society.

Pensacola, Florida, Impact 100 past president Debbie Ritchie puts it this way: "I was a state representative in the Florida House of Representatives, and believe me I see firsthand that I can do more to change my community through my philanthropic work with

Impact 100 than all my voting days in the House. And it's so reward-ing to see results of your work right in front of you. You know that what you are doing is making a difference."[40]

Of the three sectors, nonprofit, corporate, and government, the nonprofit philanthropic sector is closest to the "pulse of soci-ety" with the ability to most readily discern and respond to society's most urgent needs for a sustainable and vibrant community.

The contemporary definition of "formal public institutions" includes those in the nonprofit sector, sometimes called the third sector, or as Peter Drucker defines it, the "social sector." And it is the philanthropic sector in which boom-generation women are the trailblazers of a new frontier, bringing with them the idealism authors Strauss and Howe identify as a "call to destiny, a righteous-ness of conviction, and an impatience to lead society."[41] This cohort of women also shares a common time in history and similar experi-ences during their formative years, two of the major criteria for ele-vating the intensity of social capital in a community. They grew up in the euphoric era following World War II believing they were the generation that could change the world. Indeed, they have and will continue to do so. It has been 40 years between the time leading-edge boomers applied for their learner's permit to drive and their more recent application for an AARP card, and during that time, women have fine-tuned their peer-personality talents. From young adulthood on, the process of distilling and defining the essence of their values has better prepared them to reenergize social capital, perfect the art of association and adapt the practice of enlightened self-interest to modern-day social networking. "In democratic coun-tries, the science of association is the fundamental science. Progress in all other sciences depends on progress in this one," writes Tocqueville.

> Nothing in my view is more worthy of our attention than America's intellectual and moral associations. The political and industrial associations of Americans leap to the eye more read-ily, but these others escape our notice, and if we do not rec-ognize them, we misunderstand them because we have almost never seen anything analogous. It is essential, however, to rec-ognize that they are as necessary to the American people as political and industrial associations, and perhaps more so.[42]

Intellectual and moral associations provide the venue for women to gather as the season arrives for them to lead the compassionate resolution of their consciousness revolution. Their ability to optimize the practical application of the "six degrees of separation" theory allows them to reach out and build the network necessary for collaboration and communication of their message to a chosen destination. It is both the independence and the interdependency of this vibrant and dense social capital (see Exhibit 6.1) that fosters "a radius of trust," a term attributed to economist Lawrence Harrison, currently Senior Research Fellow and Adjunct Lecturer at the Fletcher School at Tufts University. And as each social capital association extends its matrix through bridging social capital

Trust bonds women to strategically leverage time, talent, and treasure creating a dense and productive network of social capital.

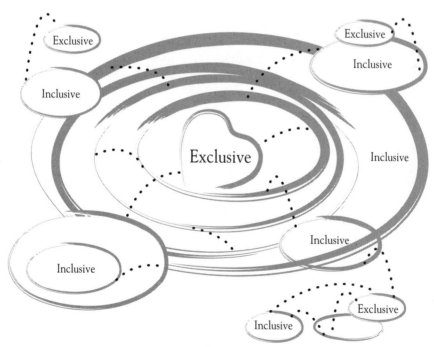

Exhibit 6.1 Social Capital
Illustrations by Elizabeth Huggins-Thompson.

networks to embrace another bonded social capital association the radius of trust increases and the group extrapolates in number far more quickly and efficiently.

The need to weave this fabric of trust from local community to world community has never been greater. Time is running short to discover the true Age of Aquarius as our nation descends into its winter of discontent. Putnam makes the case that social capital "has many features that help people translate aspirations into realities,"[43] and these features have corresponding benefits. In this decade and for several to follow, the paramount benefit to society is the fulfillment of women's hopes, dreams, and desires for a more compassionate, just, and egalitarian world community, starting with their own hometown, their community as home. The features of social capital that Putnam identifies correlate with women's natural bonding strengths, consensus leadership style, and genuine altruistic character. These attributes are becoming more prominent and dominant in society as women choose to engage in a community, but not just any community, rather a democratic community where the practice of enlightened self-interest and diversity is embraced respectfully, whether it is a political, corporate, or philanthropic community or a social network. Putnam's features and benefits include:

Feature	Benefit
Accelerate the flow of information	Advance intellectual capital
Provide venue for personal engagement	Improve health and happiness
Identify ways for collective problem solving	Create more harmony
Expand awareness of interdependence	Strengthen cooperation
Encourage transparency	Build trust and networks

How does this all relate to women's wealth and giving? Part of the answer comes by looking through the rearview mirror back into history, specifically to the Progressive Era (1880–1915), a time of "dramatic technological, economic, and social change [that] rendered obsolete a significant stock of social capital."[44] Here was a time when a coterie of women restocked America's social capital mostly by using their time and persuasive talents. As mentioned earlier, many historians refer to women's social reform activism during this era as the foundation of contemporary women's philanthropic culture. Out of the need to restock social capital, women used the opportunity structures available to them at the time to effect positive social change. Women, led by Nobel Peace prize recipient Jane Addams, suffragette Susan B. Anthony, journalist Ida Tarbell, educator Mary McLeod Bethune, and black millionaire businesswoman Madame C. J. Walker, emerged as major leaders for social reform. Their accomplishments permanently changed the society of their day and in doing so altered the future role of women in the civic, political, and business world forever.

A *New York Times* editorial titled "The Women of Thirty," published on Sunday, August 29, 1920, claimed: "Women in fighting for the vote have shown a passion of earnestness, a persistence, and above all a command of both tactics and strategy....Hitherto the distinctively feminine instincts and aspirations have centered in winning the right of suffrage, but now that it is won, a vast united force has been let loose."[45] This "force" succeeded in winning the first minimum wage and maximum hours for women workers, public health programs for pregnant women, improved educational opportunities for children and adults, the creation of the Children's Bureau headed by Julia Lathrop in 1912 and the Women's Bureau in the Federal Department of Labor during the Taft presidency.

Separated by two world wars, the civil rights and feminist movements, political and social turmoil around the world, and a widening disparity between rich and poor, the boom-generation prepare to pick up the gauntlet from their Progressive Era foremothers to work with the fervor of exuberance, enthusiasm, and idealism for a better world. While there is much similarity in the two eras between the state of society and the demise of social capital, this time around, however, boom-generation women are adding a new element to the equation: abundant financial capital and the freedom to direct its destination. Yet while being true to their foremothers, they still pause to reflect on Jane Addams's sage advice before embarking on their contemporary romance with philanthropy.

> In this readjustment, in this reorganizing world, with its uncharted problems, with its tremendous romances—because it is a very romantic thing to see a world being made over before your eyes, and have a possible part in it—women's

organizations, to my mind, will be useful, very much in proportion as they keep their philosophy more or less pragmatic, very much in proportion as they discover from life itself, what lessons we may best learn and best transmit.[46]

Construct Your Own TLC

1. Leverage: Can you imagine yourself gifting or raising $1 million for a project or cause you are deeply committed to? What would it be? Write about it.

2. Reflect on your current associations in your community and identify:
   a. Two experiences you have of trust-transparency:
      With volunteers
      With staff
   b. Two experiences of how you leverage:
      Time
      Talent
      Treasure

3. Social capital is both bonding and bridging. Identify in your own community one way in which you are part of each and how they connect to create a more diverse community:

   a. Bonding social capital activity I do is _____
   b. Bridging social capital network I am part of is _____

4. What is your definition of community? How has that definition evolved or changed over the past 40 years?

5. Ask three friends or colleagues how they define community. Encourage them to talk about their experiences of connection by asking: If we were having this discussion 10 years from now, what would you have to do from today on to realize the community you envision?

CHAPTER 7

Plan Elements

MAKING THE MATCH

We are not permitted to choose the frame of our destiny. But what we put into it is ours.

—Dag Hammarskjold (1905–1961)

According to economist Kenneth Boulding:

> The human condition can almost be summed up in the observation that, whereas all experiences are of the past, all decisions are about the future. The image of the future therefore, is the key to all choice-orientated behavior. The character and quality of the images of the future which prevail in a society are therefore the most important clue to its overall dynamics.[1]

This generation of archetype boomers is decisive, visionary, and idealistic, the exact characteristics necessary for embracing a bold vision and an even bolder image of the future. And boomer women are making their philanthropic choices in just this manner. According to a recent Foundation Center report, women's giving is growing more rapidly than giving overall, in spite of recent economic uncertainty. Since 1967, the data collected by Giving USA show that although philanthropic giving is affected by recessionary times, donations do not tend to decline as much as markets and other financial assets. A recent survey by Barclays Wealth, of 500 wealthy individuals in the United Kingdom and the United States, reveals that while three-fourths of those interviewed have become more discerning in their giving, they also said that they would be likely to cut back on luxury items rather than reduce their donations to causes they regularly support.[2] Sarah C. Libbey, president of the Fidelity Charitable Gift Fund, citing the 2009 Fidelity "Gift Fund" study of charitable givers, says, "Women are using a broad circle of influences in their charitable giving, and they are passionate about instilling the value of philanthropy in the next generation."[3]

The outcome of women's financial independence and financial clout has developed into a more democratic model of giving as a long-term investment in the community. How women envision the quality of life in their community for the next generation impacts their current decisions. As they realign their priorities to focus on issues of sustainability, economic parity, and creative solutions, it "changes the face of philanthropy," says Christine Grumm, president and chief executive officer (CEO) of the Women's Funding Network. "We're not talking about making a difference for half the world's population; we're talking about all of it."[4] How courageous women stay the course once a decision is made will provide the inspiration for others to join in the creation of long-term perspectives for a better society.

Numerous comments from our interviewees emphasize how leading by example and restating the values behind their actions encourages, empowers, and reassures others to lead from their heart in their giving and in designing a giving plan. Boomer Alice Krause, founder of the News on Women Web site uses her site (www.newsonwomen.com) to promote the achievements of women not mentioned much in the conventional press. Krause posts news stories that reinforce the breadth and depth of the accomplishments of women in the workforce, many of whom are in leadership positions and changing the face of philanthropy.

> I don't think people are creative when they measure women's progress. We get a lot of coverage of the statistics, which, while I am sure they are true, don't give the real story. What I do is try to put a face on the story, show the women who have these

great jobs, who are promoted and have great experience and need to be well-known enough across the nation to become candidates for some of these CEO positions. We don't want to hear anymore that there aren't women for these jobs. That's a big lie. There maybe are not enough, but there are lots of extremely capable women.[5]

So far, the process of giving has been discussed as an introspective search to identify, confirm, and acknowledge what is important to you and the life you live. You have read stories of women, just like yourself, who search for their truth, their core values, and find answers through philanthropic endeavors. These women are confident enough to ask: Where is my *eudaimonia*, who am I really, and what choices do I make? By now you have a holistic picture of who you are and the confidence to ask and answer the same questions and, as a result, can become a virtuous philanthropist at this stage in your life. By working through the exercises, you now have a more complete sense of what you want to do in the community in which you live and in the world that you leave for others. It is an exciting time to become comfortable, confident, and trust in your abilities. It is a process that truly distinguishes you as an empowered woman who is a torchbearer: prudent, courageous, consistent, fair, and compassionate, with a love of humankind to carry out your personal mission for a better world. One of the ways to accomplish this is with a well-thought-out giving plan that encompasses your values.

Plan Overview

A giving plan is a set of core values transformed into action, relating to choices that direct available resources in the most efficient manner possible based on those values. Core values center the soul; they guide the heart to be creative and compassionate and guide the mind to be strategic and efficient. In the process of creating your plan, strategic decisions fueled by compassion allow for choices that are consistent with the principles you cherish for living a purposeful life, principles that demonstrate by your actions and engagement that you accept ownership and make a commitment to virtuous philanthropy. "Creating and using a giving plan will give you a sense of control, purpose, and direction," writes Tracy Gary in her book *Inspired Philanthropy*:

> . . . and will inspire you to become more proactive in organizing, managing, and in general taking charge of your financial life. A thoughtfully developed and conscientiously implemented giving plan will tell you where your philanthropic hours and dollars are and will be going, and because it reflects your personal priorities and dreams for creating a better world, it will be an active ally in supporting the issues that are most important to you.[6]

No matter if the gift is large or small, the number of hours volunteered few or many, this plan is a best effort at a certain time in your life. It is a reflection of who you are and what you value. It puts into action the moral virtues of prudence, sound judgment, and common sense. It gives you the courage to lead with conviction. A strategic plan is an honest, truthful, and fair assessment of your abilities and capabilities to implement your mission statement. You become an empowered leader, you connect with the community, and you shift focus from giving to sharing, from doing to being, from transactions of valuables to transformation of values. The love in your heart combines with the energy from your soul, connects you to humanity, and inspires you to have faith in your hopes, dreams, and desires.

But having a plan is just half of the process. Full ownership includes implementation, follow-through, and realistic evaluation while still allowing for flexibility and change. Being a virtuous philanthropist is having the courage to believe in and act on your mission in spite of adversity, doubt, or fear. It is having the moral fortitude to stand up for choices you believe in and advocate strongly for the causes and issues you know must be addressed to bring about a more just, humane, and caring world. It is championing the return of harmony, reason, and moderation for social issues such as healthcare, poverty, the environment, family and children, and the arts. It is having the confidence to take personal responsibility for nurturing and fulfilling your mission statement. It is empowering, transformative, and life changing.

Choosing a Partner

Over 1.5 million nonprofit organizations and institutions in the United States are part of the social sector.[7] Their very diverse goals and services are far reaching and include but are not limited to health services, education and research, religious organizations, social and legal services, civic and fraternal organizations, arts and culture, and foundations. Take a look around your local community, spend one-on-one time talking to community leaders, learn more about how nonprofit organizations impact and enrich the quality of life for every person. Ask others why they have chosen to invest of themselves in a particular organization. And while organizations and institutions may differ in size, budget, and service, they share in common the fact that carrying out their mission depends to a great degree on private charitable contributions in the form of time and money—your time and money, and that of like-minded citizens.

How do you identify the organizations that are compatible with your mission, and how do you evaluate those you choose to support? This may be the most time-consuming part of your journey; however, the rewards are significant, most especially the peace of mind and joy you receive from sharing in a responsible relationship for the success of an organization's mission that mirrors your values and beliefs. How do you choose to make a strategic investment in the future of an organization? What insight will give you the confidence to know you have made a wise decision about how to allocate your time, talent, and treasure?

Your philanthropic autobiography will prompt you along the way to keep your focus. This would be a good time to review where you stand today. You know how much time and money you will commit to for the next year. You know which organizations you currently support that will remain obligations, and you have a clear picture of the values and vision you urgently see and passionately feel that you want to impact with new contributions. Let us look at five areas that can provide some guidance to help you choose organizations that could best use your resources with the greatest impact.

The ultimate question for you to answer is whether the organization passes the REAL test, presented in Chapter 5. Is it relevant to your values and your beliefs? Does it engage your emotion? Will your action be effective and efficient? Does it speak to your heart and your desire to leave your legacy of a better world to the next generation? Consider these five points:

1. Size and location of the organization.

   Consider how much time and money you have to commit, and then decide where it will have the most impact. Is there a local organization where you can be proactive with your time and money, or would you prefer to support a regional or national organization? Could you become more involved with an organization you currently support, perhaps through service on a committee or on the board? How could you go about getting more involved? How will you monitor the impact of your resources? What are your expectations?

2. Scope and method of work.

   Does the organization clearly articulate and communicate its mission? What is the fundamental philosophy by which it carries out its objectives? Does it focus primarily on research to solve or prevent a problem; advocacy and education to improve or change a situation; or direct assistance to individuals for immediate relief? Is it a systemic long-term commitment or a short-term immediate need that requires funding? Are you prepared to remain a committed donor for several years if necessary?

3. Evaluation and reporting.

   Does the organization present clear and accurate reporting of how money is raised and spent? Does it have a valid way to report the impact and benefit of its services, either by statistics or in stories? How well does the organization carry out its mission? Is there a duplication of similar services in the area? Do you get timely and complete answers to all your questions and concerns? How do you feel when you are at the organization's office or on site visiting a project? Does the organization abide by the Donor Bill of Rights and is it clearly on display at their facility? (Review the Bill of Rights at the end of the chapter.)

4. Community citizenship.

   Who is on the board of directors? Who attends fundraising events? What is the relationship of the staff and employees to the community in which they live? Is there diversity of staff, board, and volunteers that is representative of the community and the constituency served? Do the organization's members participate and collaborate with other citizens for the greater good of the entire community? How does the organization acknowledge and recognize donors and volunteers? What is its volunteer retention rate? Whom can you talk to whose judgment you trust and is already a supporter of the organization? Is the organization a chapter of a national organization? If so, what is the fiscal and governing relationship?

5. Efficient management and fiscal strength.

   Does the organization rely on one type of funding source, on just a few individuals, or does a broad base of support from individuals, foundations, corporations, grants, and other sources supply consistent revenue sources? Who prepares the financial statements and audit when required? What policy and procedures manuals are used for board and volunteer education and training? How long has the professional staff been in place? Is there a system for staff advancement and continuing education? Does the organization have a strategic three- to five-year plan for growth and fiscal responsibility? What is its leadership record in fundraising campaigns for its operating, capital, and endowment programs? Are the administrative costs and fundraising expenses in line with accepted national norms (considered excessive when over 25% of the total budget)? If not, is there a specific reason for the departure?

Evaluation Tools

Three techniques most women donors use to make their funding decisions include:

1. Their personal assessment by site visits, getting to know the staff, attending events, reading annual reports and how literature generated by the organization "speaks female"
2. Anecdotal information from community members as to the organization's culture and respect for mind as well as money
3. Industry charity rating organizations

All three are necessary to get a full picture of the dynamics within and without the organization. The first two techniques convey the personality of the organization. As you are getting to know its personnel and attending events, pay specific attention to their communication style and technique.

Speaking Female

You can tell a lot about how the organization builds relationships by the methods it uses to convey its message and mission. Both the written and the spoken language are gender specific. Linguistics professor Deborah Tannen uses the terms "rapport-talk" and "report-talk" when describing the difference between how women and men communicate.[8] This is not to stereotype but to highlight equally valid styles. The "rapport-talk" language and conversation style preferred by women includes a combination of both facts and feelings as a way to establish relationships. According to neuroscientific research, more cross-talk exists between a woman's emotional intuitive right side and the rational, factual left side of her brain. This cross-talk helps the listener get a mental image and visualize what she is listening to or reading. When the organization "speaks female," it uses more stories and pictures and fewer bullet points in its printed literature. It utilizes testimonials from women and stories about women's leadership and volunteer activities. The organization relates its stories and the impact it has on the community it serves by providing information that easily creates a picture in your mind and a passion in your heart. It inspires you to see how you can help make a difference. When you read the literature or talk with current donors and volunteers, you will recognize the rapport-talk when your heart tells your mind, "Yes, I want to know more about the people and the purpose of this organization. I want to get involved. I am empowered." If an organization can accomplish this, you have truly connected to its story.

Organization's Culture

Being a virtuous philanthropist is more than just writing a check, no matter how large; it is also about supporting and working in a community rich in respect, resolve, and responsibility. It is about serving in an organization where individuals acknowledge that diversity strengthens the "ties that bind" all members in a common purpose. This is facilitated when there are opportunities for you to openly discuss your ideas and your values as they relate to the organization's mission and philosophy. Respect for your ideas and values has to do with your comfort zone when it comes to speaking freely and being honored for the validity of your ideas as well as the significance of your purse. And it is how you will decide whether you will put your time and talent into building a long-term relationship with the organization. Some consider this the try-out phase of their evaluation. It is a time to talk with the supply side as well as the demand side—those who give and those who receive and evaluate the congruency between both. It is a good way to let the organization know you are serious about your stewardship and that you would like to be involved in the evolution of your involvement and commitment. It is a way to find out how open, receptive, and respectful the organization is to your ideas.

Rating Organizations

Industry rating organizations interpret the fiscal strength of an organization and base their research on a standard IRS Form 990 that organizations granted tax-exempt status under 501(c)(3) of the Internal Revenue Code are required to file annually. Most faith-based organizations and nonprofits with incomes less than $25,000 a year are exempt from filing Form 990.[9] The form is a public document that you can request from the organization or review online at one of the charity rating Web sites. It provides information about the financial integrity of the organization; its funding sources; expenses for programs, fundraising, administration and executive staff salaries; and current board members. The Web site www .guidestar.org is a national database of U.S. charitable organizations. It makes available, at no charge, Form 990s for over 850,000 organizations and includes a first-rate tutorial on how to analyze the form. Charity Navigator also uses Form 990, at www.charitynavigator.org, to establish a set of financial efficiency and capacity performance categories to provide a four-star rating system for over 5,000 charities, each of which receives $500,000 or more in public support. The American Institute of Philanthropy, at www.charitywatch.org, is a nonprofit charity watchdog and information service that rates the financial performance of more than 500 major American charities including child protection, cancer, senior citizens, environment, and crime prevention. The Better Business Bureau Wise Giving Alliance, at www.Give.org, reports on nationally soliciting charitable organizations that are the subject of donor inquiries and evaluates the charity in relation to voluntary standards for charity account-ability, so as to encourage fair and honest solicitation practices.

Making Your Decision

Using the tools and techniques suggested for evaluating charities is only part of the process. You still need to take action, you need to get involved. Consider each of the following categories that relate to the organization's culture as you begin to gain more information in working with the organizations you have selected.

Engagement

Does it engage my interest, skills, and time in meaningful and respectful activities? Are there ways I would like to engage my fam-ily and friends in helping with the mission? Would I feel confident and comfortable asking others to give their time, talent, and treas-ure? Can I identify opportunities to leverage my financial gifts to further the mission? Am I willing to take responsibility for helping the organization in unstable economic times as well as in a rosier economic climate?

Organizations that create an environment for virtuous phi-lanthropy are those that have a culture where women can engage their values—the spiritual skills that direct the living of purposeful lives, and the beliefs that guide and energize women to continue the quest for their *eudaimonia*. Boom-generation women are simul-taneously both receivers and givers. They are a vibrant conduit to engage and assimilate diversity of thought and deed.

Expedience

Does the organization have a clear definition of its mission and a strategic plan to carry it out, with a realistic timetable that is com-patible with my goals for results? What will I need as tangible evidence and benchmarks of progress toward the goals it is sup-posed to be accomplishing? What will I consider reasonable suc-cess in achieving systemic change? What are the ways in which my resources will make an impact? Is the organization flexible enough to change direction to meet changing community needs in a timely manner?

Organizations that create an environment for virtuous philanthropy expedience are those where action speaks louder than words, where opportunities exist to seek solutions in an efficient time frame. Goals will be quantitative (meet the budget goal, match the challenge grant) as well as qualitative (greater happiness, lasting friendships).

Experience

Will my experiences expand my knowledge of the issues I care about? Will I become more aware of opportunities to increase my ability to make a difference? How can I share my experiences, expertise, and values with others? How can we learn from each other as we work toward common goals? What leadership opportunities may be available for me to use my talents and skills?

Organizations that create an environment for virtuous philanthropic experiences are those where women can mentor others and stretch themselves. Wisdom passed on through stories opens the door to critical thinking from other generational perspectives, both older, the G.I. generation and the Silent generation, and younger, Generation X and Y. Life experiences can serve as a catalyst for intergenerational synergism and innovative solutions, which helps to enhance reflective self-discernment.

Empowerment

Does working and supporting this organization allow me to bring clarity and focus to the philanthropic issues that are important in my life? Can I fully use my leadership skills to be assertive and inspire others to take risks and accomplish goals important to the fulfillment of the mission? Can I lead the learning? Does it inspire me to continue my quest for creative solutions to societal issues I feel are important to embracing the love of humankind? In supporting this mission, can I fully and openly express my gratitude for the blessings received in my life that I want to share with others?

Organizations that create an environment for virtuous philanthropy empowerment are those with a community mind-set of shared responsibility and leadership. It is a nurturing community where women have the capacity to direct their entrepreneurial spirit and energy to implement change and make a lasting difference. It is a community where they can leverage wisdom and wealth through collaborative giving and learning.

Philanthropic Personality

Our research shows that even though women are very individualistic in their approach to giving, they tend to exhibit identifiable behavioral traits as to how they give. This is a budding area of research, and although it has yet to find its way into the mainstream, it is worthy of note. The giving styles relate to one of four flowers: rose, daisy, carnation, and lily. Some suggest that the theory is an outgrowth of the boomer flower power movement of the 1960s. No one style is dominant, and each serves in one way or another to complement the other three styles. All four styles are necessary for the full potential of virtuous philanthropy.[10]

Rose

"Rose" women make up a significant number of leading-edge boomers born between 1943 and 1955. They are forthright about their idealism. The work they do represents their willingness to take risks and be demonstrative about their giving. They are among the most loyal supporters and persuasive leaders.

Daisy

"Daisy" women are eclectic in their giving patterns. They have the ability, enthusiasm, and network to draw others into their giving arena. Many times they prefer to leverage their time and money and explore several aspects of a single funding issue.

Carnation

"Carnation" women strive to support grassroots initiatives and are likely to volunteer and get to know an organization before giving moderate to large sums of money. They prefer to do their own research and are willing to be proactive in seeking out issues that may be under the radar or out of vogue with funders.

Lily

"Lily" women tend to be more empathic givers. They are talented observers and have a keen intuition in finding the solution to a problem or issue that has personally touched their lives or the lives of family members. Quite often they will encourage their family to unite to support a cause.

Financial Acumen

Your financial situation is unique. Choosing the correct technique and vehicle to use to make your donation demands a significant amount of analysis. Every decision you make impacts your current and future lifestyle as well as your estate planning. The first move to make is to assemble a team of professionals. They can provide you with the legal and technical assistance you need to design a giving plan that reflects your intentions. If you do not already have a team, in most communities there is a local estate planning council or Partnership for Philanthropic Planning chapter www.pppnet.org that can provide you with a list of qualified professionals to interview. Seek out their knowledge and expertise. They are the technical experts who can document your vision and your legacy. Depending on your situation, they may well be able to show you alternatives that could allow you to do more than you thought possible with the assets you have or expect to receive in the future.

Professionals are there to implement what you want to do. The most important step in working with advisors and asking for advice is for you to be clear about your values and your philanthropic mission. They will need an accurate snapshot of your financial life. Two important documents provide this information, a net worth statement of what you own and what you owe and a cash flow statement of your income and expenses (see Exhibits 7.1 and 7.2). In Margaret's experience as a certified financial planner working with women's financial issues, she often counsels women who find hidden resources once they fully see and know their total financial picture. And these resources can be made available for their philanthropic goals, often leading to far greater capacity to give than was originally imagined. Depending on the complexity of your situation, you can do this yourself, using net worth and income and expense forms. Your financial advisor, bank trust officer, accountant, or attorney can also assemble and analyze your financial situation and make recommendations on how to proceed in order to achieve your philanthropic goals.

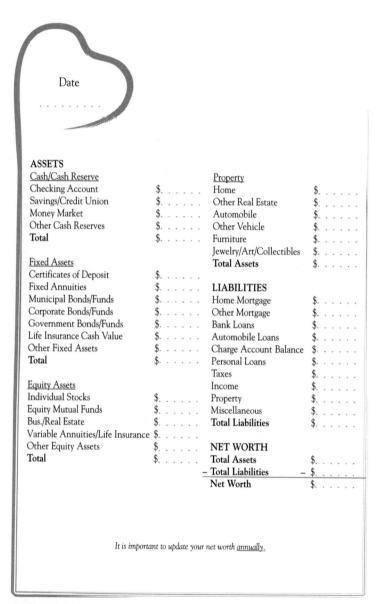

Date
. . . .

ASSETS

Cash/Cash Reserve

Checking Account	$.	Property	
Savings/Credit Union	$.	Home	$. . . . . .
Money Market	$.	Other Real Estate	$. . . . . .
Other Cash Reserves	$.	Automobile	$. . . . . .
Total	$.	Other Vehicle	$. . . . . .
		Furniture	$. . . . . .
		Jewelry/Art/Collectibles	$. . . . . .
Fixed Assets		**Total Assets**	$. . . . . .
Certificates of Deposit	$.		
Fixed Annuities	$.	**LIABILITIES**	
Municipal Bonds/Funds	$.	Home Mortgage	$. . . . . .
Corporate Bonds/Funds	$.	Other Mortgage	$. . . . . .
Government Bonds/Funds	$.	Bank Loans	$. . . . . .
Life Insurance Cash Value	$.	Automobile Loans	$. . . . . .
Other Fixed Assets	$.	Charge Account Balance	$. . . . . .
Total	$.	Personal Loans	$. . . . . .
		Taxes	$. . . . . .
Equity Assets		Income	$. . . . . .
Individual Stocks	$.	Property	$. . . . . .
Equity Mutual Funds	$.	Miscellaneous	$. . . . . .
Bus./Real Estate	$.	**Total Liabilities**	$. . . . . .
Variable Annuities/Life Insurance	$.		
Other Equity Assets	$.	**NET WORTH**	
Total	$.	**Total Assets**	$. . . . . .
		– **Total Liabilities**	– $. . . . . .
		Net Worth	$. . . . . .

It is important to update your net worth __annually.__

Exhibit 7.1 Net Worth

Illustrations by Elizabeth Huggins-Thompson.

Date

. . . .

INCOME

Salary	$.	
Investments/Dividends	$.	
Social Security	$.	
Pension	$.	
Alimony	$.	
Child Support	$.	
Other	$.	
Total	$.	

EXPENSES-Fixed

Mortgage/Rent	$. . . . .
Taxes (Property)	$. . . . .
Taxes (Income)	$. . . . .
Savings	$. . . . .
Pension Savings	$. . . . .
Insurance Premiums	$. . . . .
Life	$. . . . .
Health	$. . . . .
Auto	$. . . . .
Homeowners	$. . . . .
Disability	$. . . . .
Automobile Loan	$. . . . .
Credit Cards	$. . . . .
Other Loans	$. . . . .
Total	$. . . . .

EXPENSES-Variable

Food	$. . . . .
Utilities/Household	$. . . . .
Medical/Dental	$. . . . .
Transportation	$. . . . .
Entertainment	$. . . . .
Personal Care	$. . . . .
Education/Books	$. . . . .
Clothing	$. . . . .

EXPENSES-Variable cont'd.

Furniture	$. . . . .
Gifts/Contributions	$. . . . .
Miscellaneous	$. . . . .
Total	$. . . . .

TOTAL EXPENSES

Fixed	$. . . . .
Variable	$. . . . .
Total	$. . . . .

YOUR CASH FLOW PICTURE

<u>Average Month</u>

Total Income	$. . . . .
Total Expenses	$. . . . .

<u>Annual</u>

Total Income	$. . . . .
– **Total Expenses**	– $. . . . .
Discretionary Cash	$. . . . .

You have a negative cash flow if your expenses exceed your income.

You have a positive cash flow if your income exceeds your expenses.

An average month is 4.3 weeks.

Exhibit 7.2 Cash Flow
Illustrations by Elizabeth Huggins-Thompson.

A financial inventory provides you with the road map of what type of assets and how much money you can give. In many cases, the results will surprise you by identifying assets that you had not originally considered possible to use for philanthropy. They may also encourage you to investigate ways to reallocate current income, better reflecting your values and your charitable goals. No matter how small or large your gifts, you need to know your current financial situation before you can have a prudent and meaningful discussion with fundraisers, development officers, or financial advisors about the giving of your personal or financial assets. This is as important to do for your annual gifts as it is for your legacy and planned gifts, implemented through your estate planning. The sooner you get your financial and legal affairs, including your wills and trusts, in order, the quicker you can get on with the joy of your philanthropic endeavors. Your advisors will also explain federal and state income and estate tax consequences applicable to your specific situation as well as to all charitable giving decisions. This is a complex and delicate subject with many special rules that are subject to change.

Common Gifting Techniques

Charitable giving techniques can be as simple as writing a check or as complex as setting up a trust or foundation with the help of professional advisors. You have a wide variety of choices and many ways to fund your virtuous philanthropy. In all cases, before you make a donation, consult with your tax advisor and other legal professionals. This brief overview will make you aware of the diverse techniques to customize your gifting. The vehicles you choose will be determined by several factors, including the size of the gift; the type of asset gifted; tax treatments; your charitable estate planning; your lifestyle, health, and age; and the needs of your family. In most situations, a variety of gifting techniques are used to meet all of a donor's objectives. The next list, broken down into the categories of current giving, future giving, transfer assets but retain certain benefits, and leverage/learning giving, presents the most common gifting techniques with highlights about the features and benefits of each.

Current Giving

These assets and techniques are most commonly used by donors to fulfill annual giving obligations or special gifts. The feature is that the asset is readily accessible by the donor, and the benefit is that the asset is easily transferable to a non-profit organization:

- *Cash or check.*
- *Highly appreciated assets,* such as publicly traded stocks and mutual funds, or real estate such as your home, ranch, or farm.
- *Depreciated assets* that may be sold for a tax loss under the current tax code and the cash gifted to an organization.
- *Life insurance.* If you purchased insurance for a specific goal that is now funded, such as to protect a mortgage, you can transfer ownership of the policy to the charity, which will be the beneficiary of the value of the insurance proceeds upon the death of the insured.
- *Donor-advised fund.* A fund established at a community foundation or at a financial investment company. The donor can make recommendations where to direct contributions, and the foundation, for a fee, takes care of all management and Internal Revenue reporting.
- *Pooled income funds.* Gifts from all donors are invested together in a fund run by the charity. The donor receives annual income depending on the fund performance. Upon the death of the donor, his or her remaining assets are distributed to the charity.

Future Giving

Future giving gifts allow you to make the decision today, with the right to change your mind prior to your death. The feature is that you have the flexibility and options to adjust your giving accordingly. The benefit is you may be able to make a larger gift from accumulated assets that were needed during your lifetime:

- *Bequests in your will.* A stated amount or percentage of money to a named charity.
- *Beneficiary designation* for your annuities, individual retirement account, life insurance, or other retirement plans subject to compliance with the Internal Revenue Service and the Tax Code.

Transfer Assets but Retain Certain Benefits

These are more flexible and sophisticated methods of giving that allow you to move the asset out of your estate while still retaining partial control either over the asset or the income from the asset. The feature is that each technique has its own unique tax advantages. The benefit is that you can plan strategically and financially to achieve both your lifetime and your estate planning philanthropic goals:

- *Gift annuity.* You give cash, stock, or other types of property to charity and in return you receive payments of income for life.
- *Charitable remainder trust.* You donate cash, appreciated stock, or other assets to a charity via a tax-exempt trust (CRT) and receive income payments from the trust for life or a term of years. As the remainder beneficiary, the charity receives all of the remaining funds at the donor's death or the end of the trust life.
- *Charitable lead trust.* You donate assets to the trust (CLT) and the charity receives a fixed income stream for a term of years or the life of the donor; thereafter, the balance of the trust is transferred back to the donor or to a designated beneficiary.
- *Family foundation.* A private foundation in which the donor retains substantial control over the investment of the assets, administration and designation of its grants, and involves the next generation in charitable decisions. Family members often serve as officers and board members.
- *Private foundation.* A professionally managed organization with a large asset base, in most cases donated by one person, family, or corporation and managed by trustees and staff. It is required to make annual grants equal to 5% of the market value of the assets.
- *Corporate foundation.* A company-sponsored, independent entity with assets contributed by a for-profit business.
- *Charitable gift funds.* Asset management companies such as Fidelity and Vanguard have established gift mutual fund vehicles similar to but not exactly like donor-advised funds. Donors make a gift to the fund, receive tax benefits, and make charitable contributions from their personal account in the fund. It makes charitable giving simple and effective at a low management fee.
- *Giving circles.* A pooled fund of designated amounts of money by a group of individuals who research and decide where to donate their funds collectively.

Leverage/Learning Giving

Participating in a giving circle provides a venue for a diverse membership base to combine their contributions and to participate in the allocation of the funds in their community. It is a common meeting ground for women from many walks of life who share core values. They can learn more about community issues, how to give wisely, and share equally in grant-making decisions. For more information, see Sondra Shaw-Hardy's *Creating a Women's Giving Circle.*[11]

How to Volunteer Time and Talent

Many times becoming a volunteer is the first opportunity to learn more about how an organization operates and carries out its mission. Volunteering is personal and means something different to each person. Perhaps one of the most critical elements to being a volunteer is to remember that you have a choice as to how to direct your time and energy, how to share your enthusiasm, your compassion, and your skills. How you volunteer will depend on how much time you have, your values and mission statement, and what level of involvement is appropriate for your lifestyle. And for boom-generation women, volunteering provides an outlet to engage in meaningful experiences when starting a new chapter in life. It is an important component to fulfillment of *eudaimonia* and the practice of virtuous philanthropy. Volunteering happens 24 hours a day, every day, as people connect to people and build stronger communities, in the process becoming activists to effect social change.

"The whole structure of volunteering is about to be reinvented," Edgar Bronfman writes in his book, *Third Act: Reinventing Yourself After Retirement.* He predicts "a virtual tidal wave of skilled professionals, talented individuals and top drawer executives who are ready to do good."[12] By tradition, many people first like to volunteer for an organization or a project before they commit to a significant financial contribution, but with boomers retiring and Internet access, that is changing. There are now efficient Web sites and search engines—such as the Points of Light Foundation, the Volunteer Center National Network, Action Without Borders, and Volunteer Match—(see Resource Section for Web sites) that connect people with opportunities to serve in their local community or worldwide. At the beginning of 2009, President Obama and First Lady Michelle

Obama urged people to help in the nation's recovery by volunteering. The government-run Corporation for National and Community Service is directing the United We Serve program in hopes of involving millions of new volunteers.[13] In recent years, national organizations, such as the Experience Corps, have become proactive in identifying community-based issues, establishing a local affiliate unit, and recruiting and training volunteers to work on solutions. Today, in 19 cities across the country, 2,000 corps members tutor and mentor elementary school children who struggle with reading.[11] Other trends include workplace volunteering, where employees receive a few hours of paid time off each month to participate in community service, such as the former Wachovia Bank's "Time Away from Work" program. The bank also supports the Single Volunteer program that brings individuals together for service events, and the concept of a regular family volunteer event or vacation. However, for the most part, local volunteer recruitment happens when one person asks another to help out for a cause or event that other friends and family members are supporting. Volunteer efforts vary from helping prepare tax returns, serving on a board of directors, writing grant proposals, chairing a multimillion-dollar fundraising campaign, delivering Meals on Wheels, being an after-school tutor, serving as a officer of a civic organization, giving service at the local fire and rescue department, signing up for a local trash at the beach cleanup day, playing in the community band, or building a house. There is no limit to the need or a minimum for the deed. At a volunteer orientation meeting several years ago, the trainer ended the session with this quote from St. Francis of Assisi: "A single sunbeam is enough to drive away many shadows."

Why Volunteer?

Make a difference	Respond to emergencies
Be a role model	Recover from disasters
Be a good citizen	Improve the environment
Improve your community	Teach someone
Help someone	Spread a message
Meet new people	Give someone a new start
Save lives	Inspire others to help
Share your knowledge	Prevent accidents
Learn new skills	Help children
Build homes	A reason all your own
Support a cause	

Source: copyright 2006 Points of Light Foundation, reprinted with permission.

Find Your Match

1. Five areas to analyze as you review the culture of an organization: Write one specific question you will ask:
   a. Size and location of the organization (impact)
   b. Scope and method of work (mission)
   c. Evaluation and reporting (transparency)
   d. Community citizenship (diversity)
   e. Efficient management and fiscal strength (stability)

2. Identify one unique way in which the organization:
   a. Speaks female
   b. Respects ownership
   c. Ranks in the ratings

3. How does the organizational culture meet your need for:
   a. Engagement
   b. Expedience
   c. Experience
   d. Empowerment

4. Complete your net worth and cash flow statements. Establish a monitoring system to find hidden resources.

5. Decide which of the common giving techniques work best for you. Make a list of current and deferred giving objectives you have for one, three, and five years. Stretch your vision and your goals. Do not settle for less.

6. Take the Bolder Giving Evaluation of your giving potential to assess your readiness to implement your optimal giving plan (see Exhibit 7.3).

Your Giving Potential

If you want to systematically determine your giving potential, this questionnaire outlines some steps to take.

Questionnaire

Which of these do you have in place?

◯ A lifetime financial plan.

◯ An up-to-date will or "legacy plan" that reflects my values.

◯ A long-term giving plan.

◯ Financial professionals who support my values and philanthropy.

◯ A strong connection to causes and /or organizations I care about.

◯ A peer philanthropic community.

◯ Confidence in discussing money and values with my parents, spouse & children.

◯ Strong sources of nonmaterial satisfaction and security (e.g. friendships, community, meaningful work, creative expression, exercise, contact with nature, religious or spiritual practice).

◯ Other

What motivates you to explore your giving potential?

◯ My religious or spiritual values.

◯ My social concerns.

◯ Pressing needs in the world.

◯ I have more money than I need.

◯ I want to have a bigger impact.

◯ I believe my giving will make a greater difference now than later.

◯ I want more meaning in my life.

◯ I'm inspired by other committed givers and want to be one of them.

◯ I have lots of talent and ideas to give.

◯ I'd love to make a huge difference to a particular organization.

◯ I want to enlarge my community and have more diverse relationships

◯ Curiosity—how much *could* I give?

◯ Other

Bolder Giving In Extraordinary Times

Exhibit 7.3 Bolder Giving Questionnaire
Reprinted with permission of the Zing Foundation.

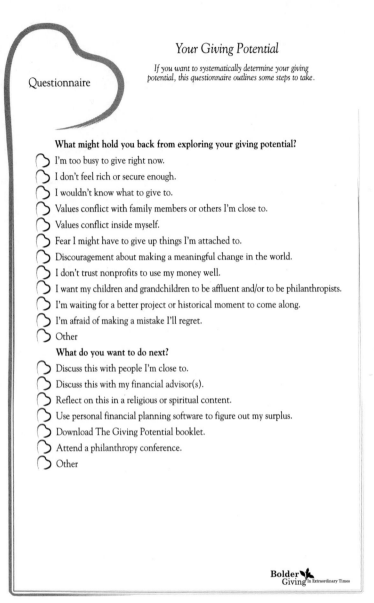

Your Giving Potential

Questionnaire

If you want to systematically determine your giving potential, this questionnaire outlines some steps to take.

What might hold you back from exploring your giving potential?

◯ I'm too busy to give right now.

◯ I don't feel rich or secure enough.

◯ I wouldn't know what to give to.

◯ Values conflict with family members or others I'm close to.

◯ Values conflict inside myself.

◯ Fear I might have to give up things I'm attached to.

◯ Discouragement about making a meaningful change in the world.

◯ I don't trust nonprofits to use my money well.

◯ I want my children and grandchildren to be affluent and/or to be philanthropists.

◯ I'm waiting for a better project or historical moment to come along.

◯ I'm afraid of making a mistake I'll regret.

◯ Other

What do you want to do next?

◯ Discuss this with people I'm close to.

◯ Discuss this with my financial advisor(s).

◯ Reflect on this in a religious or spiritual content.

◯ Use personal financial planning software to figure out my surplus.

◯ Download The Giving Potential booklet.

◯ Attend a philanthropy conference.

◯ Other

Bolder Giving In Extraordinary Times

Exhibit 7.3 continued

Donor Bill of Rights

The Independent Sector has archived nearly 100 standards, codes, and principles of nonprofit and philanthropic organizations on its Web site, www.independentsector.org. Although many of the standards were created by membership organizations as a code of ethics for their institutional members and affiliates, some were written from the donor's perspective. In 1993 a Donor Bill of Rights for Philanthropy was developed by the American Association of Fund Raising Council, Association for Healthcare Philanthropy, Council for Advancement and Support of Education, and the National Society of Fund Raising Executives, rebranded the Association of Fundraising Professionals.

Donor Bill Of Rights

Philanthropy is based on voluntary action for the common good. It is a tradition of giving and sharing that is primary to the quality of life. To assure that philanthropy merits the respect and trust of the general public, and that donors and prospective donors can have full confidence in the not-for-profit organizations and causes they are asked to support; we declare that all donors have these rights.

I. To be informed of the organization's mission of the way the organization intends to use donated resources, and of its capacity to use donations effectively for their intended purposes.

II. To be informed of the identity of those serving on the organization's governing board, and to expect the board to exercise prudent judgment in its stewardship responsibilities.

III. To have access to the organization's most recent financial statements.

IV. To be assured their gifts will be used for the purposes for which they were given.

V. To receive appropriate acknowledgement and recognition.

VI. To be assured that information about their donations is handled with respect and with confidentiality to the extent provided by law.

(continued)

VII. To expect that all relationships with individuals representing the organizations of interest to the donor will be professional in nature.

VIII. To be informed whether those seeking donations are volunteers, employees of the organization or hired solicitors.

IX. To have the opportunity for their names to be deleted from mailing lists that an organization may intend to share.

X. To feel free to ask questions when making a donation and to receive prompt, truthful and forthright answers.

Source: "Copyright 2009, Association of Fundraising Professionals (AFP), all rights reserved. Reprinted with permission."

A Lasting Footprint for a Better World

Our deepest fear is not that we are inadequate. Our deepest fear is that we are powerful beyond measure. It is our light, not our darkness that most frightens us.

We ask ourselves, Who am I to be brilliant, gorgeous, talented, fabulous? Actually, who are you not to be?

You are a child of God. Your playing small does not serve the world. There is nothing enlightened about shrinking so that other people won't feel insecure around you.

We are all meant to shine, as children do. We were born to make manifest the glory of God that is within us. It's not just in some of us; it's in everyone.

And as we let our own light shine, we unconsciously give other people permission to do the same. As we are liberated from our own fear, our presence automatically liberates others

—Marianne Williamson (1952–), *A Return to Love*
Reprinted with permission of the author

As the first contingent of the boomer generation moves from values revolution to values resolution, as they contemplate their future legacy, there are many questions still to be asked. Some may not yet have answers. Was my life here worth living? Did I make a difference? What was this struggle for? Did I make a dent in the universe?

In their time, that early boomer group helped change the face of society. Some say that as a result of their values, the boomers have turned this world into a hedonistic playground. Yet is that really the case? For the first time in history, most of the world enjoys a higher standard of living than preceding generations.

In *Democracy in America*, Alexis de Tocqueville questioned and lauded the American habits, social mores, customs, "their proclivity for voluntary associations, the nature of their religiosity, their moralism, their inordinate pride in their own institutions." Tocqueville believed that "anyone can make it here"—in the United States, that this was a land of freedom, opportunity, and equality. He writes of his observations with a sense of amazement of the "boundless skill of Americans in setting large numbers of people a common goal and inducing them to strive toward that goal voluntarily."[1] While he commended our individualism, he had his concerns. He applauded our "habits of the heart," which ennobles human beings, but was concerned that this could spiral down to mediocrity, sameness, and a loss of community. Tocqueville's words are somewhat prophetic, as we are in a challenging time, when many are concerned about our loss of community.

Yet as a people, we tend to be generous and expansive, with a need for making things better. Yes, there are still people hungry at night. Yes, there is more reported violence, we hear more about crime and upheavals and what does not work. Yet how much of that is a result of an openness in the media and of our willingness to talk about the untouchable topics? It may well be the boomer generation that fostered this conversation of openness. Yes, there is still illiteracy, yet it is not the expectation. And it is the boomer generation that has turned the world around so that for the first time in history, while there is still war, there is a stronger possibility of peaceful outcomes to those wars. It is a world where technology brings to home viewing via cell phones and Twitter a popular revolt against an election in a country thousands of miles away, as in the Iranian elections of June 2009. It is a world in which there is serious discussion and action about what can we do to help our neighbors locally, nationally, and internationally.

Congratulations, boomers—and most especially boomer women, who more than ever are at the forefront of making a difference. We marched, picketed, got jailed, provoked, studied, took issue with, were insubordinate, questioned, and challenged. And along with our male partners, we changed the world. As boomer women grew and expanded their horizons, we have searched for ways to cope with the political, social, and economic dilemmas of our age in the face of mediocrity and intolerance. Some would say we arrive at a time in our lives bankrupt in spirit, searching for meaning and a purpose—a centered life—at precisely the time when our nation is searching for the capacity for a sustainable and just society. Although there may, in fact, be significance in this convergence and a benefit to human kind as a result, we argue that boomer women are not bankrupt in spirit. Just the reverse. There is a keenness and an appreciation for what we and our country have accomplished, a sharper interest in politics and economics, and a spirit that challenges the status quo. While we may be in critical times emotionally, socially, morally, religiously, politically, and economically, the more educated and financially secure boomer women are ready to play a significant role in meeting the challenges our society faces today to reverse a spiraling down, self-destructive trend.

Although the most influential group in the social history of our country often has been perceived as problem children, and often we are branded for a supposed moral insincerity, recklessness, and immaturity, we also accomplished much to be proud of, from civil rights to social activism that changed society for the better. In the next 8 to 10 years, a boomer will enter his or her fifties every 8 seconds![2] Five years ago—even three years ago—most Americans entering this midlife period were relatively secure and happy. That may well have shifted due to the economic and political upheaval of the last couple of years. Still, happy or not, when a person enters midlife, there is a shift, a realignment of one's perception of self. People's thoughts turn not to what was accomplished to date but to what still remains to be accomplished in the time left. There is a quickening of the spirit and a searching of the heart to fulfill suspended dreams. This is how Susan Lloyd, of Nokomis, Florida, a participant at one of Margaret's workshops sums it up: "It's a time to sort through some of many things that are relevant in my life and so many of the thoughts I have churning in my head. It's a time to sit back and say 'wow'; I'm not the only one."[3]

A Model for Future Generations

The boom generation often has been branded as selfish, short-sighted, and unconcerned about legacies and the future. Yet we are seeing a shift that is reflected in our interviewees' responses. In our surveys and conversations, the women boomers reaching "that" certain age, or those who are already there, are showing a reflective side at odds with much of the research of the adolescent-behaving boomer. These women have a concern about leaving a legacy to their children. They very much want their Generation X offspring, born between 1961 and 1980, or their millennial children and grandchildren, born between 1981 and 2001, to put into place the core values their boomer parents often espoused around the dinner table.

Regardless of our economic circumstances while growing up, the fact remains that the boomer generation was perhaps the first in history to have the time and the financial freedom to think, to dream, to afford the space to change society. Our parents' generation was driven by necessity and obligation. We reaped the benefits of an era, and many of us who did not work after school or during the summer had leisure time. By and large, we were not expected to bring in income until we were adults. This changed our perspectives, for better or worse. The point is, it gave us a willingness to think about how we wanted life to be. Many of us want to make sure our core values are assimilated by our children and children's children, so they in turn can make a contribution.

All of the women we interviewed had spent some time thinking about her legacy. Perhaps in our eagerness to touch the world, or perhaps because of guilt that we were too self-absorbed, to the educated middle-class boomer women we have surveyed, age brings an urgency to talk to our children in order to articulate our vision, mission, and values. We reconsider what wealth and work ethics we want to pass on. Some studies suggest that our core values are not what influence our children; they often model their grandparents' ethos and attitudes. Still, a boomer characteristic is to reform the world, so we try.

Carol Weisman, the author of *Bringing Up Philanthropic Children*, articulated her concern when she saw her youngest son, who was just learning to walk, already getting involved in American consumerism—the "gimme-gimme" mind-set. "I could see that some major values education was needed—otherwise, my angelic, golden-haired child was going to turn into a materialistic, selfish little brat." Carol made it a big part of her family's core values to instill charitable giving. She had been taught these values around her parents' kitchen table and passed them down. Family conversations about giving and why this was so important were a part of their heritage. She said," it didn't take long for him to realize how great giving can feel." Today Carol writes about how to get children involved, so that they earmark their own money for a charity of their choice. "If giving is part of the family structure and this is what part of the expectation is, then it becomes a habit. We've always planned on where our gifts would go. This is now part of who we are. As I get older, I can't wait to fulfill my wishes to be even more generous as I can afford to. I hope that's part of the legacy I leave my son, that giving is fun."[4]

Vanessa Freytag, executive director with the Women's Fund in Cincinnati, Ohio, tells us that her role models included her mother.

> My first vivid memory is Meals on Wheels. My mother did that for a long time and she would have us go with her and I remember being a typical kid saying I didn't want to do that, I didn't want to see old people. And my mother said to me, "Don't you understand, sometimes we're the only meal they get all day, that's why we're doing this." And that thought never left me. I have two boys, young teenagers. They are very interested in helping the community. After Hurricane Katrina, my son came home from school (fifth grader at the time) and said, "Mom, I want to do something about all the people down there." "Well, what do you want to do?" "I want to raise money for them and I want to do a bake sale."
>
> He had already thought about it, how to go about it, setting up a little table on the corner of our street, etc. I decided to help him do it, yet let him do so independently. So I helped by making every kind of cookie, and a sign, had him practice what to say, he's a sweet, serious kid. I gave him my cell phone and let him go off on his own. His little brother helped him.

The adults were wonderful, some just wanting to make a donation. He said they needed to take a thank-you gift of a cookie,
even if they gave it to someone else. I was in tears, because everyone was so wonderful to him. My husband and I matched
what they raised and we took it down to the Red Cross, which is
where they wanted to donate the money. The boys felt so good.

Vanessa tells us:

It's very important to know that you're not the only person in
the world, and that no matter who you are, you have the ability
to change lives. I told them that some people change lives in
their neighborhood and that's great; some change lives in their
city, that's wonderful; some in their country . . . some people
are fortunate to literally change the world, but that all of it is
important. What's on my mind nowadays, as a boomer in the
upper end of the age scale, is we have this new opportunity to
bring together all of the players at the table. There are many
people like me in corporate America. I made more money than
I ever thought I'd make, before going on to do something that
for me was more meaningful to me, that of getting all of the
players together, those who are in need and those who serve
the needs of others . . . And we can look at the time, talent,
and treasure each brings to the table and more clearly define
what is the best role, what is the best way in which this entity,
this person, can use their skill. Collaborating, we have different adulthoods; we live a really long time. And if you can't give
now, how might you later? And in the role you're in, what can
you do? There's a way to pursue some level of this, regardless of
where and who you are.[5]

America, once a country of the young, is fast graying. The
number of boomers ready to pass on their core values is increasing. This age group is very concerned about the next generation,
and that concern is valid. Did we pass on the selfish, me-me values
of the boomer mentality? From 2010 to 2030, as boomers prepare
to retire, we recognize that the world we are passing on to our children and children's children is not what we, the boomers, inherited. Our Generation Xers will inherit a different world, a world we

made. While some of it is very good, there is a price still to be paid. The younger generation will be hard-pressed to pay for our retirement benefits. There is a real issue of dependency. Some analysts predict a generational war over this issue sometime soon. There may well be conflict among generations as a result of benefits going to aging boomers when there is a perception of scarcity, real or not.

And there is no doubt that for the near term, we are coping with the prospects of a less abundant future. What happens when economic austerity meets the future and proposed entitlements for aging boomers and the elderly? What boomers may expect is not realistic, most especially in light of current economic and demographic projections. A potential backlash is already under way, with academics, journalists, and political figures talking about how continued high levels of spending could destroy our nation's financial stability. Members of Generation X have started forcibly questioning age and need. They ask: Why should an aging millionaire receive free medical care? They argue that it is need rather than age that determines who gets what assistance. There is a growing urgency for agreement and respectful acknowledgment of the need for intergenerational mutual dependence. The model of the interdependent supportive family analogy may well be the one for the future, rather than the independent one fostered by the boomer generation. Perhaps the model we must adapt to cope with a diminishing abundance is one that was common before World War II and which stayed strong into the 1950s: a family unit where many generations lived near each other and every family member respected and helped the other, and the neighborhood, and the community raised a child.

And so we ask: What is a viable platform to host and nurture a revival of consciousness of spirit? One is sorely needed. Is this the place in time right now for a dialogue and engagement of mutual inquiry and practice among generations? And central to the core of this book: How will this impact philanthropy? Linda A.Wasserman, a Detroit, Michigan, attorney and partner with Honigman Miller Schwartz and Cohn, L.L.P., expresses her concern this way:

> I don't know what the children of these very wealthy families are thinking. There is a trend toward private foundations. Now,

I encourage my clients to do this, but often the next generation comes in and may not have the same philanthropic spirit
as their parents. They'll divide the foundation up and go their
separate ways rather than keeping it together and making a big
impact. My clients say "This money is for my children to give
away as they want." Some of my wealthier clients will leave a letter of intent, but I don't see a lot of training going on for the
next generation [Boomers, X and Y]. I worry about the mainstream charities, the zoo, the opera, the art museums, United
Way; I worry about who is going to support these in the future.[6]

Roots

We need to look back no further than the late 1960s to find the
roots of the season for women philanthropists. The feminist movement gave rise to a new way of life for women. Many had an opportunity for a college education. From college campuses to city parks,
young idealistic women challenged the conventional materialistic
paradigm and refuted the monopoly of a hierarchical power grid.
According to the 1970 U.S. Census, 79% of the freshmen of 1970
had as an important personal objective "developing a meaningful
philosophy in life."[7] Success at the time was defined primarily by
economic and financial gain, "conspicuous consumption." Women
students sought a different cognizance of what was important. It
was the beginning of a silent culture in search of a new idealism.
Fifty years later, that culture is silent no more; it is the cadre of
women in midlife replacing valuables with values. It is a generational coterie with a mandate for "conspicuous compassion" and a
revival of virtue.

During the same years women were rewriting the rules, our
nation transitioned from an industrial base to a knowledge-based
economy, with technology accelerating a global world economy.
We find ourselves part of an increasingly complex and interrelated
world, where the growing dichotomy between people of wealth and
people living in poverty affects all humanity. A study reports that
the richest 2% of adults in the world own more than half of all global household wealth.[8] More have to make due with less, and fewer
have more. Today the world is a web of interrelationships magnify-
ing the frailty on which the sustainability of our planet exists.

Concurrent with the rise of a new women's culture and the ascent of frailty of planet Earth, a new consciousness of thought has emerged. Sociologist Paul H. Ray and psychologist Sherry Ruth Anderson report how 50 million people are shaping a new agenda for the twenty-first century. This group, the Cultural Creatives, are leading-edge creators of a new culture in America in this time of epochal change. In their book, *The Cultural Creatives*, they extrapolate on the research and interviews regarding how values relate to culture and how reframing lets you look at old problems from a new angle of vision. When speaking about his work, Ray says, "Our research showed that the more the person is engaged in social activism, ecology, and social justice, the more likely they are to be engaged also in developing their spiritual lives and personal growth. This seeking for authenticity is part of what links each person's own personal growth with the concern for the big picture."[9] A significant number of Cultural Creatives are boom-generation women, whose idea of success has been refined from making a great deal of money to creating a more spiritual life, focused on creating a better future for everyone. Cultural Creatives want to leave the world a better place for the next generation. They are designing a new worldview, a new vision of what they value, what they care about in their work, their relationships, their community, and for their country. Women who care and who dare are taking action to bring their values and vision into mainstream society, and they are finding a receptive community of like-minded individuals.

Viable Platform

This receptive community is the "social sector," where more than 1.5 million nonprofit organizations provide a viable platform for the meeting of like minds, hearts, and open pocketbooks. In the early 1970s, the movement took hold on both the East and the West Coast at the same time among individual donors. In New York, Gloria Steinem started the Ms. Foundation; in San Francisco, Tracy Gary founded Resourceful Women. Advocacy for funding women's issues began in 1977, when Women & Philanthropy formed as a network and voice for positive change. The Women's Funding Network, established in the 1980s, has grown to over 145 funds with combined assets exceeding $450 million. In 1997, Sondra Shaw-Hardy and Martha Taylor formed the Women and Philanthropy Institute as an educational forum for all women donors. It is now part of the Center on Philanthropy at Indiana University under the direction of Dr. Debra Mesch and Andrea Pactor. A recent study by New Ventures in Philanthropy identified 400 giving circles throughout the country of which 57% are female members.[10]

Historically, the nonprofit environment provides a venue where creative discussion and innovation can flow more freely and openly than in the public-private sector. While it is not free of controversy, the nonprofit sector has fared significantly better than the recent greed, corruption, and grandstanding in the political and corporate sectors. Mike W. Martin writes in his book *Virtuous Giving,* "Above all, it [philanthropy] contributes to caring relationships and communities in more personal ways than by voting and paying taxes."[11] It is also a sector where the infrastructure may be at a more receptive stage for change and innovation, out of both the necessity to serve a greater population and the challenge to find new financial support for such programs. This receptivity creates a culture that allows women to leverage their abilities to the fullest. According to economist Kenneth Boulding, it becomes a special time in history when "the inputs at certain moments of 'readiness' in the development of the person produce effects which far outweigh their intrinsic importance."[12] In other words, this is the right generation of women advancing in the appropriate sector at the optimal time in history. The "social sector" is congruent with women's goals of making a difference in society and restocking social capital and serves as a common meeting ground for women to bond by asking "What do you think?" rather than "What do you do?" Women are already in significant leadership positions in the nonprofit sector, and that number is increasing rapidly. As reported in a recent Zoominfo InSite Report, cumulatively, women have the most significant numbers of chief executive officers (CEOs) in nonprofit and healthcare industries, and as partners in law firms and legal services, representing 29.6%, 22.1%, and 17.7% of the executive profiles, respectively. In the foundation field, 50% of CEOs and 70% of program officers are women.[13]

Reach Back to Go Forward

In 1902, at the height of the Progressive Era, social activist Jane Addams set the benchmark for today's boom-generation women's virtuous philanthropy. She writes in *Democracy and Social Ethics*:

> But we all know that each generation has its own test, the contemporaneous and current standard by which alone it can adequately judge of its own moral achievements, and that it may not legitimately use a previous and less vigorous test. The advanced test must indeed include that which has already been attained; but if it includes no more, we shall fail to go forward, thinking complacently that we have "arrived" when in reality we have not yet started."

Addams considers "Ethics as but another word for 'righteousness,' . . . without which life becomes meaningless."[14]

For contemporary scholars such as Strauss and Howe, the test of a generation's moral achievement includes living a meaningful life of "righteousness of conviction."[15] Idealistic in principle, women are using their acts of philanthropy as a way to test the validity of their moral achievements by how well they carry out "self-interest properly understood" as defined by Tocqueville.[16] And the foundation for philanthropy being accepted as a viable platform for such a test in the twenty-first century lies in the belief expressed by Robert L. Payton that philanthropy is "the principal means by which our ethics and values shape the society in which we live."[17] One may well ask whether philanthropy chose boom-generation women or whether an idealistic generational cohort in search of a legacy chose philanthropy to set the moral benchmark for the next generation. Our answer is: Both! In our opinion, it is destiny. Women bestowed with the zest and zeal, energy and purpose, and mobilized with greater wealth will meet their destiny through virtuous philanthropy, and leave their everlasting footprint.

Imprint for the Future

The four cornerstones that serve as the foundation for virtuous philanthropy are values, abundance, TLC, and leadership (see Exhibit 8.1). The essence of each makes up the Boom-Generation Women's Philanthropic Footprint, a holistic picture of virtuous philanthropy—equal parts of fortitude, justice, prudence and moderation, a dash of narcissism, a pinch of idealism, wrapped in heartfelt faith and hope, and seasoned with love. When all are in balance and the harmonious duality of yin merges with yang, women act in present time, creative in thought and with clear purpose. There is harmony, gratitude, and joy. There is community. There is hope for the future. There is reason to let our light shine.

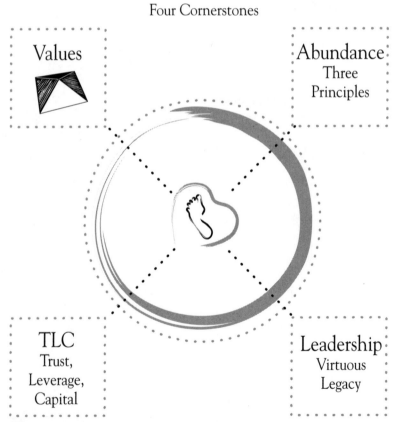

Four Cornerstones

Values

Abundance
Three
Principles

TLC
Trust,
Leverage,
Capital

Leadership
Virtuous
Legacy

Exhibit 8.1 Boom-Generation Women's Philanthropic Footprint

illustrations by Elizabeth Huggins-Thompson.

Let Your Light Shine

We are reminded of one of our favorite quotes:

> I wake up every morning both determined to change the world and have a heck of a good time doing it. Of course that makes planning rather interesting.
>
> —E. B. White

You empower yourself to be a Virtuous Philanthropist. Here are five examples of how you can "Let Your Light Shine." Enjoy your journey.

1. Sit down with your next generation, talk, share those kitchen values. Get them involved in the giving world, be a role model, share your hopes and your heart and your dreams. Let them see what really matters to you and why it matters all the way around for the future of our society.

2. Assemble your Empowerment Quartet. Write down what you recognize as your most visible strength in each cornerstone (Values, Abundance, TLC, and Leadership). Are they all of equal proportion? Do you see and feel the harmony in your word and deed each day? If not, select the cornerstone you want to change, write down one action you can take and practice it for a week. Continue the process until you find congruence in all four cornerstones.

3. In the near future, at a meeting you attend, sit down and ask the person on your left and the person on your right: "What is one thing you are grateful for today in your life?" Share that moment of gratitude with another person.

4. Virtuous philanthropy means daily practice in moderation of all seven virtues (see Exhibit 8.2). Reflect on your day, and consider how what you did and what you said were examples of the virtues and values that you identify as important to you.

5. What is one fear that you will let go of today to let your light truly shine?

Seven Covenants of Virtuous Philanthropy

Synergy among the seven covenants creates the full spectrum of women's philanthropic footprint.

A voluntary philanthropist is one who, empowered by the Three Principles of Abundance, lives a life harmonious with the seven covenants in reasonable and caring ways appropriate to her hopes, dreams, and desires for the greater good of all humanity.

1. **Courage** for a virtuous philanthropist is the ability to sustain the steadfast pursuit on one's convictions and beliefs in the face of skepticism or discouragement.

2. **Justice** for a virtuous philanthropist is the ability to respect and treat other people as moral equals, particularly when there is inequity of power or opportunity.

3. **Prudence** for a virtuous philanthropist is the ability to judge wisely and objectively in all matters pertaining to time, talent, and treasure.

4. **Temperance** for a virtuous philanthropist is the ability to exhibit a discipline in all matters so as to avoid extreme or harmful thought or action.

5. **Faith** for a virtuous philanthropist is the ability to trust in the expectation of right and proper being accomplished and the conviction it will be, without prior proof.

6. **Hope** for a virtuous philanthropist is the ability to accept risk with reasonable optimism but not absolute, for good to be achievable.

7. **Love** for a virtuous philanthropist is the ability to act beneficently and rejoice in the happiness of others.

Exhibit 8.2 Seven Covenants of Virtuous Philanthropy

Illustrations by Elizabeth Huggins-Thompson.

Epilogue: Our Hope for the Future . . . Destiny Calls a Generation

Every few hundred years in Western History there occurs a sharp transformation. Within a few short decades, society—its world view, its basic values, its social and political structures, its arts, its key institutions—rearranges itself. And the people born then cannot even imagine a world to which their grandparents lived and into which their own parents were born. We are currently living through just such a transformation.

—Peter Drucker, *Post Capitalist Society*
(1909–2005)

The noblest gift a human soul can give to one another is the gift of love. It is love from the heart that connects, listens, and responds to the pulse of a world crying out for a new spirit of humanity. Time and money alone cannot heal injustice and oppression. They provide the tools but not the passion or purpose. It is this generation of women, driven by their love of humankind, who with their *philanthropia,* impart the zeal and passion that endows women with the courage, compassion, and conviction to live their authentic lives as virtuous philanthropists.

It is the destiny of boom-generation women to engage all people in the holistic quest for a more harmonious world. It is the season for women to lift high the beacon of light and lead us through the unknown, a process of transformation from a place where we no longer can remain to a place we have not yet been but yearn to create and experience. It is a time to reach forward, to put our power to its highest and best use to help and heal a world crying for serenity and salvation. It is a dance of trust, assurance, and connection, employing the past to create the future. It is time to join hands, hearts, and heads, with fortitude, compassion, and the faithfulness to listen and act. It is the moment for you to live the Covenant, summon your sisters, and join us.

Margaret and Niki

Notes

Chapter 1

1. U.S. Census Bureau Newsroom Report, (CB06-FFSE 01-2) January 2006, Table 2a. Projected Population of the United States by Age and Sex: 2000 to 2050.
2. Michael J.Silverstein and Kate Sayre, "The Female Economy," *Harvard Business Review* (September 2009), 48, 50.
3. National Center for Women and Retirement Research, (Southampton College, Long Island University, Southampton, NY 11968).
4. John J. Havens and Paul G. Schervish, "Why the $41 Trillion Wealth Transfer Estimate Is Still Valid: A Review of Challenges and Questions,"*Journal of Gift Planning* 7, No. 1 (January 2003) 11–15, 47–50.
5. " Philanthropy Among Business Women of Achievement." Center for Women's Business Research. www.womensbusinessresearch.org
6. Tom Peters. *The Circle of Innovation* (New York: Alfred A. Knopf, Inc., 1997), 399.
7. Interview, Marie C. Wilson, New York, NY, September 2007.
8. Interview, Brenda Pejovich, Dallas, TX, March 2009.
9. Interview, Vi Nichols Chason; Stuart, FL, July 2007.
10. Daniel Yankelovich, *Uniting America: Restoring the Vital Center to American Democracy* (New Haven, CT: Yale University Press, 2006).
11 Meg Whitman, Princeton Class of '77 and her husband, Dr. Griffith R. Harsh IV, made a gift of $30 million to the university. Darla Moore has donated $70 million over the past nine years to USC's School of Business which bears her name.
12. Landon Y. Jones, *Great Expectations: America and the Baby Boomer Generation* (New York: Coward McCann, 1980). Jones is credited with coining the term "Baby Boomer."
13. William Strauss and Neil Howe, *Generations, The History of America's Future, 1584 to 2069* (New York: William Morrow, 1991), Strauss and Howe define a generation by a three-part test: (1) common age location; (2) common beliefs and behavior; and (3) perceived membership in a common generation.(p 64) The rationale to extend the time frame back to 1943 is in part because the boom generational cohort starts with the "victory babies" in 1943 (p. 301).
14. U.S. Census Bureau Newsroom Report, (CB06-FFSE 01-2) January 2006. Hans Finzel, *Help I'm a Baby Boomer* (Wheaton, IL: Victor Books, 1989).

15. J. Walker Smith and Ann Clurman, *Generation Ageless: How Baby Boomers Are Changing the Way We Live Today—And They're Just Getting Started* (New York: HarperCollins, 2007), 56.
16. U.S. Census Bureau Newsroom. Finzel, *Help I'm a Baby Boomer.*
17. Zogby International and Key Bank Survey, Reuters News Service, January 2008, 1.
18. U.S. Census Bureau Newsroom; Baby Boomer Headquarters.com.
19. Quoted in Smith and Clurman, *Generation Ageless*, xxix. According to Smith and Clurman, boomer optimism will continue through their aging years and in the process they will reinvent everything they encounter.
20. William Strauss and Neil Howe, *The Fourth Turning: What the Cycles of History Tell Us about America's Next Rendezvous with Destiny* (New York: Bantam, 1997), 65.
21. Alexis de Tocqueville, *Democracy in America*, (1835) trans. and ed. by Harvey C. Mansfield and Delba Winthrop (Chicago: University of Chicago Press, 2000).
22. *Eudaimonia* in Greek literally means "having a good guardian spirit." However, the term has a much more objective meaning. To live and experience *eudiamonia* is to be successful, to have what is most desirable, and to flourish. There is some disagreement about what sort of life is most flourishing. Some say it is a life of pleasure, others of honor, some a wealthy life, others a virtuous one. In the context of this book, *eudaimonia* is used to mean the virtuous ways an individual can achieve and express the well-being of the soul for a harmonious and fulfilling life.
23. Aristotle, "Niomachean Ethics, Book II, Chapter 1" in *The Basic Work of Aristotle*, ed. by Richard McKeon (New York: Random House, 2001), 942,
24. Robert L. Payton, *Ethics and Morals Essay* (Indianapolis: Center on Philanthropy at Indiana University, 2000), Payton Papers.org. Payton was a thought-leader in establishing the academic field of philanthropy and one of the founders of the Center on Philanthropy at Indiana University.
25. Riane Eisler, *The Real Wealth of Nations: Creating a Caring Economics* (San Francisco: Berrett-Koehler, 2007).
26. Robert William Fogel, *The Fourth Great Awakening and the Future of Egalitarianism* (Chicago: University of Chicago Press, 2000), 4.
27. Jean Shinoda Bolen, *Urgent Message from Mother: Gather the Women, Save the World* (San Francisco: Conari Press 2005), 44. Material excerpted from *Urgent Message From Mother* by Jean Shinoda Bolen, MD © BY Jean Shinoda Bolen, MD, Red Wheel Weiser, 65 Parker Street, Suite 7, Newburyport, MA 01950, 1-800-423-7087
28. Barbara Wilder, *Money Is Love* (Boulder, CO: Wild Ox Press, 1999), 15.
29. Bolen, *Urgent Message from Mother*, 74.
30. Patricia Aburdene, *Megatrends 2010, The Rise of Conscious Capitalism* (Charlottesville, VA: Hampton Roads, 2005).
31. Elizabeth Blackwell was the first woman to receive a medical degree from an American medical school in 1849 (www.About.com: Women's History site).
32. *Out of Africa* is a 1985 film based on work of Isak Dinesen, nom de plume used by Danish baroness Karen von Blixen-Finecke.
33. Interview, Donna Hall, San Francisco, CA, November 2007.
34. Interview, Marilyn Wechter, MSW, BCD, Clayton, MO, February 2009.

Chapter 2

1. Rachel Naomi Remen, MD, *Kitchen Table Wisdom* (New York: Riverhead Books, 1996), xx, VII.
2. Quoted in Alfred Lubrano, *Limbo: Blue-Collar Roots, White-Collar Dreams* (New York: John Wiley and Sons, 2004), 32.
3. Interview, Elizabeth (Betty) Lahti, Palm City, FL, November 2007.
4. Interview, Pat Stryker, Ft. Collins, CO, September 2007.
5. Interview, Patricia Fripp CPAE, San Francisco, CA, April 2009.
6. Walter Smith and Anne Clurman, *Generation Ageless* (New York: HarperCollins, 2006), xvi.
7. William Strauss and Neil Howe, *Generation: The History of America's Future, 1584 to 2089* (New York: William Morrow, 1964), 302. According to the authors, the 1943 "victory babies" are ranked among the most self-absorbed cohort in American history.
8. Quoted in Hans Finzel, *Help! I'm a Baby Boomer* (Wheaton, IL: Victor Books, 1989), 17.
9. Alexander W. Austin, *The American Freshman*, National Norms for Fall, 1974, University of California, Cooperative Institutional Research Program. In studies conducted from 1966 to 1970, 15% of the nation's institutions of higher education were selected by sampling procedures and invited to participate in the program.
10. Lynne Twist, *The Soul of Money Transforming Your Relationship with Money and Life* (New York: W.W. Norton, 2003), 5.
11. *Money* magazine, September 13, 2007, thirty-fifth anniversary issue featured a survey of 3,000 boomers conducted by the Clark, Martire, Bartolomeo polling firm. Among other things, the study pointed out that boomers are reinventing the American dream, emphasizing friends and family over making money, having fun over working hard, and making a difference in the community and the world.
12. James V. Gambone, *ReFirement: A Boomers' Guide to Life after 50* (Minneapolis: Kirk House Publishers, 2000), 27. Dr. Gambone writes about his own experiences and his work as coordinator of the 1994 United Nations Year of the Family Conference promoting intergenerational respect, caring, and cooperation.
13. Quoted in "Forever Young" article by Marilyn Harris, *Money* magazine, September 13, 2007.
14. Thomas J. Stanley, *Millionaire Women Next Door* (Kansas City, MO: Andrews McMeel Publishers, 2004), 148.
15. Abraham H. Maslow, Ph.D., American psychologist (1908–1970). Maslow is noted for his theory of motivation (1943) and conceptualization of the hierarchy of human needs.
16. Erik Erikson Ph.D., German-born psychologist (1902–1994). Known for his theory of identity development, among Erikson's greatest innovations was adding three more stages to Freud's original personality development and emphasizing that there are meaningful stages of adult psychology that have to be considered, in addition to child development.

17. Interview, Lucille Griffo, Knoxville, TN. July 2007.
18. Susan B. Evans and Joan P. Avis, *The Women Who Broke All the Rules: How the Choices of a Generation Changed Our Lives* (Naperville, IL: Sourcebooks, Inc., 1999), xvii.
19. Morris Massey Ph.D., *What You Are Is Where You Were When-The Massey Triad Revised Program #1.* DVD Video. Richardson Company Training Media, Lakewood, WA 98499
20. Carol Gilligan, *In a Different Voice* (Cambridge, MA: Harvard University Press, 1982), 2.
21. Katharine Fulton and Andrew Blau, "Cultivating Change in Philanthropy—A Working Paper on How to Create a Better Future" (Monitor Company Group, LLP, 2005), www.futureofphilanthropy.org.
22. Center for Women's Business Research. "Key Facts about Women-Owned Business," 2009. www.womensbusinessresearchcenter.org.
23. Carl Gustav Jung, Swiss psychiatrist, (1875-1961), *The Basic Writings of C.S. Jung.* ed. by Violet Stab deLaszlo. (New York: Random House, 1993) He is founder of the analytical psychology known as Jungian psychology. His concept of psychological archetypes emphasized the importance of harmony, balance, spirituality, and the appreciation of unconscious realms.

Chapter 3

1. Shelly Banjo, "Women Take Philanthropic Reins,"*Wall Street Journal* Online, May 13, 2009. Ms. Buffett is president of the NoVo Foundation, which aims to empower women and girls. The foundation received the Clinton Global Initiative (CGI) Global Citizen Award in 2008 for work to improve the lives of women and girls everywhere in the world.
2. Tracy Gary, "Women philanthropists: Leveraging influence and impact as change makers," published in *The Transformative Power of Women's Philanthropy*, ed. Martha A. Taylor and Sondra Shaw-Hardy. New Directions for Philanthropic Fundraising, No. 50, Winter 2005 (San Francisco: Jossey-Bass, 2006), 97.
3. Eric Wilson, "Her Forced Retirement,"*New York Times*, August 14, 2008.
4. Interview, Marilyn Wechter, Clayton, MO. February 2009.
5. Sondra C. Shaw and Martha A. Taylor, *Reinventing Fundraising: Realizing the Potential of Women's Philanthropy* (San Francisco: Jossey-Bass, 1995), 88–96. The Six Cs of Women's Giving as defined in their book are: Change, Create, Connect, Commit, Collaborate, and Celebrate. More recently, they added three more Cs for the twenty-first century: Control, Confidence, and Courage.
6. Colleen Willoughby, as quoted in "Giving circles: A powerful vehicle for women," an article by Jessica Bearman, Buffy Beaudoin–Schwartz and Tracey A. Rutnik published in *The Transformative Power of Women's Philanthropy*, p 109.
7. Oprah Winfrey: Commencement speech, Stanford University, Palo Alto, CA 2008.
8. Simone de Beauvoir, *The Second Sex* (New York: Penguin, 1972). Originally published in 1949. de Beauvoir, a French writer and philosopher, wrote her treatise as a detailed analysis of women's oppression and as a foundational tract on contemporary feminism.

9. Interview, Marilyn Wechter.

10. Lynne Twist, *The Soul of Money*, Part Two: *Scarcity and Sufficiency: The Search for Prosperity* (New York: W.W Norton & Company, 2003), 209.

11. Deepak Chopra, *The Seven Spiritual Laws of Success: A Practical Guide to the-Fulfillment of Your Dreams* (San Rafael, CA: Amber Allen Publishing and New World Library, 1994), 25.

12. Lynne Twist, p 209.

13. Darla Moore was the first women profiled on the cover of *Fortune* magazine and named to the *Fortune* list of the top 50 most powerful women in American business. Currently she is president of Rainwater Investments. In 2007, Moore was inducted into the South Carolina Business Hall of Fame.

14. Meg Whitman, Princeton Class of '77, She was president and chief executive officer of the online auction site eBay before resigning to run in the 2010 race for the office of governor of California.

15. Robert Putnam: *Bowling Alone: The Collapse and Revival of the American Community* (New York: Simon & Schuster, 2000). Putnam is a political scientist and takes the position that the United States is undergoing an unprecedented collapse in civic, social, associational, and political life (social capital), and has been since the 1960s. He points out: Over the last 25 years, the percentage of people attending club meetings has dropped 43%; attending and having family dinners has dropped 43%; and having friends has dropped over 35%. He believes we are becoming a nation of loners and that this impacts our fundamental way of life.

16. James V. Gambone and Erica Whittlinger, *The 75% Factor: Uncovering Hidden Boomer Values* (The ReFirement Group: Crystal Bay, MN: 2003), 4.

17. Oral Lee Brown and Caille Milliner, *The Promise: How One Woman Made Good on Her Extraordinary Pact to Send a Classroom of 1st Graders to College* (New York: Doubleday, 2005). Brown earned her bachelor of science degree from the University of San Francisco while raising three daughters and holding a management position, supervising 55 people, at Blue Cross Insurance Company. She is now a marketing entrepreneur, owner of the Nationwide Realty T.P.I. Corporation, Oakland, CA. and known for her popular dessert, the Oral Lee Famous Peach Cobbler at Cobbler's Restaurant. In 1987, she made her commitment to "give back" and adopted the first-grade class at Brookfield Elementary School in East Oakland. Of the original 23 students, 19 have graduated and are currently enrolled in college. The Oral Lee Brown Foundation provides educational assistance and scholarships for residents of the city of Oakland for the pursuit of post–high school education.

18. Thomas J. Stanley, *Millionaire Women Next Door* (Kansas City, MO: Andrews McMeel Publishers, 2004), 145.

19. Interview, Sally Hare- Schriner, Lawrence, KS, September 2007.

20. Thorstein Veblen, *The Theory of the Leisure Class: An Economic Study in the Evolution of Institutions* (New York: Penguin Classics, 1994). Chapter Four. Originally published 1899. Veblen (1857–1929) was a Norwegian-American sociologist and economist. He introduced the term "conspicuous consumption" in 1899 to depict the behavioral style demonstrated by the indulgences of a nouveau riche society emerging in the nineteenth century as a result of the accumulation of excess wealth. The term is now more widely used to apply

to individuals with discretionary income who are consumers of goods and services to show their status of wealth and power.

21. Sonja Lyubomirsky, *The How of Happiness* (New York: Penguin Books, Penguin Group, 2007). 43-44. Dr. Lyubormirsky is professor of psychology at the University of California, Riverside. Her premise is that we all want happiness, regardless of how we phrase it, and that improving our own happiness is realizable and within our own power.

22. Megan Kenny, "82-Year-old Award Winner Opened Doors for Children,"*Stuart* (FL) *News,* April 7, 2007.

23. Interview, Margaret Smith, San Francisco, CA, October 2007.

24. Interview, Jody Bond, Palm City, FL. July 2007.

25. Interview, Beverly Holmes, Springfield, MA. November 2007.

26. Interview, Sherron Long, West Palm Beach, Florida. January 2008

27. Interview, Dame Roddick, Association of Fundraising Professionals conference, San Diego, CA, March 2002. Quote: *Women's Philanthropy Institute News,* September 2001, 3.

Chapter 4

1. Kathleen D. McCarthy, *Women and Philanthropy in the United States, 1790 to 1990, curriculum guide.* Center for the Study of Philanthropy, City University of New York (Spring 1998), 81.

2. Interview, Brenda Pejovich, Dallas, TX, March 2009.

3. Interview, Suzanne Horstman, Stuart, FL, February 2008.

4. Janet L. Surrey, Ph.D., *Self-in-Relation: A Theory of Women's Development.* Paper presented at a Stone Center Colloquium, Wellesley Center for Women, Wellesley, MA, November 16, 1983.

5. Interview, Ronda Stryker, Kalamazoo, MI, October 2007.

6. Riane Eisler, *The Real Wealth of Nation: Creating a Caring Economics* (San Francisco: Berrett-Koehler, 2007).

7. Interview, Melissa Morriss-Olson, PhD, Longmeadow, MA, August 2007.

8. Interview, Anne McCormick, Hobe Sound, FL, November 2007.

9. Daniel H. Pink, *A Whole New Mind: Why Right-Brainers Will Rule the Future* (New York: Berkley, 2005), 2.

10. Sherry Buffington, *The Law of Abundance* (Dallas: QuinStar Publishing, 2008). Quote from Core Management Workshop, Dallas, TX, June 5, 2009.

11. Interview, Lucy Crow Billingsley, Dallas, TX, February 2009.

12. Robert H. Bremner, *American Philanthropy* (Chicago: University of Chicago Press, 1998), v, 2, 12.

13. John Winthrop as quoted in Robert H. Bremner, *American Philanthropy,* 7.

14. Cotton Mather as quoted in Robert H. Bremner, *American Philanthropy,* 12.

15. Kim Klein, *Fundraising for Social Change* (Berkeley, CA: Chardon Press, 2006), 14.

16. Robert H. Bremner, *Giving, Charity and Philanthropy in History* (New Brunswick, NJ: Transaction Publishers, 1996), 42, 43, 159.

17. Andrew Carnegie, *The Gospel of Wealth* (1889) (Bedford, MA: Applewood Books, 1998), 23.
18. Tracy Gary, Dallas Women's Foundation Conference, Workshop on Philanthropy for Women and Goal Setting. Spring 2009.
19. Kathleen Miller quoted in Eva Marer, "Women and Philanthropy: Inspiring and Engaging your Clients in Giving" (Council on Foundations and Community Foundations of America, 2004), 1, 2.
20. Interview, Marie C. Wilson, New York, NY, August 2007.
21. Kathleen D. McCarthy, Women and Philanthropy in the United States, 1790 to 1990, curriculum guide. Center for the Study of Philanthropy, City University of New York (Spring 1998), 58.
22. Abbie J. von Schlegell and Joan M. Fisher, *Women as Donors, Women as Philanthropists* (San Francisco: Jossey-Bass, 1993), 5.
23. Joanna L. Krotz, *Making Philanthropy Count: How Women Are Changing the World* (Indianapolis: Women's Philanthropy Institute at the Center on Philanthropy at Indiana University, 2009), 5.
24. Interview, Cam Kelly, Durham, NC, July 2009.
25. Jennifer Kahlow quoted in Amy Gage, "Making a Case for Philanthropy," Women In Business, *St. Paul, Pioneer Press*, September, 1996, Section D, p.1.
26. Anne Mosle is vice president for Programs at the W. K. Kellogg Foundation. Previously she was president of the Washington Area Women's Foundation. She serves on the National Board of Women and Philanthropy and is a member of the Children, Youth and Families Steering Committee of the Washington Regional Association of Grantmakers.
27. Sondra C. Shaw and Martha A. Taylor, "A Career Woman: A Changing Environment for Philanthropy,"*NSFRA Journal* (Fall 1991), p 42—49.
28. Gretchen Kreuter, "Women Philanthropists Pave the Way for Women in Politics,"*Women's Philanthropy Institute News* (February 2000): 1.
29. Amy Gage, "Making Case for Philanthropy" Women in Business, *St. Paul Pioneer Press* (September 1996), Section D, 1.
30. Donna E. Shalala as quoted in Anne I. Thompson and Andrea R. Kaminski, *Women and Philanthropy, A National Agenda* (Madison, WI: Center for Women and Philanthropy, 1993), 1.
31. Interview, Andrea R. Kaminski, former director, Women's Philanthropy Institute Madison, WI, March 2002.
32. Interview, Phyllis Rappaport, Boston, MA, November 2007.
33. Interview, Suzanne Horstman, Stuart, FL, February 2008.
34. Maya Thornell-Sandifor as quoted in Kristin Butler, "Local Women Change Face of Philanthropy,"*Bay Area Business Women* (December 2005): 1.
35. Thompson and Kaminski, *Women and Philanthropy,* 1.
36. Interview, Anna Lloyd, former director of the Committee of 200, Chicago, IL, March 2002.
37. Abraham H. Maslow, *Toward a Psychology of Being* (New York: Van Nostrand Reinhold Company, 1968).
38. Michael Anft and Harvey Lipman, "How Americans Give,"*Chronicle of Philanthropy Special Report,* May 1, 2003, 1.

Chapter 5

1. Petra Karin Kelly, German-born activist (1947–1992), cofounder of the Greens and the Global Women's Peace Movement.
2. Daniel H. Pink, *A Whole New Mind: Why Right-Brainers Will Rule the Future* (New York: Berkley, 2005), 35.
3. Robert William Fogel, *The Fourth Great Awakening, and the Future of Egalitarianism* (Chicago: University of Chicago Press, 2003), 3.
4. Sherry Buffington, *The Law of Abundance* (Dallas: QuinStar Publishing, 2008). Quote from Core Management Workshop, Dallas, TX, June 5, 2009.
5. Pink, *A Whole New Mind*, 2–3.
6. Linda Ellis, "The Dash Poem,"www.lindaellis.net, 1996.
7. Deborah Tannen, *You Just Don't Understand: Women and Men in Conversation* (New York: William Morrow, 1990).
8. Interview, Ronda Stryker, Kalamazoo, MI, July 2007.
9. Barry K. Baines, *Ethical Wills: Putting Your Values on Paper* (Cambridge, MA: Perseus Book Group, 2002), 10.
10. Rachael Freed, *Women's Lives, Women's Legacies—Passing Your Beliefs and Blessings to Future Generations* (Minneapolis: Fairview Press, 2003), 4.
11. Joseph Campbell, *The Hero with a Thousand Faces* (New York: Pantheon Books, 1949).
12. Jean Shinoda Bolen, *Urgent Message from Mother: Gather the Women, Save the World* (San Francisco: Conari Press 2005), 113.
13. Tracy Gary with Nancy Adess, *Inspired Philanthropy Your Step-by-Step Guide to Creating a Giving Plan and Leaving a Legacy,* 3rd ed. (San Francisco: Jossey-Bass, 2008), 2.
14. Interview, Carolyn Eychaner, Martinez, GA, January 2008.
15. Interview, Sally Hare-Schriner, Lawrence, KS, September 2007.

Chapter 6

1. Rheta Childe Dorr (1868–1948), was an author and writer for the New York *Evening Post* and a war correspondent during World War I. Steven J. Diner, *A Very Different Age: Americans of the Progressive Era* (New York: Hill and Wang, 1998), 202.
2. Interview, Wendy Steele, Traverse City, MI, October 2007.
3. Marianne Williamson, *Everyday Grace: Having Hope, Finding Forgiveness, and Making Miracles* (New York: Riverhead Books, 2002). Williamson is best known for her work on the Course in Miracles. A world-renowned lecturer, she is a fervent believer in hope and grace and that it is how we live on a daily basis that determines who we are.
4. "Open kimono" is a 1990s business phrase used to connote being open, sharing data, keep no secrets, establish trust.
5. "May the force be with you," a phrase used principally by Obi-Wan Kenobi, a character in George Lucas' films, Star Wars series, Twentieth-Century Fox, original, 1997. It became a popular expression used to wish someone well.

6. A Donor Bill of Rights was developed by the Association of Fundraising Professionals, the Association for Healthcare Philanthropy, the Council for Advancement and Support of Education, and Giving Institute: Leading Consultants to Non-Profits (formerly the American Association of Fundraising Counsel). Its purpose is to assure that a donor can have full confidence in the not-for-profit organizations and causes that they are asked to support.

7. Guidestar USA, November 2006 Report. www.guidestar.org.

8. David Halpern, as quoted in Steven M. R. Covey *The Speed of Trust,* 11.

9. Heartland Institute, *School Reform News* (February 2004), Josephson Institute of Ethics, Marina del Rey, CA, Donald McCabe, Rutgers University professor of Management.

10. Steven M.R. Covey, *The Speed of Trust* (New York: Free Press, 2006), 11–12.

11. The Sarbanes-Oxley Act of 2002 (Public Law 107-204, United States Statute 745) enacted July 30, 2002 sets the standards for all U.S. public company boards, management, and accounting firms. The law is also referred to as the Public Company Accounting and Investor Protection Act of 2002. While it does not apply to nonprofit organizations and privately held companies, most have incorporated the standards in their fiscal reporting.

12. WorldCom CEO: Bernie Ebbers, convicted of fraud, 2005. Jeffrey Skilling: former president, CEO of Enron, Inc., convicted in 2006, for the largest corporate fraud in history. Skilling was interviewed in 2002, for the McCuistion program on KERA, PBS Dallas. In citing the 64-page ethics policy Enron subscribed to, he said, "Enron prides itself on its integrity."

13. Securities and Exchange Committee Report 12-12—007, Section 44 on Sarbanes Oxley.

14. Peter F. Drucker, *Managing the Non-Profit Organization* (New York: HarperCollins, 1990), 116.

15. Patricia Aburdene, *Megatrends 2010: The Rise of Conscious Capitalism* (Charlottesville, VA: Hampton Roads Publishing, 2005, xiv.

16. "The See Through CEO," Clive Thompson. *Wired Magazine* 15:04 (March 2007). Online www.wired.com.

17. Don Tapscott and David Ticoll, *The Naked Corporation* (New York: Simon & Schuster, 2003).

18. Claire Gaudiani, *The Greater Good, How Philanthropy Drives the American Economy and Can Save Capitalism* (New York: Henry Holt, 2003), 169.

19. Interview, Wendy Steele.

20. IRS 2008 Report: The $5 billion Battle of the Sexes.

21. *The Economist* magazine (April 12-15, 2006) issue Womenomics. www .economist.com.

22. Kimberly Davis quoted in Joanna L. Krotz, *Making Philanthropy Count: How Women Are Changing the World* (Indianapolis: Women's Philanthropy Institute at the Center on Philanthropy at Indiana University, 2009), 20.

23. Minniwatts Marketing Group, June 2009. www.internationalstats.com Internet World Stats Usage and Population Statistics.

24. Kimberly Davis quoted in Krotz, *Making Philanthropy Count,* 7.

25. Cynthia Ryan, principal of the Schooner Foundation, which has a focus on human rights, peace, and security.
26. Swanee Hunt quoted in Krotz, *Making Philanthropy Count,* 16.
27. Tracy Gary with Nancy Adess, *Inspired Philanthropy your Step-by Step Guide to Creating a Giving Plan and Leaving a Legacy,* 3rd ed. (San Francisco: Jossey-Bass, 2008), 258. Quote from "Women Moving Million" May 13, 2009. www.womenmovingmillions.org.
28. Anne Mosle, vice president of Programs, W.K. Kellogg Foundation, 2007.
29. The Conference on Baby Boomers and Retirement: Impact on Civic Engagement, October 8–10, 2003, sponsored by Harvard School of Public and Health-MetLife Foundation, *Reinventing Aging: Baby Boomer and Civic Engagement* (Cambridge, MA: President and Fellows of Harvard College, 2004), Chapter 7, 33.
30. Interview, Jody Bond, Palm City, FL, July 2007.
31. Alexis de Tocqueville, *Democracy in America* (1835) trans. and ed. by Harvey C. Mansfield and Delba Winthrop (Chicago: University of Chicago Press, 2000), Book II, Chapter 8, 611.
32. Bruce Frohnen,"Compassionate Conservatism Rightly Understood, Self-Interest in a Humane Society,"*Intercollegiate Review* 1 (Fall/Spring 2000), 38.
33. Robert D. Putnam, *Bowling Alone: The Collapse and Revival of American Community* (New York: Simon & Schuster, 2000), 23.
34. Harvard School of Public Health-MetLife Foundation *Reinventing Aging,* Chapter 7, 34.
35. Jean Shinoda Bolen, *Urgent Message from Mother: Gather the Women, Save the World* (San Francisco: Conari Press, 2005), 76.
36. Putnam, *Bowling Alone,* 27.
37. Francis Fukuyama, "Social Capital and Civil Society," paper delivered at the IMF Conference on Second Generation Reforms, Institute of Public Policy, George Mason University, Fairfax, VA October 1, 1999.
38. Interview, Elaine Suess, Cincinnati, OH, August 2007.
39. Peter F. Drucker, "The Age of Social Transformation,"*Atlantic Monthly* 297, No. 3 (Spring 1994).
40. Interview, Debbie Ritchie, Pensacola, FL, April 2008.
41. William Strauss and Neil Howe, *Generations: The History of America's Future, 1584-2069* (New York: William Morrow, 1991), 405.
42. Tocqueville, *Democracy in America,* Book II, Chapter 5, 599.
43. Putnam, *Bowling Alone,* 288.
44. Ibid., 368.
45. Editorial "*The Women of Thirty,*" *The New York Times,* Sunday Section, August 29, 1929, E 2.
46. Marilyn Fischer and Judy D. Whipps, eds. *Jane Addams, Essays and Speeches,* "The Philosophy of a New Day" (London: Continuum International Publishing Group, 2003), 351.

Chapter 7

1. Kenneth Boulding quoted in David Rejeski and Robert L. Olson, "Has Futurism Failed?" *Wilson Quarterly* (Winter 2006), 20.
2. Ledbury Research, *Tomorrow's Philanthropist* (New York: Barclays Wealth, 2009). The survey contacted 500 high-net-worth individuals in United States and the United Kingdom with investable assets of over $1 million. Included were 150-plus ultra-high-net-worth individuals with investable assets of over $5 million and 20 experts in the field of philanthropy.
3. Chrysalis Research, Kirkland, WA, and Research Data Technology, Woburn, MA, The Fidelity® Charitable Gift Fund Study (2009), an online survey of 1,003 respondents who donated at least $1,000 in 2007.
4. "Foundation Donations Targeting Women and Girls on the Rise," *Financial Post,* Canada.com Network (June 27, 2009).
5. Interview, Alice Krause, New York, NY, November 2007.
6. Tracy Gary with Nancy Adess, *Inspired Philanthropy, Your Step-by-Step Guide to Creating a Giving Plan and Leaving a Legacy* (San Francisco: Jossey-Bass, 2008), 3.
7. National Center for Charitable Statistics, www.nccs.urban.org.
8. Deborah Tannen, *You Just Don't Understand: Women and Men in Conversation* (New York: William Morrow, 1990).
9. The filing threshold as of 2010 is $200,000 gross receipts and $500,000 total assets. In addition to financial data, the form allows an organization to describe its accomplishments and mission.
10. The comparison for philanthropic personalities to qualities and characteristics of flowers is part of an ongoing research project at the Institute for Women and Wealth, Lake Worth, FL. The study has used various survey and self-identification techniques.
11. Sondra Shaw-Hardy, *Creating a Women's Giving Circle: A Handbook* (Indianapolis: Center on Philanthropy, Women in Philanthropy, 2001). This 70-page primer leads you through the how to of organizing, funding and publicizing a women's giving circle. For details on creating a giving circle, contact Sondra Shaw-Hardy at www.philwomen.com. In a 2007 study, the Forum of Regional Association of Grantmakers' New Venture in Philanthropy initiative identified approximately 400 Giving Circles in the United States.
12. Edgar M. Bronfman with Catherine Whitney, *Third Act: Reinventing Yourself After Retirement* (New York: G.P. Putnam's Sons, 2002), 56.
13. The Corporation for National and Community Service conducts and supports high-quality, rigorous social science evaluation and research and assists in the development of new initiatives in volunteering and civic engagement; www .nationalservice.gov.
14. The Experience Corps is a national program that engages people over 55 in the mentoring and tutoring of young students. Services include literacy coaching and after-school supervision. There are programs in 23 cities across the

country. Their newsletter, *The Voice of Experience,* reports news and research of the positive effectives of community service; www.experiencecorps.org.

Chapter 8

1. Alexis de Tocqueville, *Democracy in America,* (1835) trans. and ed. by Harvey C. Mansfield and Delba Winthrop (Chicago: University of Chicago Press, 2000), Book II, Chapter 5, Page 595.
2. Roma Hanks, *Baby Boomer's Influence,* Harbinger (Mobile, March 16, 1999), 1.www.theharbinger.org.
3. Comment from Susan Lloyd after Margaret May Damen's "Women Philanthropists: Pebble in the Pond," workshop at Florida Planet Philanthropy Day, Sarasota, FL, 2008.
4. Interview, Carol Weisman, St. Louis, MO, February 2009. Carol, a professional speaker and consultant in nonprofit strategy, is the author of several books on philanthropy, including *Fundraising Superheroes* (2009).
5. Interview, Vanessa Freytag, Cincinnati, OH, September 2007.
6. Interview, Linda Wasserman, Detroit, MI, May 2008.
7. *Statistical Abstract of the United State Census* (Washington, DC: 2006), Table 274.
8. World Institute for Development Economics Research, United Nations University, Helsinki. www.wider.unu.edu.
9. Paul H, Ray and Sherry Ruth Anderson, *The Cultural Creatives: How 50 Million People Are Changing the World* (New York: Harmony Books, 2000). Quote from www.yesmagaazine interview by Sarah van Gelder with Paul Ray and Sherry Anderson, "A Culture Gets Creative" (Winter 2001 issue) 1.
10. The Forum of Regional Association of Grantmakers "The Impact of Giving Today," May 14, 2009.p. 4. www.givingforum.org/giving circles.
11. Mike W. Martin, *Virtuous Giving: Philanthropy, Voluntary Service, and Caring* (Bloomington: Indiana University Press, 1994), 7.
12. Kenneth Boulding first used the term "psychic capital" in 1950 to define the accumulation of positive or negative mental states as a dynamic motivating force.
13. ZoomInfo InSite Reports, "Gender in the Executive Suite" (Waltham, MA: June 2007). www.zoominfo.com.
14. Jane Addams, *Democracy and Social Ethics,* intro. by Charlene Haddock Seigfried (Chicago: University of Illinois Press, 2002), 1. Originally published 1907.
15. William Strauss and Neil Howe, *Generations: The History of America's Future, 1584 to 2069* (New York: William Morrow, 1991), 404.
16. Alexis de Tocqueville, 610.
17. Robert L. Payton, *Ethics and Morals Essay* (Indianapolis: The Center on Philanthropy at Indiana University, The Joseph and Matthew Payton Philanthropic Studies Library, Payton Papers.org, 2000), 1.

Resources

Associations

Advisors in Philanthropy (AiP)   (888) 597-6575
95 West Street   www.advisorsinphilanthropy.org
Rocky Hill, CT 06067
A membership organization for professional financial advisors. It is a forum to inspire and educate advisors to integrate philanthropy into their practice and empower their clients to leave a legacy.

Association of Fundraising Professionals   (800) 666-3863
(AFP)   www.afpnet.org
4300 Wilson Boulevard, Suite 300
Arlington, VA 22314
Represents more than 30,000 members in the United States and Europe. Local chapter events and regional and national conferences provide education and dialogue for professionals in the field of fundraising.

Board Source   (202) 452-6262
1828 L Street NW, Suite 900   www.boardsource.org
Washington, DC 20036
Dedicated to advancing the public good by building exceptional nonprofit boards and inspiring board service.

Committee of 200 (C200)   (312) 255-0296
980 N. Michigan Avenue, Suite 1575   www.c200.org
Chicago, Il 60611-7540
An international, nonprofit organization of more than 400 of
the most powerful women who own and run companies and
who lead major divisions of large corporations.

Council for Advancement and Support of   (202) 328-2273
Education (CASE)   www.case.org
1307 New York Avenue NW, Suite 1000
Washington, DC 20005
The membership organization for educational institutions and
a resource for higher-education fundraising and development professionals.

Council on Foundations   (800) 673-9036
2121 Crystal Drive, Suite 700   www.cof.org
Arlington, VA 22202
Offers conferences, publications, research, and national support services for family foundations, regional grant makers,
associations, and philanthropic affinity groups.

Entrepreneurs Foundation   www.entrepreneursfoundation.org
Various chapters throughout the United States and Israel. In
partnership with Entrepreneurs Foundations, companies
leverage their corporate assets to create customized philanthropy and community programs that meet corporate objectives and serve social needs.

Foundation Center   (212) 620-4230
79 Fifth Avenue   www.foundationcenter.org
New York, NY 10003-3076
Compiles research on philanthropy and supports education
and training for grant seekers. Information services available through the Web or at their training centers.

Funders for Lesbian and Gay Issues   (212) 475-2930
116 East 16th Street, 3rd Floor   www.lgbfunders.org
New York, NY 10003

Studies and strengthens philanthropy to advance racial, economic, and gender justice and create a healthy community
with widespread equity.

Hispanics in Philanthropy   (415) 837-0427
200 Pine Street, Suite 700   www.hiponline.org
San Francisco, CA 94104
An association of more than 450 grant makers and not-for-
profit leaders who promote the participation of Latinos in
philanthropy.

The Institute for
Divorce Financial Analysts™ (IDFA)   (800) 875-1760
24901 Northwestern Highway,   www.institutedfa.com
 Suite 710
Southfield, MI 48075
The premier national organization dedicated to the certifica-
tion, education, and promotion of the use of financial pro-
fessionals in the divorce arena.

National Association of Baby Boomer Women   (877) 226-6637
401 W. Chesapeake Avenue   www.nabbw.com
Townsend, MD 21204
A Web site, newsletter, and membership service to empower
women to explore and live their passions, by connecting,
encouraging, and supporting women personally, professionally, and spiritually.

National Association of Women
Business Owners(NAWBO)   (800)556-2926
601 Pennsylvania Avenue NW   www.nawbo.org
South Building, Suite 900
Washington DC 20004
Propels women entrepreneurs into economic, social, and politi-
cal spheres of power worldwide

National Black United Funds   (800) 223-0866
40 Clinton Street   www. nbuf.org
Newark, NJ 07102

Promotes African American philanthropy nationwide through conferences, training, and campaigns.

National Center for
Family Philanthropy (NCFP)   (202) 293-3424
1818 N Street, NW, Suite 300   www.ncfp.org
Washington, DC 20036
Encourages families and individuals to create and sustain their philanthropic mission through effective and responsible giving.

Native Americans in Philanthropy   (612) 724-8798
2801 21st Avenue South,   www.nativephilanthropy.org
Suite 132D
Minneapolis, MN 55407
Serves as a forum for Native Americans, donors, foundations, and interested philanthropists in support of Native American people.

Partnership for Philanthropic Planning (PPP)   (317) 269-6274
(formerly National Committee
on Planned Giving)   www.pppnet.org
233 McCrea Street, Suite 400
Indianapolis, IN 46225
The national organization for individuals serving people and organizations that work together to make charitable giving more meaningful. There are over 150 local councils and 10,000 members. The organization provides extensive research data and presents national conferences.

Social Venture Partners International (SVP)   (206) 728-7872
1601 Second Avenue, Suite 615   www.svpi.org
Seattle, WA 98101
Brings together worlds that typically do not overlap: grant making, volunteerism, nonprofit capacity building, and philanthropic education. Every SVP is a network of engaged philanthropists who believe that they can have a positive impact on their communities and who use innovative strategies to address complex social issues. Chapters throughout the United States and Japan.

Third Wave Foundation (212) 228-6311
25 East 21st Street, 4th Floor   www.thirdwavefoundation.org
New York, NY 10010
Forum to network and educate young women ages 15 to 30 in
   philanthropic endeavors.

United Jewish Communities (212)-284-6500
National Women's Philanthropy www.ujc.org
P.O. Box 157
Wall Street Station, NY 10263
Dedicated to the continuity, connectivity, and thriving future of
   their North American communities, Israel, and the Jewish
   people.

United Way Women's Initiative (702) 836-7112
701 Noth Fairfax Street   www.liveunited.org
Alexandria, VA 22314
National leadership council and local chapters engage women as
   philanthropic leaders, community advocates, and financial
   investors for social change.

Women Donors Network (WDN) (415) 814-1333
565 Commercial Street, Suite 300   www.womendonors.org
San Francisco, CA 94111
A philanthropic community for those who refuse to accept the
   status quo. WDN members fund progressive causes through
   independent giving and collaborative efforts.

Women's Funding Network (WFN) (415) 441-0706
505 Sansome Street,
2nd Floor   www.womensfundingnetwork.org
San Francisco, CA 94111
Forum for more than 145 public and private women's funds
   with combined working assets of $465 million. The WFN
   is a global champion for investment in women. The
   WFN optimizes the impact and success of women's funds on six
   continents.

Education and Research

The American College   (888) 263-2265
270 S. Bryn Mawr Avenue   www.theamericancollege.edu
Bryn Mawr, PA 19010
A nonprofit educational institution offering academic accredi-
    tation dedicated to leadership in innovative training
    and development of philanthropic and financial services
    professionals.

American Institute of Philanthropy   (773) 529-2300
Charity Rating Guide & Watchdog   www.charitywatch.org
3450 North Lake Shore Drive, Suite 2802E
P.O. Box 578460
Chicago, IL 60657
A nonprofit charity watchdog organization that helps donors
    make informed giving decisions.

Bay Path College   (800) 782-7284
588 Longmeadow Street   www.baypath.edu
Longmeadow, MA 01106
A pioneer in innovative undergraduate programs for women
    and professional graduate degrees for men and women
    including nonprofit management and philanthropy.

The Center on Philanthropy at
Indiana University   (317) 274-4200
550 West North Street, Suite 301   www.philanthropy.iupui.edu
Indianapolis, IN 46202
Offers the only international fundraising education program
    housed within a university.

Center on Wealth and Philanthropy,
Boston College   (617) 552-4070
140 Commonwealth Avenue   www.bc.edu
McGuinn Hall 515 Chestnut Hill, MA 02467
Offers research and publications on the spirituality and motiva-
    tions for financial giving of wealth holders who are guided
    through a self-reflective process of conscientious decision
    making about their legacy.

The Center for Women's Business Research   (703) 556-7162
1760 Old Meadow Road,
Suite 500   www.womensbusinessresearchcenter.org
McLean, VA 22102
Provides data-driven knowledge that advances the economic,
social, and political impact of women's business enterprises.

Charity Navigator   (201) 818-1288
1200 MacArthur Boulevard,
2nd Floor   www.charitynavigator.org
Mahwah, NJ 07430
America's premier independent charity evaluator, working to
advance a more efficient and responsive philanthropic marketplace by evaluating the financial health of over 5,400 of
America's largest charities.

Council of Better Business Bureau's Philanthropic Advisory Service
4200 Wilson Boulevard, Suite 800   (703) 276-0100
Arlington, VA 22203-1838   www.bbb.org
Sets standards for charitable solicitations and collects information on charitable organizations in the United States that
solicit nationally.

Guidestar Directory of American Charities   (800) 421-8656
4801 Courthouse Street, Suite 220   www.guidestar.org
Williamsburg, VA 23188
Maintains a database of more than 1.6 million not-for-profit
organizations in the United States. Reports on indica-
tors and issues in the areas of finance and fiscal stability,
programs, contributions and grants, and other related
areas.

The Institute of Noetic Science   (707) 775-3500
101 San Antonio Road   www.noetic.org
Petaluma, CA 94952
Conducts and sponsors leading-edge research into the potential
and power of consciousness, including perceptions, beliefs,
attention, intention, and intuition. It explores phenomena
that do not necessarily fir the conventional scientific models
while maintaining a commitment to scientific rigor.

The Philanthropic Initiative (TPI)   (617) 338-2590
160 Federal Street, Floor 8   www.tpi.org
Boston, MA 02110
A nonprofit advisory team that designs, carries out, and evaluates philanthropic programs for individual donors, families, foundations, and corporations.

The Wellesley Centers for Women   (781) 283-2500
106 Central Street   www.wconline.org
Wellesley, MA 02481
Conducts scholarly research and sound action programs with women's perspectives and experience at the center.

The White House Project   (212) 261-4400
434 West 33rd Street, 8th Floor   www.thewhitehouseproject.org
New York, NY 10001
A national nonpartisan organization working to advance women in business, politics, and media, including a newsletter, weblog, and news.

**The Women's Philanthropy
Institute at the Center**   (317) 278-8990
on Philanthropy at
Indiana University (WPI)   www.philanthropy.iupui.edu
550 West North Street, Suite 301
Indianapolis, IN 46202
The only organization to examine all the aspects of women's philanthropy through a value-neutral lens from distinctive structures and models to the multiple roles of women in philanthropy and in the nonprofit sector.

Social Capital

Ashoka: Innovators for the Public   (703) 527-8300
1700 North Moore Street, Suite 2000,
20th floor   www.ashoka.org
Arlington, VA 22209
Strives to shape a global entrepreneurial competitive citizen sector, one that allows social entrepreneurs to thrive and enables the world's citizens to think and act as change makers.

Board Builders   714-863-4422
8015 Maryland Avenue   www.boardbuilders.com
Suite 5A
St. Louis, MO 63105
Innovative and entertaining training workshops specializing in
fields of volunteerism, fundraising, and governance.

Bolder Giving   (781) 646-1705
The Zing Foundation   www.boldergiving.com
P.O. Box 1216
Arlington, MA 02474
Bolder Giving's mission is to inspire and support people to give
at their full potential Bolder Giving is a project of the Zing
Foundation.

Center for a New American Dream   (301) 891-3683
6930 Carroll Avenue, Suite 900   www.newdream.org
Takoma Park, MD 20912
Helps Americans consume responsibly to protect the environment, enhance the quality of life, and promote social
justice.

Changemakers   (415) 551-2363
1550 Bryant Street, Suite 850   www.changemakers.org
San Francisco, CA 94103
A community of action where all collaborate on solutions. Their
mantra is "Everyone is a Changemaker."

The Ethical Will   (612) 374-9526
1043 Grand Avenue, Suite 162   www.ethicalwill.com
St. Paul, MN 55105
A resource to create a document that provides an organized
way to articulate a person's values that honors the past, cel-
ebrates the present, and informs the future.

Inspired Legacies   (713) 527-7671
P.O. Box 66274   www.inspiredlegacies.org
Houston, TX 77266
Helps donors, advisors, and nonprofits collaborate for inspired
outcomes benefiting self, family, and society.

The Institute for Women and Wealth   (561) 202-0863
205 North K Street   www.instituteforwomenandwealth.org
Lake Worth, FL 33460
Provides workshops, inspirational speeches, and private consulting for individuals, nonprofit organizations, corporations, and foundations to effectively and efficiently align
their wealth capacity with their passion and life purpose and
design a lasting legacy of values and valuables.

Social Venture Network   (415) 561-6501
P.O. Box 29221   www.svn.org
San Francisco, CA 94129
A network of creative and innovative social entrepreneurs with
resources and ideas necessary for an individual to succeed
as a mission-driven entrepreneur.

The Strategic Initiatives Group   (214) 750-5157
P.O. Box 12852   www.strategicinitiativesgroup.com
Dallas, TX 75225
A consulting group dedicated to assisting nonprofit leaders,
directors, and their organizations to fulfill their mission
and develop successful strategies to effectively raise funds,
build board capacity and governance; and strengthen and
develop internal staff and leadership through consulting,
training, coaching, and strategic planning.

The Soul of Money Institute   (415) 386-5599
3 Fifth Avenue   www.soulofmoney.org
San Francisco, CA 94118
Offers workshops and consulting to individuals and organizations to create freedom, power, and sufficiency in their relationship with money.

The Spirited Woman   (888) 428-1234
P.O. Box 20042   www.thespiritedwoman.com
Santa Barbara, CA 93120
Provides an inspirational and informative e-newsletter for
women. Focuses on woman authors and inspirational litera-
ture and workshops.

The Women's Legacy Foundation   (612) 558-3331
P.O. Box 16202   www.life-legacies.com
Minneapolis, MN 55416
A resource to inspire women to undertake the creation of their
    spiritual ethical will.

Publications

Chronicle of Philanthropy   www.philanthropy.com
The newspaper for the nonprofit world offers news for non-
    profit organizations on grant seeking, fundraising, foun-
    dations, managing nonprofit groups, technology, and the
    nonprofit job market.

Fortune   www.fortune.com
A leading global business magazine published by Time Inc.'s
    Fortune/Money Group on business news and current
    affairs.

Harvard Business Review   www.hbr.org
A business magazine featuring current articles and case studies
    applicable to both for profit and nonprofits.

The NonProfit Times   www.NPTimes.com
A leading publication for nonprofit management.

The NonProfit Quarterly   www.nonprofitquarterly.org
A unique print magazine that leaders count on to provide them
    with values-based management information and proven
    practices.

Nonprofit World   www.snpo.org
A bimonthly magazine, published since 1983, that provides busy
    nonprofit leaders with concise and practical articles whose
    advice can be easily implemented.

Planned Giving Today   www.PGToday.com
An essential resource for gift-planning professionals. A premier
    monthly publication serving the planned giving community,

connecting readers to leading professionals in the field, and providing information about key training events and resources, fresh marketing ideas, and valuable insights.

Wired   www.wired.com

A magazine whose mission is to uncover the most surprising and resonant stories about the people, companies, technologies, and ideas that are transforming our lives.

Informative Web Sites

Scrapbooking for Beginners
www.creativememories.com
www.everything-aboutscrapbooking.com
www.scrapbooking.about.com

Tech, Distance Education, and Grant Opportunities
www.fundingalert.org
www.grassrootsfundraising.org
www.profitsources.org
www.Techsoup.org
www.womenwealthandgiving.com

Video Legacy
www.familylegacyvideo.com
www.legacyvideoproductions.com
www.timelesslegacyvideo.com

Volunteer Sites
www.civicventure.org
www.encore.org
www.experiencecorps.org
www.nationalservice.gov
www.networkforgood.org
www.pointsoflight.org
www.voa.org
www.volunteermatch.org

Bibliography

Aburdene, Patricia. *Megatrends 2010: The Rise of Conscious Capitalism.* Charlottesville, VA: Hampton Roads Publishing, 2005.

Aburdene, Patricia, and John Naisbitt. *Megatrends for Women.* New York: Villard Books, 1992.

Addams, Jane. *Democracy and Social Ethics,* introduction by Charlene Haddock Seigfried. Chicago: University of Illinois Press, 2002.

Allen, Nick, Mal Warwick, and Michael Stein. *Fundraising on the Internet.* Berkeley, CA: Strathmoor Press, 1996.

Allison, Michael, and Jude Kaye. *Strategic Planning for Nonprofit Organizations.* New York: John Wiley & Sons, 1997.

Ashton, Debra. *The Complete Guide to Planned Giving,* rev. 3rd ed. Quincy, MA: Ashton and Associates, 2004.

Autry, James A. *Love & Profit. New* York: William Morrow, 1991.

Baines, Barry K. *Ethical Wills—Putting Your Values on Paper.* Cambridge, MA: Perseus Book Group, 2002.

Barletta, Martha. *Marketing to Women.* Chicago: Dearborn Trade Publishing, 2003.

Bassoff, Michael, and Steve Chandler. *RelationShift: Revolutionary Fundraising.* San Francisco: Robert D. Reed Publishers, 2001.

Beckwith, Harry. *The Invisible Touch.* New York: Hachette Book Group, 2000.

Blanchard, Ken, P. John Carlos, and Alan Randolph. *The 3 Keys to Empowerment.* San Francisco: Berrett- Koehler Publishers, 1999.

Blanchard, Ken, and Cathy S. Truett. *The Generosity Factor.* Grand Rapids, MI. Blanchard Family Partnership, 2002.

Bode, Richard. *First You Have to Row a Little Boat. New* York: Warner Books, 1993.

Bolen, Jean Shinoda. *Crones. Don't Whine.* San Francisco: Conari Press, 2003.

———. *Urgent Message from Mother: Gather the Women, Save the World.* San Francisco: Conari Press, 2005.

Bremner, Robert H. *Giving: Charity and Philanthropy in History.* New Brunswick: Transaction Publishers, 1996.

Brinckerhoff, Peter C. *Generations: The Challenge of a Lifetime for Your Nonprofit.* Saint Paul, MN: Fieldstone Alliance, 2007.

Brizendine, Louann. *The Female Brain.* New York: Broadway Books, 2006.

Bronfman, Edgar M., with Catherine Whitney. *Third Act: Reinventing Yourself After Retirement.* New York: G.P. Putnam's Sons, 2002.

Brooks, Robert, and Sam Goldstein. *The Power of Resilience.* New York: McGraw-Hill, 2004.

Brown, Mary, and Carol Osborn. *Marketing to the Ultimate Power Consumer—The Baby-Boomer Woman.* New York: American Management Association, 2006.

Brown, Oral Lee, and Caille Milliner. *The Promise: How One Women Made Good on Her Extraordinary Pact to Send a Classroom of 1st Graders to College.* New York: Doubleday, 2005.

Buffington, S. D. *The Law of Abundance.* Dallas: QuinStar, 2008.

Buford, Bob. *Half Time: Changing Your Game Plan from Success to Significance.* Grand Rapids, MI: Zondervan, 1994.

Cameron, Julia. *The Artist's Way.* New York: Penguin Putnam, 1992.

Campbell, Joseph. *The Hero with a Thousand Faces.* New York: Pantheon Books, 1949.

Canfield, Jack. *The Success Principles.* New York: HarperCollins, 2005.

Capek, Mary Ellen S., and Molly Mead. *Effective Philanthropy: Organizational Success through Deep Diversity and Gender Equality.* Cambridge, MA: MIT Press, 2006.

Carnegie, Andrew. *The Gospel of Wealth Essays and Other Writings.* New York: Penguin Group, 2000.

Chatzky, Jean. *Make Money, Not Excuses.* New York: Three Rivers Press, 2006.

Chopra, Deepak. *Creating Affluence:The A–Z Steps to a Richer Life.* San Rafael: Amber-Allen Publishing and New World Library, 1998.

———. *The Seven Spiritual Laws of Success: A Practical Guide to the Fulfillment of Your Dreams.* San Rafael, CA: Amber-Allen Publishers and New World Library, 1994.

Clift, Elayne, ed. *Women, Philanthropy, and Social Change.* Medford, MA: Tufts University Press, 2005.

Clinton, Bill. *Giving: How Each of Us Can Change the World.* New York: Alfred A. Knopf, 2007.

Cohen, Alan. *A Deep Breath of Life.* Carlsbad, CA: Hay House, 1996.

Covey, Stephen M. R. *The Speed of Trust.* New York: Free Press, 2006.

Crutchfield, Leslie R., and Heather McLeod Grant. *Forces for Good.* San Francisco: Jossey-Bass, 2008.

Dalai Lama. *Ethics for the New Millennium.* New York: Riverside Books, 1999.

Dees, J. Gregory, Jed Emerson, and Peter Economy. *Enterprising NonProfits: A Toolkit for Social Entrepreneurs.* Hoboken, NJ: John Wiley & Sons, 2001.

Dorris, Christopher. *Creating Your Dreams.* New York: iUniverse, Inc., 2005.

Douglas, James. *Why Charity? The Case for a Third Sector.* Beverly Hills, CA: Sage Publications, 1983.

Drucker, Peter F. *The Drucker Foundation Self Assessment Tool.* San Francisco: Jossey-Bass, 1999.

———. *Management Challenges for the 21st Century.* New York: HarperCollins, 1999.

———. *Managing the Non-Profit Organization.* New York: HarperCollins, 1990.

Eisler, Riane. The *Real Wealth of Nations: Creating a Caring Economics.* San Francisco: Berrett-Koehler, 2007.

Ellis, George, Robert Wright, and David Hale Smith. *The Little Green Book of Venture Philanthropy.* Dallas: Social Venture Press, 2008.

Englund, Gregory J. *Beyond Death & Taxes.* Boston: Estate Planning Press, 1993.

Erkut, Sumru, and Wind of Changes Foundation. *Inside Women's Power: Learning for Leaders.* Wellesley, MA: CRW Special Report No 28, Wellesley Center for Women, Wellesley College, 2001.

Evans, Susan B., and Joan P. Avis. *The Women Who Broke All the Rules: How the Choices of a Generation Changed Our Lives.* Naperville, IL: Sourcebooks, Inc., 1999.

Fischer, Marilyn, and Judy D. Whippe, eds. *Jane Addams Essays and Speeches.* London: Continuum International, 2005.

Fogel, Robert William. *The Fourth Great Awakening and the Future of Egalitarianism.* Chicago: University of Chicago Press, 2000.

Freed, Rachael. *Women's Lives, Women's Legacies—Passing Your Beliefs and Blessings to Future Generations—Creating Your Own Spiritual-Ethical Will.* Minneapolis: Fairview Press, 2003.

Freedman, Marc. *Encore: Finding Work that Matters in the Second Half of Life.* New York: Public Affairs Books, 2007.

Friedman, Lawrence J., and Mark D. McGarvie. *Charity, Philanthropy, and Civility in American History.* Cambridge: Cambridge University Press, 2003.

Frumkin, Peter. *Strategic Giving: The Art and Science of Philanthropy.* Chicago: University of Chicago Press, 2006.

Fukuyama, Francis. *Trust: The Social Virtues and the Creation of Prosperity.* New York: Simon & Schuster, 1995.

Fuller, Margaret. *Woman in the Nineteenth Century.* Mineola, NY: Dover Publications, 1999.

Fulton, Katherine, and Andrew Blau. *Cultivating Change in Philanthropy.* San Francisco: Monitor Company Group, 2005.

Gambone, James V. *ReFirement: A Boomers' Guide to Life after 50.* Minneapolis: Kirk House, 2000.

Gary, Tracy with Nancy Adess. *Inspired Philanthropy: Your Step-by-Step Guide to Creating a Giving Plan,* 3rd ed. San Francisco: Jossey-Bass, 2008.

Gaudiani, Claire. *The Greater Good: How Philanthropy Drives the American Economy and Can Save Capitalism.* New York: Owl Books, 2004.

Gawain, Shakti. *Creating True Prosperity: Workbook.* Novato, CA: Nataraj Publishing, New World Library, 1998.

———. *Creative Visualization.* Novato, CA: New World Library, 2002.

Gilbert, Daniel. *Stumbling on Happiness.* New York: Vintage Books, 2005.

Gilligan, Carol. *In a Different Voice: Psychological Theory and Women's Development.* Cambridge, MA: Harvard University Press, 1982.

Goleman, Daniel. *Emotional Intelligence.* New York: Bantam Books, 1995.

Goodwin, Robert, and Thomas Kinkade. *Points of Light: A Celebration of the American Spirit of Giving.* New York: Warner Books, 2006.

Gozdz, Kazimierz, ed. *Community Building.* San Francisco: New Leaders Press, 1995.

Grace, Kay Sprinkel. *Beyond Fundraising,* 2nd ed. Hoboken, NJ: John Wiley & Sons, 2005.

Grace, Kay Sprinkel, and Alan L. Wendroff. *High Impact Philanthropy.* Hoboken, NJ: John Wiley & Sons, 2001.

Gray, Doug, *Passionate Action.* Huntersville, NC: Gray Publications, 2007.

Greenleaf, Robert K. *Servant Leadership*. New York: Paulist Press, 1997.

Gunderman, Richard B. *We Make a Life by What We Give*. Bloomington: Indiana University Press, 2008.

Gurney, Kathleen. *Your Money Personality: What It Is and How You Can Profit from It*. Incline Village, NV: Financial Psychology Corporation, 1998.

Hall, Craig. *The Responsible Entrepreneur*. Franklin Lakes, NJ: Career Press, 2001.

Hall, Holly. "Gender Differences in Giving," presented at the Women's Philanthropy Institute, Indianapolis, 2004.

———. "Power of the Purse: Fund Raisers Fail to Tap Self-Made Wealthy Women," *Chronicle of Philanthropy*, February 17, 2005.

Hanson, Janet. *More than 85 Boards: Women Making Career Choices, Taking Risks, and Defining Success on Their Own Terms*. New York: McGraw-Hill, 2006.

Hansen, Mark Victor and Robert G. Allen. *The One-Minute Millionaire*. New York: Three Rivers Press, 2009.

Hartsook, Robert F. *Getting Your Ducks in a Row*. Wichita, KS: ASR Philanthropic Publishing, 2001.

———. *How to Get Million Dollar Gifts and Have Donors*. Wichita, KS: ASR Publishing, 1999.

Hughes, James E. Jr. *Family Wealth—Keeping It in the Family*. New York: Bloomberg Press, 2004.

Jamal, Azim, and Harvey McKinnon. *The Power of Giving*. Vancouver: Tides Canada Foundation, 2005.

Johnson, Spencer. *The Precious Present*. New York: Doubleday *1981*.

Joyaux Simone P. *Strategic Fund Development*. Gaithersburg, MD: Aspen Publishers, 1997.

Jones, Landon Y. *Great Expectations: America and the Baby Boomer Generation*. New York: Coward McCann, 1989.

Kass, Amy, ed. G*iving Well, Doing Well: Readings for Thoughtful Philanthropists*. Bloomington: Indiana University Press, 2008.

Kartoff, H. Peter, ed. *Just Money: A Critique of Contemporary American Philanthropy*. Boston: Philanthropic Initiative, 2004.

Kartoff, H. Peter, with Jane Maddox. The *World We Want: New Dimensions in Philanthropy and Social Change*. Black Ridge Summit, CO: AltaMira Press, 2007.

Klauser, Henriette Anne. *Put Your Heart of Paper*. New York: Bantam Books, 1995.

Kornfeld, Eve. *Margaret Fuller: A Brief Biography with Documents*. Boston: Bedford Books, 1997.

Kouzes, James M., and Barry Z. Posner. *A Leader's Legacy*. San Francisco: Jossey-Bass, 2006.

Kreeft, Peter. *Back to Virtue: Traditional Moral Wisdom for Modern Moral Confusion*. San Francisco: Ignatius Press, 1992.

Krotz, Joanna. *The Guide to Intelligent Giving*. New York: Sterling/Hearst, 2009.

Lawson, Douglas. *Give to Live*. San Diego: Alti Publishing, 1991.

Levitin, Daniel. J. *The World in Six Songs: How the Musical Brain Created Human Nature*. New York: Penguin Group, 2008.

Lubrano, Alfred. *Limbo: Blue-Collar Roots, White-Collar Dreams*. Hoboken, NJ: John Wiley & Sons, 2004.

Lyubomirsky, Sonja. *The How of Happiness.* New York: Penguin Books, 2007.

MacIntyre, Alasdair. *After Virtue,* 3rd ed. Notre Dame, IN: University of Notre Dame Press, 2007.

Mancuso, Joseph R. *How to Write a Winning Business Plan.* New York: Simon & Schuster, 1985.

Markova, Dawna. *I Will Not Die an Unlived Life.* San Francisco: Conari Press, 2000.

Martin, Mike W. *Virtuous Giving: Philanthropy, Voluntary Service, and Caring.* Bloomington: Indiana University Press, 1994.

McCarthy, Kathleen D., ed. *Lady Bountiful Revisited: Women, Philanthropy and Power.* New Brunswick, NJ: Rutgers University Press, 1990.

———. *Women, Philanthropy & Civil Society.* Bloomington: Indiana University Press, 2001.

McKeon, Richard, ed. *The Basic Works of Aristotle.* New York: Modern Library, 2001.

Merrill, Roger A., and Rebecca R. Merrill, *Life Matters.* New York: McGraw-Hill, 2003.

Miedzian, Myriam, and Alisa Malinovich. *Generations: A Century of Women Speak about Their Lives.* New York: Atlantic Monthly Press, 1997.

Moore, Thomas, ed. *The Education of the Heart.* New York: HarperCollins, 1996.

Mundis, Jerrold. *Making Peace with Money.* Kansas City, KS: Andrews McMeel Publishing, 1999.

National Foundation for Women Business Owners. *Philanthropy among Business Women of Achievement. Research Report* Committee of 200, Sponsored by Merrill Lynch, 1999.

Neederman, Jacob. *Money and the Meaning of Life.* New York: Doubleday, 1991.

New, Cheryl Carter, and James Aaron Quick. *Grantseeker's Toolkit: A ComprehensiveGuide to Finding Funding.* New York: John Wiley & Sons, 1998.

Nichols, Judith E. *Global Demographics.* Chicago: Bonus Books, 1995.

Orman, Suze. *Financial Guidebook.* New York: Three Rivers Press, 2006.

———. *You've Earned It, Don't Lose It.* New York: Newsmakers Press, 1998.

Palmer, Parker J. *Let Your Life Speak: Listening for the Voice of Vocation.* San Francisco: Jossey-Bass, 2000.

Pederson, Rena. *What's Missing?* New York: A Perigee Book, 2003.

Perry, Gail. *Fired-Up Fundraising: Turn Board Passion into Action.* Hoboken, NJ: John Wiley & Sons, 2007.

Pink, Daniel H. *A Whole New Mind: Why Right-Brainers Will Rule the Future.* New York: Penguin Group, 2005.

Popcorn, Faith, and Marigold Lys. *EVEolution—The Eight Truths of Marketing to Women.* New York: Hyperion, 2002.

Price, John Randolph. *Empowerment: You Can Do, Be, and Have All Things!* Carlsbad: Hay House, 1992.

Prince, Russ Alan, and Karen Maru File. *The Seven Faces of Philanthropy.* San Francisco: Jossey-Bass, 1994.

Putnam, Robert D. *Bowling Alone: The Collapse and Revival of American Community.* New York: Simon & Schuster, 2000.

Quinn, Daniel. *Ishmael: An Adventure of the Mind and Spirit.* New York: Bantam Books, 1992.

Rafferty, Renata J. *Don't Just Give It Away: Making the Most of Your Charitable Giving.* Worcester, MA: Chandler House Press, 1999.

Rath, Tom. *Strengths Finder 2.0.* New York: Gallup Press, 2007.

Rath, Tom, and Barry Conchie. *Strengths-Based Leadership.* New York: Gallup Press, 2008.

Ray, Paul H., and Sherry Ruth Anderson. *The Cultural Creatives: How 50 Million People Are Changing the World.* New York: Harmony Books, 2000.

Raymond, Susan U. *The Future of Philanthropy, Economics, Ethics and Management.* Hoboken, NJ: John Wiley & Sons, 2004.

Remen, Rachel Naomi. *Kitchen Table Wisdom.* New York: Riverhead Books, 1996.

Roazzi, Vincent M. *The Spirituality of Success: Getting Rich with Integrity.* Dallas: Brown Books, 2002.

Roberts, Cokie. *Founding Mothers: The Women Who Raised Our Nation.* New York: HarperCollins, 2004.

Roddick, Anita. *Business as Unusual.* London: Thorsens, 2000.

Roundtree, Cathleen. *On Women Turning 50, Celebrating Mid-Life Discoveries.* New York: HarperCollins, 1993.

Schervish, Paul G. *Taking Giving Seriously.* Indianapolis: Center on Philanthropy at Indiana University, 1993.

Sharma, Robin S. *The Greatness Guide.* New York: HarperCollins, 2006.

———. *The Monk Who Sold His Ferrari.* New York: Harper-Collins, 1997.

Shaw-Hardy, Sondra C. *Creating a Women's Giving Circle.* Indianapolis: Women's Philanthropy Institute at the Center on Philanthropy at Indiana University, 2000.

Shaw-Hardy, Sondra C., and Martha A. Taylor. *Reinventing Fundraising: Realizing the Potential of Women'sPhilanthropy.* San Francisco: Jossey-Bass, 1995.

Shaw-Hardy, Sondra C., and Martha A. Taylor, eds. *The Transformative Power of Women's Philanthropy.* New Directions for Philanthropic Fundraising, The Center on Philanthropy. San Francisco: Jossey-Bass, 2006.

Shim, Jae, and Joel G. Siegel. *Financial Management for Nonprofits.* New York: McGraw-Hill, 1997.

Smith, J. Walter, and Ann Clurman. *Generation Ageless: How Baby-Boomers Are Changing the Way We Live Today—and They're Just Getting Started.* New York: HarperCollins, 2007.

Stanley, Thomas J. *Millionaire Women Next Door.* Kansas City, MO: Andrews McMeel Publishing, 2004.

Strauss, William, and Neil Howe. *The Fourth Turning: An American Prophecy.* New York: Broadway Books, 1997.

———. *Generations—The History of America's Future, 1584 to 2069.* New York: William Morrow, 1991.

Susanka, Sarah. *The Not So Big Life.* New York: Random House, 2007.

Tannen, Deborah. *You Just Don't Understand: Women and Men in Conversation.* New York: William Morrow, 1990.

Tocqueville, Alexis de. *Democracy in America (1835).* ed. Harvey C. Mansfield and Delba Winthrop. Chicago: University of Chicago Press, 2000.

Tolle, Eckhart. *A New World: Awakening to Your Life's Purpose*. New York: Penguin Group, 2006.

———. *The Power of Now*. Novato, CA: New World Library, 1999.

Twist, Lynne. *The Soul of Money: Transforming Your Relationship with Money and Life*. New York: W.W. Norton, 2003.

Veblen, Thorstein. *The Theory of the Leisure Class: An Economic Study in the Evolution of Institutions*. New York: Penguin Classics, 1994.

von Schlegell, Abbie J., and Joan M. Fisher. *Women as Donors, Women as Philanthropists*. San Francisco: Jossey-Bass, 1993.

Ward, Francine. *Esteemable Acts*. New York: Broadway Books, 2003.

Weisman, Carol. *Fundraising Superheros*. St. Louis, MO: F. E. Robbins & Sons, 2009.

———. *Raising Charitable Children*. St. Louis, MO: F.E. Robbins & Sons, 2006.

———. *The Secrets of Successful Fundraising*. St. Louis, MO: F.E. Robbins & Sons, 2000.

Wilde, Stuart. *The Little Money Bible*. Carlsbad, CA: Hay House, 1998.

Wilder, Barbara. *Embracing Your Power Women, 11 Steps to Coming of Age in Mid-Life*. Boulder, CO: Wild Ox Press, 2005.

———. *Money Is Love*. Boulder, CO: Wild Ox Press, 1999.

Williams, Karla A. *Donor Focused Strategies for Annual Giving*. Gaithersburg, MD: Aspen Publishers, 1997.

Williamson, Marianne. *Everyday Grace*. New York: Riverhead Books, 2002.

———. *A Return to Love*. New York: HarperCollins, 1992.

Winget, Larry. *You're Broke Because You Want to Be*. New York: Gotham Books, 2008.

Witter, Lisa, and Lisa Chen. *The She Spot*. San Francisco: Berrett-Koehler, 2008.

Yankelovich, Daniel. *United America: Restoring the Vital Center to American Democracy*. New Haven, CT: Yale University Press, 2006.

Zander, Rosamund Stone, and Benjamin Zander. *The Art of Possibility*. New York: Penguin, 2000.

Zenger, John H., and Joseph R. Folkman. *The Extraordinary Leader*. New York: McGraw-Hill, 2009.

Zogby, John. *The Way We'll Be*. New York: Random House, 2008.

About the Authors

Margaret May Damen and Niki Nicastro McCuistion have the experience, education, and hands-on working knowledge of what it takes to implement strategies nonprofit organizations and for-profit corporations can effectively use to achieve successful results in highly competitive economic environments. Over the last 30 years they have worked with hundreds of organizations and individuals, men, and women, developing initiatives for fundraising, governance and leadership, conducting board retreats, workshops, and coaching CEO's and their boards.

Frequent conference speakers at numerous national and international forums they are known for inspiring and motivating an organization's team in revenue development, goal-setting and implementing cutting edge initiatives and ideas. Separately, each has written and authored numerous articles, books and learning materials on leadership, governance, and fundraising. Now working together for the first time, they have pooled their strengths in this transformational work, *Women, Wealth and Giving*, based on their research conducted over the past four years of 1,500 baby boomer women.

They are continuing this study with additional surveys and interviews nationwide to identify future trends and to develop cutting edge workshops and strategic consulting to assist individuals, organizations and their leaders achieve lasting results. Their Web site, www.womenwealthandgiving.com offers additional readings and insights.

Margaret May Damen, CFP®, CLU®, ChFC®, CDFA™, is a charismatic speaker and seminar leader with a warm and engaging style that gives audiences a refreshing and practical vision of how to live and leave a legacy unique to their passion and purpose of making a difference in the world. The publication of her first book in 1990, *Money$ense* *for Women,* began her focus on women's financial and philanthropic issues. Today her workshop series, *The Life You Live Is the Legacy You Leave,* and *You Are the Pebble in the Pond,* inspire and empower men and women to excel in meaningful individual and family philanthropic giving by using tools from her *10 Steps to Living the Three Principles of Abundance.*

Margaret is President and CEO of the Institute for Women and Wealth, holds a Bachelor and Masters Degree from Boston University, and has had a successful career in education, finance, and philanthropy. She has held various positions in nonprofit and corporate leadership, from Associate VP for Development for Boston University, Director of Public Relations at the New England Conservatory of Music, Executive Director of Arts/Boston, and Senior Financial Advisor with American Express Financial Advisors. She has conducted workshops and consulted with national organizations including, CARE, The Humane Society of the United States, The Philadelphia Foundation, The Raymond F. Kravis Center for the Performing Arts, The United Way of Martin County Foundation, and the Women's Philanthropy Institute at the Center on Philanthropy at Indiana University. In addition, she has served on numerous nonprofit boards, from the Planned Giving Council of Palm Beach County, and the Treasure Coast Planned Giving Council, to the national Partnership for Philanthropic Planning (PPP). She is listed in "Who's Who in Finance in America," and is a recipient of the Boca Raton, Florida, chapter Brandeis Women of the Year Award and the Executive Women of the Palm Beach's Leadership Award. Margaret is a flutist and a member of the Sigma Alpha Iota International Music Fraternity.

Her talent and ability to speak from the heart combined with her financial and philanthropic experience has helped hundreds of individuals and organizations, private and public, unlock "their wealth within," connect with their values and live a purposeful life and legacy. For more information on her consulting and speaking availability, contact her at mmdamen@earthlink.net; and through her Web site: www.instituteforwomenandwealth.org.

Niki Nicastro McCuistion, CSP, strategist, speaker, and performance coach is known for inspiring transformational change within organizations and with individuals, working with them to develop and implement strategies that lead to more informed and balanced choices, personally and professionally. Her cutting-edge information combined with a strong business and nonprofit background and her no-nonsense, yet humorous and compassionate style give value and solutions to daily business and people challenges. She knows what it takes to get results and does so with her clients with integrity and style.

Over the last 25 years, Niki has spoken to hundreds of groups and consulted with organizations as diverse as General Motors to Cas-Argentina, Hewlett-Packard to the World Affairs Council and Avance, and the Society for Hispanic Engineers as well as the United States Marine Corp. She has earned the highest professional award the National Speakers Association bestows the certified speaking professional (CSP) designation and has received the J. Charbonneau award for contribution to the speaking profession. Niki has been honored as a Malone Fellow by the NCUSAR and as an Ambassador for Peace, by the International Peace Federation.

Her hands-on background in marketing, sales, and training, with a major real estate franchise to president/CEO of the Foundation for Responsible Television, combined with a master's in Philanthropy and Development, from St. Mary's University in Minnesota and an MBA in Leadership and Governance from the University of Dallas, give her sound business tools and an ability to move organizations forward successfully. Niki is the executive producer/producer of the syndicated PBS TV business program *McCuistion,* now in its twentieth year. With her leadership the program has earned over 50 major awards for excellence in programming and journalism. She is the author of several business books on sales, leadership and coaching, and the filmmaker for The Roots of War . . . the Road to Peace.

Her unique approach and intuitive ability to help individuals and organizations connect with their personal and professional mission and purpose make her a sought-after speaker and consultant. For more information on her consulting and speaking availability, contact her at nikin@nikimccuistion.com and visit her Web site, www.nikimccuistion.com.

Stay in Touch/Contact Us with Your Story

Dear reader:

Your story is important to us . . .

Our research for *Women, Wealth, and Giving* has inspired us to make this work an on-going project. We're going to continue this study and its success depends on you. In the course of our research, we have met and interviewed many dynamic women who are living the *Three Principles of Abundance* and encouraging others to follow the *Seven Covenants of Virtuous Philanthropy.* Truly they are inspiring a whole generation of boomer women to follow their heart and live a purposeful life.

We'd like to hear your story. If you have an experience, advice to share, a comment, a question, or resources to recommend, let us know. You can reach us at www.womenwealthandgiving.com.

Thank you for all you do each and every day to make the world a better place.

Carpe Diem!

Index